THE CATHOLIC UNIVERSITY OF AMERICA
CANON LAW STUDIES
No. 309

INVESTMENT OF CHURCH FUNDS

A STUDY IN ADMINISTRATIVE LAW

BY

Harry J. Byrne, A.B., J.C.L.

A Priest of the Archdiocese of New York

A DISSERTATION

*Submitted to the Faculty of the School of Canon Law
of the Catholic University of America in Partial
Fulfillment of the Requirements for the
Degree of Doctor of Canon Law*

THE CATHOLIC UNIVERSITY OF AMERICA PRESS
WASHINGTON, D. C.
1951

Nihil Obstat:

JOHN ROGG SCHMIDT, J.C.D.,
Censor Deputatus.

Imprimatur:

✠ FRANCIS CARDINAL SPELLMAN,
Archbishop of New York.

New York, July 22, 1949.

Printed by
THE PAULIST PRESS
401 WEST 59TH STREET
NEW YORK 19, N. Y.
◆ 51

TABLE OF CONTENTS

CHAPTER VIII

INVESTMENT OF FUNDS GIVEN FOR PIOUS CAUSES
(2): PROPERTY SUBJECT TO THE PROVISION OF
CANON 533

CHAPTER IX

INVESTMENT OF FUNDS GIVEN FOR PIOUS CAUSES
(3): ENDOWMENTS OF PIOUS FOUNDATIONS....

CHAPTER X

FOREWORD

PROPERTY by its nature is capable of two fundamentally different uses. On the one hand, property may be expended in such a way that it is consumed in the supplying of current necessities. On the other hand, property may be put to a use that is productive of income, or converted into property that is productive of income. Money may be consumed by expenditure for immediate needs, or it may be used as capital productive of income.

In the fulfillment of its mission, the Church must make use of temporal resources. The most efficient use of these material resources sometimes calls for their immediate expenditure, sometimes calls for their placement in uses productive of income. The determination as to which of these two modes of using property is to be followed is not left entirely to the discretion of immediate administrators. The canon law, having purposes in view that are broader and more universal than those seen by an immediate administrator who might be led to sacrifice future interests under the pressure of immediate necessity, establishes legal administrative patterns according to which the administrator must carry on the affairs of his office. The canon law on property administration preserves a proper proportion between present and future interests of the juridic person involved. The law protects the broader and future interests of this ecclesiastical person from the dangers inherent in complete discretionary power of administrators acting under the pressure of immediate and, frequently, urgent needs.

Those provisions of law which restrict the alienation of church property furnish protection against the loss of productive and other resources. Those provisions of law which require investment of certain funds establish these funds as elements that are to be productive of income, generally, although not always, on a stable and permanent basis. In this way sterile preservation of funds is avoided, and in those cases wherein the funds are designated for stable and permanent investment there is protection for the future interests of the juridic person through the prevention of undue expenditure for mere present advantage. Both the law regarding

vii

alienation of property and the law regarding investment have for their purpose the use of property most advantageous for the ecclesiastical juristic person in its continuing existence and for the religious and charitable activities carried on by that person.

The conversion of funds to productive use constitutes investment. It is the purpose of the present study to examine those provisions of the present canon law which furnish administrative norms regarding the investment of church funds. The law will be seen to indicate the obligation of investing certain funds, the qualities that must characterize ecclesiastical investments, and the legal formalities prescribed for acts of investment.

The canon law regarding investment of church funds must be examined in its present actuality and in its historical antecedents. Investment as it is known today and as it appears in the *Codex Iuris Canonici* is a feature of relatively modern economic life. Yet the productive use of property in any age has for its purpose the acquisition of some sort of income from that property. Productive use of church property in any age is one means to the acquisition of income for the support of the Church's activities. Productive wealth under the feudal economy of the Middle Ages did not have the fluidity and mobility that characterize productive wealth today. The problems of church law in governing the productive use of material resources were quite different in such a background than they were after the disintegration of the feudal system of property tenure.

It is not surprising to find, therefore, that the earliest sources of the present canon law respecting investment as indicated in the footnotes to the Code date from the late sixteenth and early seventeenth centuries. Accordingly, to view historical antecedents of the present law as they existed in the twelfth century *Decretum* of Gratian and in the subsequent collections which were to make up the *Corpus Iuris Canonici*, it became necessary in the study of this period to widen considerably the scope of the subject treated to the extent of treating more general trends and features of the law of property administration which were still later in canonical history to appear in the particular and specific legislation regarding investment.

The present study approaches the law contained in the *Corpus Iuris Canonici* with the purpose of examining underlying principles regarding the productive use of property. Since productive property consisted in those times almost exclusively of land, these principles must be sought in law dealing with property in land. Accordingly, the first chapter consists of an exclusively historical analysis of the law of the *Corpus Iuris Canonici* in an effort to discover patterns of law which will have a relevancy to the more specific law of later periods and of the present regarding the investment of church funds. This first chapter consists of two articles. The first of these treats the ecclesiastical unit of ownership of productive property and the legal protections furnished to its ownership. The second article discusses various dispositions made of ecclesiastically owned property in order to derive income from it.

After the period covered by the *Corpus Iuris Canonici*[1] the rôle of land as almost the unique form of productive wealth had been challenged. Money had taken on the quality of increased productivity over and above its character as a medium of exchange. This is demonstrated by the introduction of the practice of purchasing for a sum of money the right to receive a certain annual yield or income,[2] and by the increasing use of extrinsic titles to permit the acceptance of interest charges on loans of money.

Ownership and tenure of land also had undergone a radical change in the break-up of the feudal system.[3] Previously the king had been regarded as the owner of all the land of the nation, its *usufruct* alone being passed down through the various elements in the feudal hierarchy.[4] With the destruction of feudal tenure, the ownership itself of landed property became more mobile. The in-

---

[1] The latest law included in the *Corpus Iuris Canonici* consists of decretals from the pontificate of Sixtus IV (1471-1484).

[2] See pp. 15-20 regarding this contract of the purchase and sale of the *census*.

[3] In England, for example, a large part of the agricultural land was out on lease by the end of the fifteenth century. Cf. *Encyclopedia Brittanica* (24 vols., 1946), article "Land Tenure," Vol. XIII, p. 677.

[4] Jarrett, *Social Theories of the Middle Ages* (Westminster, Maryland: Newman Bookshop, 1942), p. 131.

creased productivity of money and the increased mobility of land tenure were factors underlying the new approaches made by ecclesiastical authorities to the perennial problem of deriving income and of safeguarding its sources in order that the activities of the Church be supported.

With money having the quality of increased productivity, investment in its modern character was able to appear. Productive use of property was no longer largely limited to property in land. Accordingly, after the study of the period covered by the *Corpus Iuris Canonici,* it becomes possible to restrict the scope of analysis to the proper scope of the present study, viz., the investment of church funds.

The origins of the present law regarding investment lie in considerable measure, as will be seen, in the jurisprudence of the Roman Congregations. An effective principle of unity in studying the responses of the Congregations is had in linking them with the present law. Inasmuch as investment provisions apply to a variety of types of funds, a topical consideration of them seemed imperative. A further division on the basis of historical periods did not appear to be advantageous. Accordingly, the historical development of investment legislation from the time of the Council of Trent to the promulgation of the Code will be treated incidentally and in conjunction with the present law.

Thus only the first chapter is exclusively historical. Succeeding chapters consist of canonical commentary upon the present law regarding investment with pertinent provisions of the law from the Council of Trent to the Code viewed in their relation to the present law.

This study of the present canonical enactments respecting investment is a thoroughly legal study. Investment is of its nature an act of property administration. Investment can prudently and efficiently be made only on the basis of the wise judgment of skilled men. In modern economic affairs the management of investments is a professional task. Investment decisions must be made after consideration of a great variety of factors including canonical and civil legal aspects, the investment needs of the particular juristic person involved, and the entire state and condition of the investment

market and the business world. The present study is in no way—
and it is important that this be emphasized—a study of all the factors involved in the making of investment decisions and the formu-
lating of investment policies by ecclesiastical administrators. Its
scope is strictly confined to the area of canonical factors to be considered by administrators and to the canonical formalities required
in making investments. It aims to present the pertinent canonical
factors involved in investment in their legal details. It attempts
to indicate, without treating details, the areas in which pertinent
civil law, canonized by canon 1529, must be looked to for its
directives.

It is beyond the scope of the present work to consider investment factors other than those created by the canon law. Similarly
it is beyond the scope of this work to formulate judgments of value
regarding specific provisions of law. The study simply intends to
present the canonical provisions respecting investment as they exist,
and not the great variety of other factors that must be considered
in the making of any investment decision. Entrance into the areas
of these other factors that have been indicated could be made only
on the basis of a study of investment in its economic, and not merely
canonical, aspects.

The writer wishes to express his thanks to His Eminence Francis
Cardinal Spellman, Archbishop of New York, for the opportunity of
pursuing graduate study in Canon Law.

CHAPTER I

THE EMPLOYMENT OF ECCLESIASTICAL PROPERTY IN PRODUCTIVE USES AS FOUND IN THE *CORPUS IURIS CANONICI*

PREREQUISITE to any consideration of the administrative disposal of property to secure certain ends is a knowledge of the particular mode of ownership of such property. For property administration, in any stage other than a primitive one, must be carried on as a complex. There must be a complex of holdings so that the periodic needs of one element of the complex may be met by the produce of another element. The farmer buys feed for his poultry with money realized from the sale of crops that he has raised. The produce of any one type of property can be "reinvested" in the same type or in other types, and thus the produce itself takes on a quality of further productiveness of its own. This makes possible the conservation of such property holdings as well as their expansion and the acquisition of new property elements.

The number and the variety of these elements are factors in the material prosperity of the owner. Different property elements are co-ordinated in a smoothly functioning productive relationship by a unity of administration deriving from the unit of ownership. Ownership by an individual is the most widely encountered unit of property ownership. The partnership, the corporation, and the socialistic state are further examples of other property complexes set up to achieve a variety of ends. There is this end common to them all: a greater productivity from the different property elements than could be realized from them in the relative isolation of separate and unrelated ownership.

The end to be achieved will affect the form that the property complex takes; and that form viewed in its actuality, especially in its legal actuality, will give evidence of the purpose desired. This is the value in a historical study of positive law, namely, that it reveals something of the ends desired by the legislative authority in

1

its historical continuity, and of the means taken by that authority to secure those ends in an environment constantly subject to stabilizing influences of legal creations, yet constantly changing before the nameless energies hidden in material things.

The value to the study of property law as fashioned and used by the Church to care for its own holdings lies in an awareness of what the law can achieve, and of the means to such achievement, in the way of protection of what is owned and in the further aggrandizement of property to serve its ultimate mission. In studying the employment of ecclesiastical property in productive uses as regulated by the law contained in the *Corpus Iuris Canonici,* the scope of the property complex itself must first be considered. This will be evident from the unit of property ownership. The way will then be clear for a study of the more particularized enactments of law providing for the productive disposal of the various elements of property.

ARTICLE 1. THE UNIT OF OWNERSHIP—BASIS OF PRODUCTIVE USE

A canon of the sixth century Council of Agde (506), contained in the *Decretum* of Gratian, distinguished between the title of ownership of goods as held by a cleric and the title of ownership as held by the church to which the cleric was attached.[1] Alexander IV (1254-1261) in a decree vigorously asserted the right of ecclesiastical ownership of goods against civil authorities who denied or delimited that right.[2] From this decree it is evident that the right inhered, not in the individual clerics, but in churches and in other ecclesiastical moral personalities. This basis of ownership of ecclesiastical goods in moral persons will be much in evidence throughout the various laws of which notice will be taken in this study.

---

[1] C. 3, C. XII, q. 3; Mansi, *Sacrorum Conciliorum Nova et Amplissima Collectio* (53 vols. in 60, Paris, 1901-1907), VIII, 325 (hereafter cited as Mansi).

[2] C. 1, *de immunitate ecclesiarum, coemiteriorum, et aliorum locorum religiosorum,* III, 23, in VI°; Potthast, *Regesta Pontificum inde ab anno post Christum MCXCVIII ad MCCCIV* (2 vols., Berolini, 1874-1875), n. 16308 (hereafter cited Potthast).

There was a relative independence in the ownership of goods by each moral personality, and in their administration as well. This independence was protected in the law apparently as a practical corollary of the right of the moral person to its very existence. For example, the interests of the ecclesiastical moral person were protected even when some alienation of its property would have benefitted some other ecclesiastical moral person. Legislation prohibiting alienation of ecclesiastical possessions, or establishing certain solemnities for validly effecting alienation, provided for no exception in the case wherein another ecclesiastical moral person would have been the intended recipient of such property. In fact, such alienations to ecclesiastical moral persons were sometimes specifically mentioned as being equally subject to the prohibition. Gratian included in his collection a law—its origin is variously ascribed—which prohibited, unless consent of the bishop was had, any estrangement of tithes or offerings outside of the baptismal church in which they were made, and this prohibition was declared to be effective even when the estrangement was to favor another church.[3] So, too, a council of Lyons specifically prohibited a bishop or an abbot from giving land of one church to another, even though both churches were subject to his jurisdiction.[4] It was also provided that, if the superior wished to make exchanges of lands belonging to different churches, he could do so only with the consent of the interested parties on each side.

In the same vein, the bishop could not arbitrarily confer the proprietary rights of one church upon other churches or upon monas-

---

[3] C. 55, C. XVI, q. 1. The law is ascribed in Gratian to Pope Anastasius without any indication as to which of the popes bearing this name was meant. Friedberg (1837-1910) indicated, however, that its asserted origin was spurious, since the text derived rather from Benedict the Levite, who had drawn upon the seventh canon of the Council of Gangra (340/341). Ives of Chartres (1040-1117) in his *Decretum* cited the legislation as *ex concilio apud Sanctum Medarum, cap. 1 (ex conc. Gangren., c. 7)*. Cf. Migne, *Patrologiae Cursus Completus, Series Latina* (221 vols., Parisiis, 1844-1864), CLXI, 850 (hereafter cited Migne, *PL*).

[4] C. 1, X, *de rebus ecclesiae alienandis vel non*, III, 13; Ives, *Decretum*, III, 29, as in Migne, *PL*, CLXI, 205.

teries, even though he enjoyed the *ius patronatus* of the churches involved.[5]

Innocent III (1198-1216) in his declaration of the foregoing ruling quoted from a letter of Pope Leo I (440-461) to the bishops of Sicily [6] which indicated that for such a conferral there was to be some resulting advantage, and that the chapter was to treat of the matter and furnish its consent. Innocent pointed out elsewhere that the bishop could neither confer parish churches nor any income from these on a monastery under his jurisdiction unless he had the consent of his chapter.[7]

There were also in the law other regulations which affected the grants made to monasteries from the holdings of other ecclesiastical persons. A bishop could not confer upon a monastery which he had founded more than two per cent of the possessions of his church, nor more than one per cent upon some secular church to which he wished to show some favor, perhaps because he wished to be buried there on his death.[8]

The holdings of ecclesiastical moral persons were also protected against administrators' acts of placing heavy liabilities upon them to their disadvantage. In the course of ordinary administration, an administrator could not reap all the advantages of a contract during his own term while unduly extending its obligations as they touched the property beyond his term. Celestine III (1191-1198) enacted just such a prohibition when he forbade a cleric to give in perpetual lease the lands of the church in exchange for a lump sum of money received by himself.[9]

---

[5] C. 8, X, *de his quae fiunt a praelato sine consensu capituli*, III, 10; Potthast, n. 1447.

[6] This is found also in c. 52, C. XII, q. 2; Jaffé, *Regesta Pontificum Romanorum ab condita ecclesia ad annum post Christum natum MCXCVIII* (2 ed., correctam et auctam auspiciis G. Wattenbach, F. Kaltenbrunner, P. Ewald, S. Loewenfeld, 2 vols. in 1, Lipsiae, 1885-1888), n. 415 (hereafter cited as Jaffé).

[7] C. 9, X, *de his quae fiunt a praelato sine consensu capituli*, III, 10; Potthast, n. 2350.

[8] From the IX Council of Toledo (655). Cf. c. 74, C. XII, q. 2; c. 9, X, *de his quae fiunt a praelato sine consensu capituli*, III, 10; Mansi, XI, 27.

[9] C. 9, X, *de rebus ecclesiae alienandis vel non*, III, 13; Jaffé, n. 10690.

Similarly, according to a decree of Alexander III (1159-1181) a prelate could not burden the possessions of his church beyond his own lifetime without the authorization of the bishop.[10] The glossator added the note that, whenever some annual payment to be made from the resources of a church was agreed upon in a settlement, there existed a presumption that the obligation to make this payment was of a character personal to the cleric, and not real as attaching to the goods of the church.[11] Alexander III provided similarly in a case involving tithes, a portion of which had been conceded to a monastery by the rector of the church to which they were legally due.[12] He ordered that any settlement made by the prelate thus alienating the goods of his church did not oblige his successor unless the consent of the Holy See had been given. The glossator here also clearly indicated that any settlement involving possessions arrived at between administrators was purely personal unless it had been confirmed by the Holy See.[13]

Not only did the law conserve and protect the holdings of the moral person, but it also conduced to and favored the increase of such holdings. The III General Council of the Lateran (1179) in its fifteenth canon enacted that goods accruing through a benefice could not be willed to others by the cleric holding the benefice.[14] Such goods were to remain with the church to which the benefice was attached. The glossator in his commentary on this provision declared that whatever a cleric acquired *intuitu ecclesiae* pertained to that church.[15] So, too, whenever something was purchased with funds belonging to the church, the thing purchased belonged to the church.[16] This same provision, deriving from the *Capitularia* of

---

[10] C. 5, X, *de transactionibus,* I, 36; Jaffé, n. 8898.

[11] *Glossa* ad *casus.*

[12] C. 8, X, *de transactionibus,* I, 36; Jaffé n. 9162.

[13] *Glossa* ad *casus.*

[14] C. 7, X, *de testamentis et ultimis voluntatibus,* III, 26; Mansi, XXII, 226.

[15] *Glossa* s.v. *acquisita.*

[16] *Glossa* s.v. *construxisse.*

Archbishop Hincmar of Rheims (845-882), is to be found in the Decretals of Gregory IX (1227-1241).[17]

The favored position granted by ecclesiastical law to juristic persons in the Church and to their tenure of property is further exemplified in a canon dating from the II Council of Toledo, held in 527. This canon provided that any improvements made by a cleric on the property of the church were to be his during his lifetime, but on his death were to revert to the church, and were not to pass to another either by normal right of succession or by will of the beneficiary.[18]

Normally one who enjoyed the rights of the *dominium utile* over property was entitled to compensation for any improvements he made on that property, as, for example, one who established a vineyard on a previously uncultivated field.[19] With a cleric in his benefice the situation was quite different. Any improvements he made served him for his lifetime, and this even if he was removed from his benefice. On his death, however, as has been seen, they ceded immediately to the church without any compensation to the heirs.[20] Thus was improvement of ecclesiastical property encour-

---

[17] C. 4, X, *de peculio clericorum,* III, 25. It bears the adscription of the Council of Rheims (813). This law with the same adscription is to be found in the *Decretum* of Ives, III, 96, in Migne, *PL,* CLXI, 217. Friedberg noted that it is borrowed from canon 19 of the *Capitularies* of Hincmar, and that it appears in Regino of Prüm, I, 223. This last is evidently an error. The law in question with the adscription to c. 19 of Hincmar's *Capitularies* appears in Regino's work in I, 220. Cf. Migne, *PL,* CXXXII, 232. Fournier (1855-1935) and Le Bras list several apocryphal canons appearing in the work of Regino. This is not one of those so listed. Cf. Fournier et Le Bras, *Histoire des Collections Canoniques en Occident depuis les Fausses Décrétales jusqu'au Décret de Gratien* (2 vols., Paris, 1931-1932), I, 259-262.

[18] C. 5, X, *de peculio clericorum,* III, 25; Bruns, *Canones Apostolorum et Conciliorum Saeculorum* IV, V, VI, VII (2 vols., Berolini, 1839), I, 209. Cf. also *Glossa* s.v. *obitus.*

[19] C. (IV, 66) 3, in *Corpus Iuris Civilis,* II (Editio Stereotypa Decima, Berolini, 1929), p. 191. This reference to the Justinian Code was made by the glossator s.v. *requisita,* ad c. 4, X, *de locato et conducto,* III, 18.

[20] Panormitanus (Nicholaus de Tudeschis), *Commentaria in Quinque Libros Decretalium* (5 vols. in 7, Venetiis, 1588), VI, p. 171(b), sec. 1 (hereafter cited *Commentaria*).

aged while at the same time the title to such improvement was safeguarded for the juristic person.

In the Roman law concerning property, which was the basis of the ecclesiastical legislation under discussion, there were numerous specifications of the general principle *accessorium sequitur principale.* However, when temporal affairs of the church were involved and the interested parties were clerics, there again appeared the favored position of the ecclesiastical moral person. Normally the ownership of a structure built upon land belonging to another passed to the owner of the land.[21] If, however, a cleric built a structure upon his own land, with the resources of the church, then in favor of the church the law required that the ownership of the land cede to the ecclesiastical moral person owning the building.[22]

While protecting and advancing the temporal interests of the ecclesiastical moral person, the law also protected this moral person against even the supervisory action of legitimate superiors when carried to unwarranted lengths. In a case wherein certain diocesan statutes forbade a monastery to sell claims upon its future income from tithes to any persons save parish priests, Innocent III countered with a grant of full permission for the monastery to rent these tithes to whomever it would, free to choose the best purchaser.[23]

Thus does the mode of ownership used by the Church in holding its temporal possessions show the ecclesiastical juristic person in its material aspect as an economic unit. This unit was protected in large measure against the failure, inculpable or otherwise, of its

[21] D. (1, 8) 6, in *Corpus Iuris Civilis,* I (Editio Stereotypa Tertia Decima, Berolini, 1920), 39. This reference to the *Digest* of Justinian was made by the glossator s.v. *construxisse,* ad c. 13, C. XII, q. 2.

[22] C. 41, C. XVII, q. 4 and also *glossa* s.v. *construxisse,* ad c. 13, C. XII, q. 2.

[23] C. 2, X, *de locato et conducto,* III, 18; Potthast, n. 7802. Since the present discussion concerns the tenure of income-producing property and its contractual dispositions, a fuller treatment of tithes, while it would be valuable in many ways, is not strictly pertinent, for tithes constituted a form of income deriving from the property of others and not from the property of the Church. The legislation here cited is used merely for the purpose of emphasizing the relative independence enjoyed by the ecclesiastical moral person in handling freely its own material affairs.

administrators to serve its best interests. It was protected against the excess of intermediate supervisory authority. And the protection furnished by the law to ecclesiastical tenure of property was a protection not merely of the ecclesiastical quality of that tenure, but it extended also to the protection of the ownership of these goods as held by the particular juristic person.

Going beyond mere protection and conservation, the law made positive provision that the normal productive results of well administered property by the very mode or manner of its tenure were not only used for the support of current work, but were also "reinvested" in the principal revenue-producing holdings. Thus property by its revenue supported the ministers of the Church and their work. But at the same time part of the accruing property was being redirected back into productive principal. It has been seen regarding the improvements made upon property how the mode of ecclesiastical property tenure effected this in some degree. Much of the material seen has consisted of corollaries to the general rules on alienation. These have been included in an effort to show how the ecclesiastical law attempted to protect the tenure of income-producing property. The next section will attempt to show some of the ways in which, under the ordinance of law, this property was applied to productive uses through the contractual dispositions made by its administrators.

ARTICLE 2. CONTRACTUAL DISPOSITIONS OF CHURCH PROPERTY

In the economy of the earlier Middle Ages, productive wealth was almost exclusively a matter of land. Through the generosity of the faithful the Church received grants of land to be used in meeting the temporal needs arising in its mission. It was the purpose of administrators to derive income from the property in their care while protecting this property as a source of income, and also to provide for the increase of such revenue-producing holdings. This last was an important concern, in order that the Church might expand its work to an even greater degree, and also that it might make its operating resources independent in some measure of the fluctuating will or ability of the faithful to make donations. Through the possession of revenue-producing holdings the Church would be cushioned partially at least from the effects of temporary economic distress in some locality. It was of importance to the community that the work of the Church be carried on at a constant pace, not only in its spiritual administrations but also in the variety of charitable and educational endeavors that were in its hands. Stable and periodic income was necessary to achieve this.

This section will treat of the means provided by the Church in its law for the realization of current operating resources and for the increase of revenue-producing holdings through various dispositions of its property.

A. *Long-term Lease* (emphyteusis)

A convenient disposal of property in order to derive income from it was the contract of rental. The long-term lease, or contract of emphyteusis as it was termed in the Roman law, received considerable treatment in decretal law. The contract of *emphyteusis* involved the grant of the *dominium utile* of uncultivated immovable property with the obligation of cultivating it and rendering some annual return.[24] This grant was made *in perpetuum* or for a long period of time. The *dominium directum* remained with the one making the grant.

The considerations made for the grant most frequently took the form of a payment to be made annually by the lessee. Because of the risk that was involved for the ecclesiastical owner in a careless contracting of *emphyteusis* over its lands, namely, the risk that the title to ownership would become obscured in the passage of time and open the way to a possible consequent loss of the title, it is found that the law of the decretals sometimes forbade it as a prohibited form of alienation,[25] sometimes subjected it to certain solemnities and guarantees. Such regulations affected not only land, but also precious articles such as jewels, the income of the churches and

[24] Scotus-Kahl-Brissonius-Heineccius, *Vocabularium Juris Utriusque* (2. ed., 4 vols., Neapoli, 1760), II, 109.

[25] Cf. canon 15 of the IV Council of Constantinople (the eighth ecumenical council) as found in c. 13, C. XII, q. 2; Mansi, XVI, 168-169.

rustic *mancipia*.[26] These *mancipia* were the accessory implements, cattle, and tools used on the land and closely associated with its productivity.

The privilege of enjoying the use and the usufruct of property was held out by the law as an incentive toward making that property productive. Where forested lands had been made arable and had been cultivated, these lands could be given in perpetual *emphyteusis* to those who themselves or whose parents had cleared the land. The church in return was to be paid an annual sum by those who enjoyed this grant.[27] One who made further improvements on land held in *emphyteusis* created a legal interest for himself which was protected by the law. The glossator in commenting on the legislation just referred to pointed out that those who held such rights of usufruct were not to be expelled from their holdings after they had made further improvements upon them.[28] Rather, they had a right to be paid for these improvements.

However, the church as the owner of the land had the first right to purchase these improvements and to incorporate them into the original holding. If the church did not wish to buy these, or if it allowed two months from the notice of their offering at sale to elapse, they could then be sold through open sale to any purchaser.[29] While the tenant was thus encouraged to make improvements through the provisions of the law, the interest of the ecclesiastical owner was adequately protected.

The usufructuary lost his general contractual right, and with it also his specific right to the improvements he had made on the property, if he failed to make his annual payment over a period of two years.[30] This two-year limit was a special limit provided in favor of an ecclesiastical owner.[31] In this way the income to the church

---

[26] C. 13, C. XII, q. 2. See also c. 5, X, *de rebus alienandis vel non*, III, 13, for a prohibition on alienation including perpetual emphyteusis of lands and their *mancipia*.

[27] C. 7, X, *de rebus ecclesiae alienandis vel non*, III, 13; Jaffé, n. 9197.

[28] *Glossa* s.v. *nisi forte tunc*, ad c. 7, X, *de rebus etc.*, III, 13.

[29] Panormitanus, *Commentaria*, VI, p. 138(b)-140(a).

[30] C. 4, X, *de locato et conducto*, III, 18.

[31] *Glossa* s.v. *per biennium*, ad c. 2, C. X, q. 2.

from the land was guaranteed. The lessee was also obliged to keep
the property in good condition. If it deteriorated while in his possession, he was liable for the damages, could not seek payment for
any improvements he may have made and, finally, could be expelled
from the property.[32]

The one enjoying the lease could improve his holdings, for example, by preparation for cultivation, and sub-lease them out to
others. However, as a protection for the church's tenure of the
land, there was a prohibition against such a sub-lease to all more
influential parties who could not easily be brought to court.[33] For
such to enter upon the property through a lease with a weaker party
holding the direct ownership would have been a risk to the holder
of the title. It was the risk of might obscuring or overcoming
right.

This was a protection furnished in law not only for the church's
ownership; it was a general provision of the law whereby all ownership of private persons was protected against the inroads of the
more influential whose holding of lesser rights would be prejudicial
to the direct title of ownership. Hence the church as a more
powerful party could not lease any property which had been im-
proved by the one who had leased it from the owner immediately,
when that owner was merely a private person. However, this im-
proved right could be donated to the church, not indeed to be held
by the church to some possible prejudice to the owner, but only in
order that the church could receive the price realized from the improvement made upon the property.[34]

B. Short-term Grants (precariae)

For the advantage of the moral person whose goods they cared
for, ecclesiastical administrators could make temporary grants of
the *dominium utile* over properties owned by the moral person. Legal
norms regulating such grants are to be found especially in a consti-

[32] C. 2, C. X, q. 2.
[33] *Glossa* s.v. *prohibentur,* ad c. 4, X, *de locato et conducto,* III, 18.
[34] Panormitanus, *ibid.,* p. 139(a), sec. 10.

tution of the early Roman Emperors Leo (457-474) and Anthemius (467-472). This law was included in the Code of Justinian,[35] and its force continued in matters of ecclesiastical administration so that it found its way into the collection of Gratian.[36] It was provided therein, in order to insure primarily the advantage of the church, that neither the administrator nor his relatives could be the recipients of such grants.

To protect the church's title to the property involved in the transaction, the law required that the time of the grant's duration, whether for the life of the recipient or for some shorter period, be agreed upon and drawn up in writing. When that period of time had elapsed, the property was to be returned to the church with the same value and income as when it was conferred. It was not to have any added encumbrances upon it, and it had to be possessed of its tenants along with all its accessory implements of production including cattle. To insure the productive value of the land, it was provided that title to these accessories remained perpetually with the ecclesiastical owner. The law as contained in Gratian's collection and as reported by its glossators applied the name *precariae* to certain temporal grants of usufruct provided for in the Code of Justinian.[37]

To encourage conferral of property upon the church by the faithful there was in use the practice, ratified by law, of conceding to the donor for life the usufruct of what was given, the naked title of ownership alone passing to the ecclesiastical person at the time of the transfer. When a person thus gave the ownership of a field to the church while retaining for his lifetime its usufruct, the church in return conferred upon him, again for his lifetime, the right of usufruct of another additional field of equal value. If the handing over of title was legally unlimited, so that it conferred complete and full rights upon the church at the time of the donation, the original owner was given in consideration of this the usufructuary rights

---

[35] C. (1, 2) 14, in *Corpus Iuris Civilis*, II, 13-14.

[36] C. 2, C. X, q. 2.

[37] *Glossa* s.v. *nam haec usus,* ad c. 2, C. X, q. 2.

of three fields, each equal in value to what he had transferred to the church.[38]

The word *precariae* was used in designation of the temporary grants of a *dominium utile*. It appears in several slightly different senses throughout the law as contained in the *Corpus Iuris Canonici*. One of the glossators listed three such significations.[39]   First, it was used in designation of a contract entered at someone's petition for a five-year period.   It normally could not be revoked until the expiration of that time.   This contract could then be renewed for another five-year period, and indeed any such contracts involving temporary grants of usufruct made by the church were subject to such a renewal every five years.[40]   The requirement for such a renewal sought the protection of the church's title to the property, lest in the passing of time the existence of the contract be forgotten.[41]   The contractual element on the part of the recipient of the *precaria* was his agreement that an annual payment would be made by him and by his heirs if the renewals were continued to them.[42]

The second use of the term *precariae* was described by the glossator as in the designation of a donation made by the church to someone, the property to be held for the lifetime of the recipient.   This was the type of grant made to a cleric to support him and his service to the church.[43]   Most properly understood this conferral was rather a donation of usufruct,[44] but because of the safeguards provided for the protection of the church's title, and also in view of other similarities to the contract of *precaria*, this term likewise was here applied.

---

[38] From can. 22 of the Council of Meaux (845) as in Mansi, XIV, 823; c. 4, C. X, q. 2.

[39] *Glossa* s.v. *precariae*, ad c. 1, X, *de precariis*, III, 14.

[40] From can. 22 of the Council of Meaux (845) as in Mansi, XIV, 823; c. 5, C. X, q. 2; c. 1, X, *de precariis*, III, 14.

[41] *Glossa* s.v. *renoventur*, ad c. 1, X, *de precariis*, III, 14.

[42] Hostiensis, *In Tertium Decretalium Librum Commentaria* (Venetiis, 1581), p. 55(a).

[43] C. 72, C. XII, q. 2.

[44] *Glossa* s.v. *sub precariae*, ad c. 72, C. XII, q. 2.

The third use of the word *precariae* was in indication of the contract already described above, whereby a donor transferred direct ownership of something and received from the church in return double or triple usufructuary rights depending on the type of his donation.[45] This type of the contract of *precaria* applied only to property in land.[46]

All types of *precariae* obliged the recipient to the usual care demanded of anyone enjoying usufructuary rights, in order that there occur no deterioration of the property.[47] Any grants of *precariae* which were made injudiciously by an administrator of ecclesiastical goods could always be revoked by his successor in office.[48]

A similar term, *precarium,* appeared also in the law. A *precarium* was a temporary grant of usufruct, but, unlike the *precaria,* it was always revocable at the will of the grantor.[49] It was similar to the *commodatum,* but differed in that it was revocable at the will of the grantor.[50]

In all leases on lands and properties, whether of long duration or of shorter length, the owner—in this study, the ecclesiastical moral person—was free from the obligations of upkeep and maintenance. These obligations fell upon the tenant, who had to return the property in at least as good condition as when it had come into his care.[51] This was an obvious advantage to the Church, which was thus kept free of the necessity of being intimately involved in business details. And, as has been seen, the law encouraged the improvement of the leased property.

[45] C. 4, C. X, q. 2.

[46] Hostiensis, *op. cit.,* p. 55(a).

[47] C. 72, C. XII, q. 2; c. 2, C. X, q. 2.

[48] C. 6, C. X, q. 2; c. 2, X, *de precariis,* III, 14; The *Correctores Romani* in the Roman edition of Gratian added to the canon in question the comment that the more ultimate source of this legislation was not to be found in any of the councils of Carthage, as was alleged. It did appear, however, in Teutonic law in the *Hlotharii Constitutiones Olonnenses—Monumenta Germaniae Historica, Leges,* Tom. I (edidit Georgius Pertz, Hannoverae, 1835; reprinted Leipzig, 1925), *Hludowice I Capitularia,* p. 249.

[49] Decretal of Gregory IX—c. 3, X, *de precariis,* III, 14; Potthast, n. 9633.

[50] *Glossa* s.v. *precarium,* ad c. 3, X, *de precariis,* III, 14.

[51] C. 2, C. X, q. 2.

C. Exchange of Property

Church property could figure in exchanges with consequent advantages to the Church. The advantage could lie in the fact that property of greater value was received, or in the greater convenience of location of the property received. Whatever may have been the motive, administrators were able to make use of exchange to achieve a greater utility from the goods in their care. This exchange could be made with the civil authority.[52]

Celestine III (1191-1198) granted the faculty to the Archbishop of Ravenna of alienating, despite the general prohibition, or of exchanging less useful possessions of the church for those of greater use and value, provided that he had the consent of his chapter. The commentator Panormitanus (1386-1453) pointed out that, if the prelate could not arrange a good exchange, he could sell his property and convert the money received to a more useful possession. The price took the place of the thing itself, and thus such a direct sale fell within the limits allowed by this legislation.[53] It was necessary, however, that this price be converted into a more useful holding. Abuse of the power to exchange possessions and the dangers consequent upon one man's judgment in these matters were inhibited by requiring the consent of interested parties on both sides.[54] Any exchanges made unwarrantedly when the church was vacant were null.[55]

D. Purchase and Sale of Annuities

The word *census*, in canon law, is susceptible of three different significations. It may indicate an annual tax that must be paid to an ecclesiastical superior. As such it occurs in the name of the

---

[52] C. 2, C. X, q. 2; c. 1, X, *de rerum permutatione*, III, 19.

[53] Panormitanus, *Commentaria*, VI, p. 120(b).

[54] C. 1, X, *de rebus ecclesiae alienandis vel non*, III, 13; from a Council of Lyons contained in the *Decretum* of Ives, III, 29, as in Migne, *PL*, CLXI, 205.

[55] C. 44, C. XII, q. 2; from can. 21 of the Council of Meaux (845), as contained in Mansi, XIV, 823.

title, *De censibus, exactionibus, et procurationibus,* which appears
in three of the collections that form part of the *Corpus Iuris
Canonici.*[56]

The word was also used in designation of an annual rent paid for
some consideration. This consideration could, for example, be the
right to the full use and usufruct of property of the church, for the
grant of which the church received an annual payment.[57] Another
contractual element in consideration of which the annual payment of
census was made consisted in the right of receiving certain specified
goods accruing as income to the church over a certain period of
time.[58] Perhaps the advantage to the church of such an arrangement as this lay in the fact that it was thereby released from the
necessity of handling and converting to more useful forms of property or to money what was given to it in the way of goods. For
much of the tithes and offerings that came to the church consisted
of produce raised or of other goods of a not easily negotiable nature. There may well have been another advantage to the church
from contracts of this kind through the fact of receiving in one
sum and at one time what would normally have accrued only gradually in the course of the year.

The third signification of the word *census* indicates the right itself of receiving a certain periodic income deriving from the property of another, as for example the right of receiving the income
from rents or tithes. By accommodation, the word *census* came
to be applied to the contract in which this right was bought and
sold. Such a contract could be *reservativus,* that is, when the one
who disposed of some property limited the disposition by reserving
for himself for the future some income deriving therefrom. The
contract could, on the other hand, be *consignativus,* that is, when a
person sold to another the right of receiving an income deriving

[56] III, 20, in VI°; III, 13, in Clem.; III, 10, in Extravag. com.

[57] Hostiensis, *In Tertium Decretalium Librum Commentaria,* p. 55(a).

[58] C. 4, X, *ne prelati vices suas vel ecclesias sub annuo censu concedant,*
V, 4; cf. also *Glossa* s.v. *praefatam ecclesiam:* "*Ecclesia, i.e., obventiones eccle-
siae possunt ad tempus locari, sive concedi pro certo censu annuatim reddendo.*"
Cf. also decretal of Innocent III in c. 2, X, *de locato et conducto,* III, 18;
Potthast, n. 7802.

from the property of the seller.[59]   Such a contract was the one that involved the purchase and sale of annuities.   Ecclesiastical persons were to be found as parties to these contracts.   Sometimes the church established annuities on its own property; sometimes it purchased annuities from others as an investment of its money.

The *Corpus Iuris Canonici* contains many laws which prohibited and penalized usurious practices.[60]   The changes and evolution that the economic system was undergoing gave rise to the need of greater funds of money than were available from current production.   However, the Church laws against usury, based on moral grounds, but also protecting the interests of society from exploitation, forbade the taking of interest on money.

For evading the law and its penalties various devices were resorted to.   For example, a person wishing to borrow a sum of money would legally sell a piece of his land or some right over it, but at the same time agree to repurchase it later for a higher price than the sum he had received when he sold it.   This higher price in effect constituted a repayment of the original sum plus a consideration or interest for the use of the money.   Such a device was labeled usurious by the law.[61]

So strict was the prohibition against the taking of interest that, if a loan was made and certain properties were given to secure the loan, the produce and fruits of those properties, if received by the one loaning the money, had to be deducted from the total amount of the debt.   The contract termed *antichresis,* whereby the loaner could receive as interest the produce of the land which he held as security, was strictly prohibited.[62]

---

[59] Gulielmus Redoanus, *Solemnis Tractatus de Alienationibus Rerum Ecclesiarum* (Placentiae, 1589), p. 98.

[60] The fifth title of the fifth book in both the collection of Boniface VIII and that of Clement V is named *De Usuris.*   In the collection of Gregory IX, title 19 of the fifth book has this title.

[61] A provision of Innocent III in c. 4, X, *de pignoribus et aliis cautionibus,* III, 21; Potthast, n. 1957.   Cf. also a decretal of Innocent in c. 5, X, *de emptione et venditione,* III, 17; Jaffé, n. 10738.

[62] C. 4, X, *de pignoribus et aliis cautionibus,* III, 21.   Cf. also another provision of Innocent III in c. 5 of the same title; Potthast, n. 3869.

One of the devices that managed to evade the prohibitions against usurious contracts, while yet securing a return on money, was the purchase and sale of revenues from certain properties. Inasmuch as it was a contract of sale and in view also of the element of doubt in the return, the receiving of a greater amount than was expended for the original purchase was not looked upon as usurious.[63]

Later ages were to witness the Church's approval of certain titles to interest on money loaned. Traces of this evolution as rooted in the evolution of economic society itself can be seen in the law of the *Corpus Iuris Canonici*. The matter of the purchase and sale of annuities is evidently such a trace. The Collection of the *Extravagantes Communes* contains a decretal letter which Pope Martin V (1417-1431) issued in the year 1425, and which rather completely pictures the practice of dealings in annuities.[64] It is the earliest official acceptance by the Church of dealings of this kind,[65] although, as the decretal indicates, they had been in use for over a hundred years. This acceptance, coming so late in decretal law, is significant.

For a lump sum of money a person could purchase an annuity to be paid each year to him. The amount of the initial payment was established in proportion to what the annuity would return to him annually and to the duration of the time over which the payments were to be made.

The person desirous of selling such an annuity was the one who experienced the need for some larger sum of money than was currently available to him. To obtain such a sum he was willing to obligate his income for the future. The decretal letter indicates that among this class of persons were to be found the civil head of the community (*princeps*), the local overlord (*baro*), the soldier, the citizen, and the townman. These attached the obligation of the annuity payments to the income deriving from their goods, their towns,

---

[63] Cf. T. P. McLaughlin, "The Teachings of the Canonists on Usury," *Mediaeval Studies*, I (1939), 81-147, esp. pp. 120-122 and 136. This article touches on the various devices employed for the purpose of evading the law on usury.

[64] C. 1, *de emptione et venditione*, III, 5, in Extravag. com.

[65] McLaughlin, "art. cit.," *ibid.*, p. 122.

lands, fields, houses, and inheritances. The goods so designated in the contract were obligated perpetually for the payment of the annuity. If these perished for any reason, the obligation became a personal one on the seller.

It appears that the ones interested in purchasing such annuities were those who possessed funds which they had built up by accumulation and for which they had no immediate use. It was to the advantage of such persons to provide a regular income for themselves. The decretal letter indicates that among those who were accustomed to purchase annuities were ecclesiastical persons, secular groups, societies, towns, and cities. As to ecclesiastical persons, the letter indicates that through such annuities were financed ecclesiastical benefices, collegiate groups, canonries and prebends, dignities, personages, offices, and altars.

Martin in his letter indicated that the practice of dealing in annuities was of over a hundred years' standing and had been accepted as a custom with no indication of anything contrary to it. As a reasonable usage, observed, warranted through legal prescription, and approved by the conventions of those who employed it, its purpose appeared to be the common utility of the people, both of those who offered the annuities for sale and those who purchased them. The very insistence in the letter on the reasonableness of the practice and its long-standing usuage, in view of the traditional hostility to anything smacking of usury, seemed to indicate that arguments could be alleged as to the usurious nature of the contract. This suspicion is confirmed by the letter's reference to those who, upon having sold annuities and benefitted from this sale, thereupon wished to benefit further by escaping payment through insistence that the contract was fundamentally usurious. Their claims were rejected by the Pope, and the contract was declared to be perfectly licit and legitimate. It was furthermore shown that in the past the statutes and penalties established by local ordinaries for enforcing the payment of annuities were freely submitted to, which fact indicated the full and universal acceptance of the legitimacy of the contract.

Possibly in order to forestall the impression of a too close similarity with usurious contracts, the decretal letter emphasized the right of the seller of annuities to buy back in whole or in part what he had sold, and at the same price. He could thus always free himself and his goods of the obligation of the annuity payments. His right in this matter was not conditioned upon the assent of the other party, nor did it expire through the passage of any time limits. On the other hand, he could never be forced to repurchase the obligation in favor of the original buyer even when the obligated goods had become completely destroyed.

Thirty years later, Calixtus III (1455-1458), in a decretal letter to the deans of the churches of Magdeburg, Nüremburg, and Halberstadt, recapitulated the authorization for such contracts. This letter was incorporated in the collection known as the *Extravagantes Communes*.[66] The letter indicated more fully than the previous one that the income of many churches, monasteries, hospitals, and ecclesiastical benefices were known to derive from such annuities.

The advantages to the Church of the financing of its individuals and its moral persons through the purchase of annuities are rather readily apparent. Over the years a greater sum was realized than was initially expended. The initial outlay rendered the funds involved productive instead of allowing them to remain sterile. A periodic and regular payment of income was also assured. So, too, the investing of money in such a manner freed the ecclesiastical administrators from the need of attending to the multitude of details that would have been required in directly converting holdings to profitable uses. They were also freed from the necessity of intimately engaging in business matters from the discharge of which the Church wished its clerics to remain aloof.

SUMMARY OF CHAPTER

It has been seen in the first article of this chapter how the law of the Church governed ecclesiastical property-holding units both in protecting their tenure of productive properties and in securing for them any improvements that might be made on such properties. A variety of legislation which related in considerable measure to mat-

---

[66] C. 2, *de emptione et venditione*, III, 5, in Extravag. com.

ters of alienation accomplished this protection of tenure. Regarding improvements made upon church properties it has been seen how the ecclesiastical juristic person enjoyed a secure position in the law. This secure and favored position was evident not only when the improvement automatically ceded to the church at some time, as, for example, upon the death of a beneficed cleric who had made improvements on the property attached to his benefice, but also when the church, like all legal owners, was given the opportunity before others of purchasing any improvements made upon its land by a tenant.

The second article attempted to show the dispositions made of church property under the law for the sake of providing regular income, as, for example, through the variety of leases that were granted. It also appeared in the study of these dispositions how security of tenure was insured and how improvement of the property, gauged to make it more productive, was encouraged.

The general principles underlying the Church's law of property administration in the *Corpus Iuris Canonici* appeared to be chiefly four: first, that productive property be safeguarded against dissipation and loss; secondly, that this property be applied to income-producing uses; thirdly, that income be derived regularly and periodically in such a way that future benefit was not sacrificed for present advantage; fourthly, that the further improvement of the property, and consequently its productivity, be encouraged. These general principles, appearing in the particular form which they took in the law contained in the *Corpus Iuris Canonici,* have a marked relevancy to the later and present canon law respecting investment of church funds. Thus there is demonstrated a historical continuity in the canon law regarding property administration despite significant differences at different periods of time in the nature and qualities of the property elements involved and in the techniques used in their administration.

CHAPTER II

INVESTMENT IN ECCLESIASTICAL PROPERTY ADMINISTRATION: GENERAL NOTIONS

ARTICLE 1. INVESTMENT

INVESTMENT has been defined as "the act of directing the employment of funds into capital or into claims to income." [1] It has also been described as meaning primarily the purchase of income-yielding property in order to get an annual income, rather than to make profits from fluctuations in capital value.[2] The investment of money has been canonically defined as the expenditure of money for acquiring productive real estate, or the change of a sum of money into another form of ownership, e.g., into stocks or bonds of states or commercial corporations.[3]

The Code of Canon Law requires that certain funds be invested in order that various works of the Church may be materially supported from the income accruing. This purpose of obtaining a source of regular and periodic income may be carried out in a variety of ways, viz., through the purchase of real estate to be rented or leased, or through the purchase of claims to income, such as stocks and bonds.[4] Some authors declare that bank deposit at interest

---

[1] *The Encyclopedia of the Social Sciences* (15 vols., New York: Macmillan, 1932), article "Investment," Vol. VIII, p. 263.

[2] Kirschman, *Principles of Investment* (Chicago and New York: A. W. Shaw Co., 1924), p. 13.

[3] Coronata, *Institutiones Iuris Canonici* (2. ed., 5 vols., Taurini: Marietti, 1939-1947), I, n. 559 (hereafter cited *Institutiones*).

[4] Bouscaren-Ellis, *Canon Law* (Milwaukee: Bruce, 1948), p. 773; Coronata, *Institutiones*, II, n. 1071(a); Heston, *The Alienation of Church Property in the United States*, The Catholic University of America Canon Law Studies, n. 132, (Washington, D. C.: The Catholic University of America Press, 1941), p. 73.

22

constitutes investment.[5]   Other authors declare that bank deposit at interest does not constitute investment in its juridical sense.[6]

Larraona declares that the term *investment* is used in a strict and proper sense and in a wide sense.   In its strict signification, *investment* signifies a true conversion of money, at least relatively permanent, into goods which are to be conserved as principal, that is, as a capital source from which income is to be derived.   This conversion of money, he continues, can be made into immovable property or into movable property, as, for example, stocks, bonds, other pecuniary titles of industrial or commercial societies, and certificates of public indebtedness.   In its wide sense, Larraona goes on, the term *investment* is used in designation, not of a permanent conversion of money into productive goods, but rather of its mere deposit with a bank in order that it may be kept secure and in the meantime yield interest.   He declares that such interest-bearing deposit does not constitute investment in its juridical sense.[7]

It appears that bank deposit at interest possesses a quality of investment in that it is productive of income, while at the same time it does not possess the quality essential to the proper notion of investment, viz., that a true conversion of money into some other form of property be made.   Yet it appears that bank deposit at interest could be selected as a means of making a sum productive of income.   Deposit at interest may be the most advantageous manner of effecting this productivity at a time of great insecurity and instability in the investment market, and when the preservation and safety of the sum is of extraordinary importance.   The question

[5] Oesterle, *Praelectiones Iuris Canonici* (Tomus I, Romae: in Collegio S. Anselmi, 1931), p. 277; Prümmer, *Manuale Iuris Canonici* (4. et 5. ed., Friburgi Brisgoviae, 1927), p. 260; Heston, *The Alienation of Church Property in the United States*, p. 73.

[6] Vermeersch-Creusen, *Epitome Iuris Canonici* (3 vols., Mechliniae-Romae: Dessain; Vol. I, 6. ed., 1937), I, n. 652 (hereafter cited *Institutiones*); Coronata, *Institutiones*, I, n. 559; O'Brien, *The Exemption of Religious in Church Law* (Milwaukee: Bruce, 1943), p. 254; Bouscaren-Ellis, *Canon Law*, p. 251; Larraona, "Commentarium Codicis," *Commentarium pro Religiosis* (henceforth cited *CpR*), XII (1931), 437.

[7] Larraona, "Commentarium Codicis," *CpR*, XII (1931), 436-437.

arises as to when and to what extent does deposit at interest come under canonical rules regarding investment.

McManus has provided a distinction which rather neatly solves the problem.[8] Bank deposit at interest may be made for the purpose of achieving administrative convenience in the paying of bills and in the carrying on of current business affairs. In such a deposit the accruing interest is rather an incidental and not a primary consideration. On the other hand, if bank deposit at interest is made, not as an administratively convenient way to hold and manage funds, but on a rather permanent basis as a specific mode of acquiring income from the funds in preference to other modes, as, for example, the purchase of bonds, then such bank deposit must be regarded juridically as an act of investment.

A satisfactory conclusion and working principle seems to be had in the view that bank deposit at interest does not by its own nature constitute investment in a canonical sense, but that only in the circumstances indicated is it to be considered canonically as investment. The important consideration is not whether or not bank deposit at interest theoretically is equivalent to investment, but rather whether or not a particular deposit at interest in its actual circumstances is to be considered as equivalent to the notion of investment in a particular canonical rule respecting investment.

It seems necessary to refine to some extent Larraona's concept of investment in its juridical sense. He speaks of it as being a conversion of money, at least relatively permanent, into productive goods.[9] This notion of permanence has been implied as being essential to the juridical notion of investment by other authors, who declare that certain canonical prescriptions regarding investment apply only to permanent investment, and not to temporary invest-

[8] McManus, *The Administration of Temporal Goods in Religious Institutes,* The Catholic University of America Canon Law Studies, n. 109 (Washington, D. C.: The Catholic University of America, 1937), p. 94.

[9] Larraona, "Commentarium Codicis," *CpR,* XII (1931), 436.

ment.[10] The reasonableness of this distinction and the consequent restriction of the canonical notion of investment to permanent investment is difficult to appreciate. It is true that when the law orders the investment of certain funds, this investment is to be by the very nature of the situation on a rather permanent basis.[11] However, many of the canonical provisions regarding investment establish requirements for another person's consent to an act of investment.[12] Since all investments are characterized by some degree of risk,[13] and some investments by a much greater degree of risk than others, the requirement for the consent of others has undoubtedly among its purposes the minimizing of risk. This element of risk is no less present in a temporary investment than it is in a permanent investment.

The proper notion of investment appears to be verified in the conversion of money into income-producing property. Although some permanence is presupposed if income is to be derived, the act of investment seems to be essentially constituted by the indicated conversion made for the sake of obtaining income. Even if this obtaining of income was to be for a limited period of time pending some other disposition of the principal itself, there does not appear to be any reason for not considering the immediate act of conversion, as, for example, the purchase of bonds, as an act of investment subject to pertinent canonical norms for investment. The canons, where they treat of investment, speak of investment without qualification as to whether a temporary or permanent disposition of the funds is involved. When the law does not distinguish or provide a reasonable basis for a distinction, it does not seem that a distinction is to be made.

[10] Vromant, *De Bonis Ecclesiae Temporalibus* (Louvain, 1927), p. 246, nota 2; Prümmer, *Manuale Iuris Canonici*, p. 260; Schaefer, *De Religiosis ad normam Codicis Iuris Canonici* (3. ed., Romae: S.A.L.E.R., 1940), n. 197; Nebreda, "Quaestiones Selectae De Iure Administrativo Ecclesiastico," *CpR*, VII (1926), 265.

[11] This is true, for example, regarding the investment made under the provisions of canons 1415, § 2, 1531, § 3, and 1547.

[12] See, for example, canons 533, 549, 1523, 4°.

[13] See p. 33 below.

If by temporary investment the indicated authors mean temporary deposit at interest, there does not appear any difficulty in regarding such deposit as not equivalent to investment, and therefore not subject to a rule respecting investment. There is some evidence to indicate that the "temporary investment" spoken of by some authors is to be understood as referring to temporary bank deposit at interest.[14]

Thus the strict and proper canonical notion of investment appears to lie in the conversion of money into income-producing property, or into claims to income, regardless of the permanence of this disposition of the funds. The purchase of bonds with funds that are to be expended in three years for church construction is equally an act of investment as is the purchase of bonds with the endowment funds of a pious foundation.

Interest-bearing deposit with a bank as productive of some return may be regarded normally as an investment only in a wide and non-canonical sense of the term. When such deposit is made in certain circumstances chiefly for income and in preference for various reasons to investments properly so called, it must be considered as equivalent to the term investment in pertinent canonical legislation.

ARTICLE 2. STABLE CAPITAL

Income-producing property obtained by an ecclesiastical juristic person by purchase, through donation, or in any other legitimate way, may on the one hand be constitutive of a permanent and stable capital source of income, or on the other hand it may exist as a free and unstable property element disposable according to the judgment of the proper ecclesiastical administrator subject to the pertinent norms of law.[15] Assets which are established as a permanent source of income, or ecclesiastical patrimony, are designated by the expression "stable or fixed capital"; assets which are not permanently established in this fashion are termed "free or unstable

---

[14] See pp. 114, below, where this question is discussed in its relation to a particular canon.

[15] "Quaesita Varia," n. 18, *Periodica,* XI (1922), (157).

capital." [16] An important canonical aspect of this distinction lies in the fact that property elements which constitute ecclesiastical patrimony, or stable capital, are subject to the canonical regulations for alienation, while transactions involving free or unstable capital are not subject to these regulations.[17]

While the very nature of stable capital as a productive source of income indicates the necessity for investment if the property is not in some productive form, it is important to note that not every investment establishes capital as stable and fixed. The impression that all investment has this effect has unfortunately been given by some authors. For example, "stable, fixed, or *invested* capital" has been distinguished from "unstable, free, or *uninvested* capital." [18] Similarly, some authors have declared that certain rules established for investment apply only to acts of permanent, and not of temporary, investment.[19] These views are suggestive of the implication that investment in its canonical sense consists exclusively of permanent investment, and of the further implication that, if a true investment is made, it is permanent for the very reason that it is an investment.

Yet an act of investment of itself does not constitute property as stable capital or patrimony. Money by its nature as a medium of exchange is regarded primarily as a *res fungibilis,* the purpose of which is that it be expended.[20] But, money may also be placed in productive uses through investment. When it is placed in in-

[16] Doheny, *Practical Problems in Church Finance* (Milwaukee: Bruce, 1941), pp. 43, 45; Heston, *The Alienation of Church Property in the United States,* p. 72.

[17] Heston, *The Alienation of Church Property in the United States,* pp. 72-73.

[18] Doheny, *Practical Problems in Church Finance,* pp. 43, 45.

[19] Vromant, *De Bonis Ecclesiae Temporalibus,* p. 246, nota 2; Prümmer, *Manuale Iuris Canonici,* p. 260; Schaefer, *De Religiosis,* n. 197; Nebreda, "Quaestiones Selectae de Iure Administrativo Ecclesiastico," *CpR,* VII (1926), 265.

[20] Vermeersch-Creusen, *Epitome Iuris Canonici* (3 vols., Mechlinae-Romae: Dessain; Vol. II, 6. ed., 1940), II, n. 852; Bouscaren-Ellis, *Canon Law,* p. 772; De Meester, *Juris Canonici et Juris Canonico-Civilis Compendium* (4 vols., Brugis, 1921-1928; Vol. III, 1926), III, 403 (hereafter cited *Compendium*).

vestment or designated for this, it may then become part of the stable capital.[21] However, investment of itself does not establish property as stable capital. That it become stable capital in the proper canonical sense, it must be incorporated as such by action of competent ecclesiastical authority.[22]

It does not seem necessary that this requisite action of a competent superior must consist in an express declaration that the property involved is henceforth an element of stable capital. Bouscaren-Ellis declare that the very act of placing funds in permanent investment under the authorization of a superior constitutes these assets as stable capital.[23] On the other hand, if there was no intention of permanently establishing funds as a capital source of income, the funds or the productive assets purchased with them would remain as free capital.[24] Thus stable capital is not constituted by investment alone, but is constituted by a proper incorporation of the property into the permanent capital resources of the ecclesiastical body. Not all invested capital is stable capital or, in other words, permanent patrimony.

As the status of funds which constitute stable capital restricts superiors from expending them in non-productive uses, this status should not be easily presumed. Rather, it is something which must be established in view of the obligations and restrictions attaching to stable capital.[25] Funds which are placed in reserve for the

[21] Doheny, *Practical Problems in Church Finance,* pp. 43, 45; Vromant, *De Bonis Ecclesiae Temporalibus,* n. 281, (3).

[22] Bouscaren-Ellis, *Canon Law,* pp. 772-773; Doheny, *Practical Problems in Church Finance,* p. 43; Heston, *The Alienation of Church Property in the United States,* p. 73. For a similar pre-Code understanding of this point see Ferraris, *Bibliotheca Canonica, Iuridica, Moralis, Theologica necnon Ascetica, Polemica, Rubricistica, Historica* (ed. novissima, 9 vols., Romae, 1885-1899), I, 177 ("Alienatio," art. 1, n. 6) (henceforth cited *Bibliotheca*).

[23] *Canon Law,* p. 773.

[24] See "Quaesita Varia," n. 18, *Periodica,* XI (1922), (158) (d), wherein it is declared that funds placed for a time in a bank or converted into securities until an opportunity is had for their expenditure do not thereby lose the quality of goods which can be freely disposed of. This is an indication that these funds are not an element of stable capital, although invested, and are not subject to the rules for alienation.

[25] Heston, *The Alienation of Church Property in the United States,* p. 75.

express purpose of purchasing immovable property, or of building a church or some other ecclesiastical structure, share the inalienable quality of the object for which they are intended,[26] and thus are considered stable assets.

As has already been intimated, the chief significance of the distinction between stable and free capital lies in the applicability or non-applicability of the laws respecting alienation of ecclesiastical property. Assets incorporated in the stable capital of an ecclesiastical organization cannot be alienated without the solemnities prescribed by law for alienation, while those assets which constitute free or unstable capital are not subject to these strictures.[27] Cash funds which constitute a stable capital element are therefore subject to the restrictions placed upon alienation.[28] The consumption of these funds through expenditure is thus considered as a form of restricted alienation. Expenditure of them in making an investment is not such an act of alienation, although the law may establish certain controls. An act of investment is not an act of alienation.[29]

The significance of the distinction between stable capital and free capital for the present study lies in its investment implications. The very nature of stable capital indicates a necessity for its productive disposition. Thus real estate holdings must be leased or

[26] Reiffenstuel, lib. III, tit. XIII, n. 15; Ojetti, *Synopsis Rerum Moralium et Juris Pontificii* (3. ed., 4 vols., Romae, 1909-1914), I, 175 (n. 300); Ferraris, *Bibliotheca*, I, 177.

[27] "Quaesita Varia," n. 18, *Periodica*, XI (1922), (157); Heston, *The Alienation of Church Property in the United States*, pp. 72-73; Cleary, *Canonical Limitations on the Alienation of Church Property*, The Catholic University of America Canon Law Studies, n. 100 (Washington, D. C.: The Catholic University of America, 1936), p. 9.

[28] This is implied by those authors who point out that consumption of money through expenditure is not considered as restricted alienation as long as the money is not part of the stable capital. See Vromant, *De Bonis Ecclesiae Temporalibus*, n. 281; Coronata, *Institutiones*, II, n. 1070; Vermeersch-Creusen, *Epitome*, II, n. 851. A pre-Code understanding of certain cash funds as subject to the law regarding alienation is given by Schmalzgrueber, lib. III, tit. XIII, n. 51.

[29] Coronata, *Institutiones*, I, n. 559. See also Vermeersch-Creusen, *Epitome*, II, n. 852.

used in some productive way if they are to be a sources of income. When funds have the complexion of stable capital, these funds must be invested if they are to have a productive quality. Furthermore, once funds are permanently invested with proper authorization, they are then considered as stable capital and are subject to all the provisions of law regarding alienation,[30] with the exception of the faculty granted by canon 1539, § 2, regarding the conversion of securities.

Among the legal requirements to which stable capital is subject is the provision that the proceeds of its alienation must be reinvested.[31] Thus the funds constituting such proceeds retain the quality of stable capital which characterized the alienated property. In requiring the reinvestment of these funds, the law is merely ordering that their quality as income-producing capital be given effect. Accordingly, there are important investment considerations to be examined regarding funds derived from alienation. Investment considerations will be involved regarding other funds pertaining to stable capital by reason of their designation or establishment as a permanent source of income to be kept intact. Among such funds are to be numbered endowments of benefices and of other non-collegiate moral persons, endowments of pious foundations, dowry funds, annuity funds, and certain kinds of trust funds. Various canonical provisions respecting the investment of different funds pertaining to stable capital will be seen under their proper headings.

Obviously investment is not limited to stable capital. Free capital elements may be temporarily invested to the advantage of the moral person pending some other permanent disposition. Pertinent canonical provisions variously subject investment of this type to certain controls and safeguards.

ARTICLE 3. INVESTMENT AND SPECULATION

The law of the Church on property administration is characterized by the protection it offers for the Church's property tenure. The

---

[30] Bouscaren-Ellis, *Canon Law*, p. 773.

[31] Canon 1531, § 3.

canons subjecting alienation to certain formalities [32] are the most obvious examples of this safeguard. There is also need for protection of funds that are to be placed in investment. Despite safeguards, legal or otherwise, there is a certain amount of risk inherent in any economic venture, and when the Church makes dispositions of its funds in income-producing activities, it is placing these funds in an area where some degree of risk is inevitable. The degrees of risk to be encountered range widely between the two obvious extremes. It is the purpose of canonical legislation to minimize these risks as well as to help in the acquisition of a satisfactory income.

In the productive use of funds one of two ways of obtaining income may be intended. There is the motive of obtaining periodic income deriving from the productive property purchased, as, e.g., a bond; on the other hand, there is the motive of purchasing something, e.g., real estate or stock in commercial enterprises, with the hope, not of periodic income, but of profit from change in capital value. In the first motive there is hope of regular income; in the second, hope of profit upon resale. This difference is the primary difference between investment and speculation.[33]

This difference is indicated in Kirschman's definition of investment given above. It may be compared with a definition of speculation which is said to consist "in buying and selling commodities, or securities, or other property in the hope of a profit from anticipated changes in value." [34] The element of risk will also be related to the motive, the risk generally being greater where there is possibility of greater increase in value. Thus speculation as distinguished from investment is characterized by the hope of profit rather than of regular periodic income and, generally, by the assuming of greater risk.[35]

[32] Canons 1530-1534.

[33] Kirschman, *Principles of Investment,* p. 13.

[34] Emery, *Speculation on Stock and Produce Exchanges of the United States,* Columbia University Studies in History, Economics, and Public Law, n. 7, (New York, 1896), p. 96.

[35] Kirschman, *Principles of Investment,* pp. 13-14.

The Holy See itself has indicated that speculation is a form of business activity prohibited in clerical and religious affairs, and in ruling speculative practices out it used the Italian equivalent of the phrase "playing the market." [36] "Playing the market" is a reference to the purchase of securities with the purpose of deriving, not a regular income from the investment over a long period, but rather a hoped for quick increase in capital value and the consequent profit upon resale.

Such speculative practices may also work in the other direction through the activity of "short-selling." "Short-selling" consists in the selling of securities that one does not own but rather borrows in the hope that the price of the security will fall after the sale of the borrowed security. It is planned to buy similar securities after the price has fallen. These securities will replace those that were borrowed for the short sale. The difference between the selling price of the short-sale and the new price involved in the purchase of securities to replace the borrowed ones represents the profit in the transaction. Minor items of expense must be deducted from this. For example, a speculator thinks the price of XYZ stock will drop in the immediate future from its present price of 100. He borrows one hundred shares from a broker and sells them at the present price of 100, realizing $10,000. The price falls ten points. He now purchases 100 shares at 90 at a cost to himself of $9,000 and returns the shares he has borrowed. He has made a profit of $1,000 on the transaction, less brokerage charges and the charge to borrow the securities.[37]

Short-selling is completely speculative and as such cannot be employed in ecclesiastical property administration.

The Code, by canons 142 and 592, prohibits to clerics and religious certain business activities, among which speculative prac-

---

[36] S. C. S. Off., resp. 15 apr. 1885—*Codicis Iuris Canonici Fontes* (9 vols., Romae, 1923-1939), n. 1091 (hereafter cited *Fontes*) ; S. C. de Prop. Fide, 7 iul. 1893—*Fontes*, n. 4925.

[37] If any dividends should be declared upon the borrowed stock before its loan is repaid, the borrower is also liable for payment to the loaner in an amount equal to the dividends.

tices are included.[38] Authors generally indicate that ecclesiastical investments are not to be characterized by speculative qualities.[39] Canon 1539, § 2, also indicates that in the transactions therein indicated there is to be no appearance of trade or business. Speculation as essentially a form of trading for profit would thus be prohibited.

Speculation is illicit in ecclesiastical administration for another reason, viz., the excessive degree of risk generally present.[40] The purpose for which stable church assets are to be employed is the production of income periodically in support of ecclesiastical activities, and not the reaping of an increase in the value of the assets themselves through risk-bearing speculative activities. In a very similar manner and for evidently the same reasons, American civil law has forbidden speculation with funds whose principal must be kept intact for trust purposes.[41]

Thus speculation as opposed to investment is not to be practiced in ecclesiastical property administration. It must, however, be noted that all investment operations regardless of their nature are attended with some degree of risk.[42] It is true that investment as opposed to speculation regards primarily the element of stability in the value of the productive property or the claim to income, and anticipation of regularity in the income produced. However, the factor of promise of increase in the value of the capital is a legitimate and indeed an important consideration for any investor, other things being equal.[43] Thus it is not possible to draw a definite line between investments that have speculative qualities and those that

[38] Beste, *Introductio in Codicem* (3. ed., Collegeville, Minnesota: St. John's Abbey Press, 1946), pp. 357-358; Bouscaren-Ellis, *Canon Law*, p. 119.

[39] Vermeersch-Creusen, *Epitome* II, n. 861; Berutti, *Institutiones Iuris Canonici* (6 vols., Taurini-Romae, Marietti; Vol. IV, 1940) IV, n. 189 (hereafter cited *Institutiones*); Vromant, *De Bonis Ecclesiae Temporalibus*, n. 332.

[40] Beste, *Introductio in Codicem*, pp. 357-358.

[41] *Dickinson's Appeal*, 152 Mass. 185, 25 N. E. 99, 9 L.R.A. 279 (1890); *English* v. *McIntyre*, 29 App. Div. 439, 51 N. Y. S. 697; *Davis* v. *Davis Trust Co.*, 106 W. Va. 228, 145 S. E. 588. See also p. 164 of the present study.

[42] Kirschman, *Principles of Investment*, p. 15.

[43] Taylor, *Investments* (New York: Alexander Hamilton Institute, 1929), pp. 48-49.

do not.[44] It is the degree of speculative characteristics and their prominence as a motive to the investor which determine whether or not a particular investment is essentially speculative.

The canonical prohibition of speculation in ecclesiastical administration is not to be understood as requiring that all risk and all speculative consideration be eliminated. Such complete elimination is not consonant with the nature of modern investment. As has been seen, true investment may well be made with proper consideration given to many investment factors, including the prospective increase or decrease in the value of an investment. This is a true investment factor which must be considered. As long as the investment is made with the prospect of and primarily for periodic income, and not for purposes of profit after resale, the investment cannot be termed speculative. Thus, if securities were purchased apart from the intention of selling them at a later date for speculative considerations, it would not be illicit for an ecclesiastical administrator to sell these, even at a higher price, and to purchase other securities.[45] Efficient administration and investment management would suggest, and not inhibit, the liquidation of an investment that has become poor when a better investment can advantageously be made.

The present study is a study of canonical legislation affecting investment practices. It does not pertain to its scope to examine all the considerations, of which the prospect of an increase in capital value is one, which are involved in the selection of investments in the face of the varying requirements which exist in different situations. This is a task requiring highly professional ability, and

[44] Taylor, *Investments,* p. 6.

[45] See Berutti, *Institutiones,* IV, n. 189; Vermeersch, *Periodica,* II (1911), 74. Battandier (1850-1921), when treating of the investment of dowries of women religious appeared to go too far in his expression of permitted investment practices: "Une supérieure générale devra donc soigneusement s'abstenir de pareilles opérations, comme aussi de jouer à la Bourse. Elle pourra bien acheter les titres quand ils sont bas, les revendre quand ils sont hauts, c'est evident, mais ce n'est pas ce qu'on appelle jouer à la Bourse." *Guide Canonique pour les Constitutions des Instituts à Voeux Simples* (6. ed., Paris, Libraire Lecoffre, 1923), p. 147.

is performed in modern economic affairs most efficiently by special business organizations equipped for it. However, when the canon law indicates certain factors which will have an impact upon investment policies and practices, it is the purpose of this study to present these factors in their canonical status for whatever use must be made of them by those who are charged with investment decisions. It is with this purpose that the canonical complexion upon speculative practices in ecclesiastical affairs has been presented.[46]

ARTICLE 4. INVESTMENT AS AN ACT OF EXTRAORDINARY
ADMINISTRATION

The activities necessary in the administration of ecclesiastical property fall within two categories, viz., those termed ordinary administration and those termed extraordinary administration. Acts of ordinary administration include whatever is necessary for the preservation of church property, the activities necessary to collect income from such property, payments for current needs, the making of ordinary repairs, and the ordinary deposit of money in a bank account.[47]

Acts of extraordinary administration include acts which do not occur periodically, and are at the same time of more than ordinary importance.[48] Among such acts have been listed the acceptance or rejection of inheritances, legacies, donations, or foundations; the purchase, sale, or exchange of immovable property; pawning or mortgaging of immovable property, burdening it with servitudes, leasing it for a period greater than three years; the sale, exchange, or pawn of objects of art, of historical documents and of other movable property of importance, or otherwise diverting the same from their purposes; the borrowing of large sums of money, the making of compromises (settlements) and other onerous contracts; the building, destroying, or rebuilding of ecclesiastical

[46] It is to be noted that the prohibition of speculative practices in ecclesiastical temporal affairs is not to be understood as a judgment regarding the intrinsic moral status of speculation.

[47] Bouscaren-Ellis, *Canon Law,* p. 770.

[48] Berutti, *Institutiones,* IV, n. 173.

structures, or the making of extraordinary repairs on them; the establishment of cemeteries; the establishment or suppression of parochial institutions; the imposition of a *per capita* tax; the raising of funds by a special drive; the donation to others of church property.[49]

The significance of the distinction between acts of ordinary administration and those of extraordinary administration lies in the fact that for the validity of the latter a special permission of the local ordinary is required, and it should be in writing,[50] although this last feature does not affect the consideration of validity.[51]

Immediately there arises the question whether investment is an act of ordinary or of extraordinary administration. Investment is an action that does not occur at regular intervals, in the way, for example, that payments from investments are periodically collected, or after the fashion that current expenses are met. Furthermore, an investment decision appears to be of more than ordinary importance. The safety itself of the invested money depends upon the placing of investments according to wise and prudent judgments. The realization of income both in its amount and in its regularity also depends upon a skillful selection of investments. Accordingly, both on the score of a lack of regularity and also on the score of the more than ordinary importance attached to investment decisions, investment appears to be an act of extraordinary administration.

As has been seen from the Instruction of the Sacred Congregation for the Propagation of the Faith of July 21, 1856, cited above, the purchase of immovable property is considered an act of extraordinary administration. Hence an investment made in real estate would evidently be such an act of extraordinary administration. The purchase of securities has similarly been declared an act of extraordinary administration.[52] Thus purchases of immovable property or of securities have been regarded as acts of

---

[49] S. C. de Prop. Fide, instr. 21 iul. 1856—*Fontes*, n. 4841.

[50] Canon 1527, § 1.

[51] Vermeersch-Creusen, *Epitome*, II, n. 848.

[52] Berutti, *Institutiones*, IV, n. 173.

extraordinary administration. But investment in its proper canonical sense consists exclusively in such conversions of property. Deposit at interest, although productive of income, does not of itself constitute investment in its proper sense.

Various provisions in the Code specifically require the consent or consultation of superiors or of others before an investment is made.[53] It is true that a reason for these formalities as prescribed by law may lie in the special nature of the funds or assets involved. It is also undoubtedly true, however, that the act of investment itself is considered of sufficient importance to require these formalities, and therefore is evidently outside the limits of ordinary administration.[54]

It seems to be quite clear that, if an investment is made definitively of funds pertaining to stable capital as opposed to a merely temporary or administratively convenient disposition of funds, this investment is to be considered as an act of extraordinary administration, as is also any change of investment and the conversion of securities mentioned in canon 1539, § 2.[55] However, there has been advanced the view that investment is an act of ordinary administration when made for a short period of time with money which does not pertain to stable capital.[56]

This declaration appears reasonable only if by such a short-term investment a bank deposit at interest is understood. But such a deposit does not constitute investment in its proper sense. If investment in its proper signification is made in immovable property or in securities even for a short length of time and with funds that are not destined to constitute permanent patrimony, the various factors of safety, productivity, ready marketability, etc., must be considered as in a permanent investment. Hence even such a temporary investment as opposed to deposit appears to transcend the limits of ordinary administration.[57]

These considerations appear to warrant the conclusion that

---

[53] Canons 533; 549; 1415, § 2; 1523, 4°; 1539, § 2 and 1547.
[54] See Bouscaren-Ellis, *Canon Law,* p. 772, for an approach to this position.
[55] Vromant, *De Bonis Ecclesiae Temporalibus,* n. 173.
[56] Vromant, *loc. cit.*
[57] See Larraona, "Commentarium Codicis," *CpR,* XII (1931), 438.

an act of investment in its proper sense constitutes an act of extraordinary administration whether the investment is permanent or
merely for a limited period of time. Declaration by particular law [58]
seems to be based on such a view. The act itself has the extraordinary quality which the particular legislation merely recognizes
and declares. It is not as though the legislative act made an act
of ordinary administration into an act of extraordinary administration.

If the amount of money involved in an investment were relatively small, the investment of it would not seem to have a sufficient importance, in view of the small amount, to be considered
as an extraordinary activity. This opinion has been enunciated regarding canon 533. It has been declared that investments of small
amounts are exempted from the requirement for the local ordinary's
consent demanded by that canon.[59]

Deposit at interest is itself an act of ordinary administration.[60]
However, if stable capital is to be invested, the decision to place it in
deposit at interest in preference to converting it into more lucrative
forms of investment appears to be a decision of importance and
magnitude which transcends the limits of ordinary administration.[61]

[58] E.g., *Synodus Altunensis Prima* (privately published, 1923), n. 128;
Acta et Decreta Synodi Dioecesanae Toletanae Primae (privately published,
1941), n. 333.

[59] Creusen-Garesché-Ellis, *Religious Men and Women in the Code* (4th
English edition, Milwaukee: Bruce, 1940), p. 119.

[60] Berutti, *Institutiones,* IV, n. 173.

[61] A more detailed study regarding the status of deposit at interest in its
relationship to investment is made on pp. 112-115.

CHAPTER III

ALIENATION AND INVESTMENT

ARTICLE 1. REINVESTMENT OF PROCEEDS FROM ALIENATION: CANON 1531, § 3

THE laws regarding the alienation of church property serve as a protection to the income-producing stable capital of an ecclesiastical body.[1] When a just cause is present, and other specified formalities have been carried out, alienation can be effected. The law in permitting alienation does not, however, permit stable capital to be placed in non-productive use or to be expended. Canon 1531, § 3, requires that the money received from the alienation of church property be cautiously, safely, and usefully invested for the advantage of the Church.[2] Thus in permitting alienation, the law is merely permitting a change in the mode in which stable capital is disposed in productive use.

Among the sources of the present law of canon 1531, § 3, indicated in the footnote of the Code to this canon, is a decision of the Sacred Congregation of the Council,[3] in which permission was given for the alienation of a house belonging to a chaplaincy. It was ordered that the price received was to be reinvested in stable property or in a *census* purchased from pious places or from the Papal States according to the judgment of the bishop.

---

[1] Alienation has been extensively discussed in two Catholic University of America Canon Law Studies: n. 100, Cleary, *Canonical Limitations on the Alienation of Church Property,* Washington, D. C.: The Catholic University of America, 1936, and n. 132, Heston, *The Alienation of Church Property in the United States,* Washington, D. C.: The Catholic University of America Press, 1941.

[2] Canon 1531, § 3. Pecunia ex alienatione percepta caute, tuto et utiliter in commodum Ecclesiae collocetur.

[3] S. C. C., *Maceraten.,* 14 mart., 4 apr. 1789—*Thesaurus Resolutionum Sacrae Congregationis Concilii* (167 vols., Urbini et Romae: 1718-1908), LVIII, 44-46, 49 (hereafter cited *Thesaurus*); *Fontes,* n. 3864. Cf. also S. C. C., *Asculana,* 7 et 21 iun. 1788—*Thesaurus,* LVII, 98-100, 102; *Fontes,* n. 3859.

Another decision of the same Congregation emphasized that the permitted alienation was not to interrupt the regular receipt of income.[4]   A house whose revenue constituted part of the income of a canonry could be alienated, but the price received was to be reinvested in unencumbered, safe, and fruitful property which paid a return of at least four per cent annually. That there be no interruption of income to the canonry, the Congregation provided that, if payment in full was not made immediately, the purchaser had to pay annually four per cent of the unpaid amount to compensate for the delay in investing caused by the failure to make immediate payment in full.   As a further protection against the loss of the productive property concerned, it was also provided that the title of ownership was to be reserved to the canonry until the full price had been paid.

In missionary lands the persecution of the Church by hostile inhabitants often made the Church's tenure of its productive property unsafe.   Accordingly, a decree of the Sacred Congregation for the Propagation of the Faith [5] declared that the Vicar Apostolic could sell or exchange ecclesiastical properties when, under the stress of persecution, there was no other way available for saving these for the Church.   The Congregation declared that such alienation was permitted only for the purpose of more safely investing the price received.

The emphasis on reinvestment appeared also in a letter of the same Congregation to a Vicar Apostolic in China.   In this letter it was declared that the Vicar had acted correctly in alienating certain property, but that there yet remained the consequent obligation of reinvesting the price received.[6]

The same Congregation for the Propagation of the Faith in an Instruction to the Patriarch of Armenia established certain condi-

---

[4] S. C. C., *Nullius Sublacen.*, 16 iun., 7 iul., 18 aug., 1781, 11 maii, 13 iul. 1782—*Thesaurus*, L, 103-105, 110, 136; LI, 71, 97; *Fontes* nn. 3816, 3819, 3822, 3824.

[5] S. C. de Prop. Fide, 27 aug. 1832—*Collectanea Sacrae Congregationis de Propaganda Fide* (2 vols., Romae, 1907), I, n. 827 (hereafter cited *Collectanea*); *Fontes*, n. 4753.

[6] S. C. de Prop. Fide, litt. (ad Vic. Ap. Cochinchin.), 31 mart. 1836— *Collectanea*, I, 484, nota 1; *Fontes*, n. 4763.

tions which were to be fulfilled when any ecclesiastical possessions were sold.[7] Among other things it was demanded that the alienation occur only when there was present some definite necessity for it, or when some utility was to be derived from it. It was also required that the price received was to be paid in full at the time of entering the contract, and was to be reinvested in an honest, safe, and licit investment. If it was not immediately invested, the sum, in order that its dissipation be prevented, was to be deposited in a public bank or in the custody of a suitable person. A written receipt was to be kept by the patriarch or by the bishop in whose jurisdiction was the church to which the alienated goods had belonged. When an exchange of properties was authorized and an additional money sum accrued to the church to balance any inequality of value between the properties exchanged, this additional sum had to be invested and was subject to the same regulation regarding deposit as described above.

The present law of canon 1531, § 3, requires the reinvestment of the proceeds from alienation. The consumption of the principal of this money by expenditure requires the permission of the Holy See or a dispensation from the law.[8] This rule is undoubtedly applicable in those cases wherein, under the terms of canon 1532, the Holy See is the legitimate superior for permitting the alienation. But does the same principle which requires a dispensation from the Holy See apply when a local ordinary can permit the alienation? When the local ordinary is the superior concerned according to canon 1532, it seems that he can merely permit a certain alienation without dispensing from the actual provisions of the law, especially of canon 1531, § 3. Canon 1532, § 2, empowers the local ordinary to permit certain acts of alienation; it does not empower him to dispense from the law regarding alienation of which canon 1531, § 3, is an integral part. The power to dispense appears to follow the general principles of dispensation as embodied in canon

---

[7] S. C. de Prop. Fide, instr. (ad Patriarch. Armen.), 30 iul. 1867—*Collectanea*, II, n. 1310; *Fontes*, n. 4867.

[8] S. C. C., *Dioecesis N.* (Donariorum Votivorum), 12 iul. 1919—*AAS*, XI, 418. See also Pistocchi, *De Bonis Ecclesiae Temporalibus* (Taurini: Marietti, 1932), p. 401.

81, and although a superior may permit certain alienations, a dispensation from the Holy See is required if the proceeds of alienation are to be expended and not reinvested.[9]

A response given on February 17, 1920, by Cardinal Gasparri, President of the Commission for the Interpretation of the Code, to the Bishop of Orense declared that the money received from the alienation of ecclesiastical property did not all have to be invested, but expenditure could be made of it, as long as the rulings of canons 1530, § 1, 2°, and 1477, § 2, were properly observed.[10] This response has been understood to indicate that the ordinary cannot only permit alienations to the extent determined in canon 1532 but can also permit the money received from such alienations to be expended in non-productive uses.[11]

In view of the clarity of the law itself, and in the light of the explicit interpretation furnished in the 1919 response of the Sacred Congregation of the Council,[12] as also because of the vagueness of Gasparri's response if it was meant as an interpretation of law, and the fact that this same response of Gasparri is not to be found in the contemporary volumes of the *Acta Apostolicae Sedis,* it seems necessary to conclude that the local ordinary can merely permit alienation in certain cases under canon 1532, § 2, and cannot under the general law normally dispense from the requirement enacted in canon 1531, § 3.

[9] Vromant, *De Bonis Ecclesiae Temporalibus,* n. 285; Cleary, *Canonical Limitations on the Alienation of Church Property,* p. 70.

[10] This response is quoted in Beste, *Introductio in Codicem,* pp. 763-764, and he cites as its source Ferreres, *Theologia Moralis,* editio 21[12?], I, n. 1089, nota. The response does not appear in the *Acta Apostolicae Sedis* for the years 1920, 1921, and 1922. (Beste's citation of Ferreres indicates the 21st edition. Various considerations seem to indicate that the 12th edition was here intended.)

[11] Beste, *Introductio in Codicem,* pp. 763-764. Bouscaren-Ellis similarly seem to understand that the superior permitting the alienation can also permit the non-productive expenditure of the proceeds: ". . . such money *may not be spent,* unless permission to spend it was obtained at the time permission was granted to alienate the property." (*Canon Law,* p. 776.)

[12] This response did not merely indicate what could be done in the submitted case, which could well have been the import of Gasparri's response, but it expressly declared an interpretation of canon 1531, § 3.

According to the canon the investment of the proceeds from alienation is to be made cautiously, safely, and usefully. Authors point out that the reference of the canon to caution has particular reference with regard to the civil law, viz., that under the civil law no opportunity be given for usurpation by theft or by confiscation.[13] To achieve this end, dioceses in some places maintain depositories in which securities are to be kept, and the administration of these securities is in the hands of the diocesan council of administration.[14]

The safety of the principal and the production of income are factors to be considered in all investments. The prohibition of speculation, which has been seen [15] as applying to all ecclesiastical investments, is obviously applicable in the reinvestment of proceeds from alienation. This prohibition exists because of the threat to the safety of the principal which marks speculative practices, and because of the fact that speculation is a form of *negotiatio* that is prohibited to clerics and religious by canons 142 and 592. Regarding the quality of usefulness on the part of the investment, simple deposit for safe-keeping is to be distinguished from investment for income.

If payment is made for alienated property at intervals over a period of time, the money should normally be invested as it is received. The responsible administrator should not wait until the entire sum is paid before he makes the investment.[16]

Persons making reinvestment:

Under the terms of canon 1531, § 3, the proceeds received from the alienation of church property must be reinvested. The canon does not indicate what person is to make the selection of the investment, nor does it indicate any special formalities surrounding

[13] Vermeersch-Creusen, *Epitome,* II, n. 853; Beste, *Introductio in Codicem,* p. 763; Pistocchi, *De Bonis Ecclesiae Temporalibus,* p. 402.

[14] Such a plan was provided for in a circular letter of June 20, 1929, of the Sacred Congregation of the Council to the Italian bishops respecting the administration of beneficial and other ecclesiastical property according to the norms of canon law and the concordat with Italy.—*AAS,* XXI (1929), 390. See also Berutti, *Institutiones,* IV, 519, nota 2, and Pistocchi, *De Bonis Ecclesiae Temporalibus,* p. 402.

[15] See pp. 30-35.

[16] Pistocchi, *De Bonis Ecclesiae Temporalibus,* p. 402.

the investment in these circumstances.[17]   In order to assure the
superior of the wisdom of a contemplated act of alienation, the petitioner of the requisite authorization may well indicate how the
proceeds are to be reinvested.[18]   In such an event the grant of permission, if made, may itself indicate that the reinvestment is to be
made as described in the petition.[19]   In other cases the superior may
himself determine the mode of reinvestment.[20]   The original donor of
the property may also provide norms regarding the reinvestment of
the proceeds in the event that alienation becomes advisable.[21]

If no determination of the reinvestment or of a person to select
the new investment is made by the superior who authorizes an
act of alienation,[22] or by the original donor, then it appears that
the general norms of administration will apply.   Accordingly the
administrator of the property would be charged with the duty of
making the investment.[23]   Since the investment in this case is an
act of extraordinary administration, the administrator must first

---

[17] It is to be noted that investment is an act of administration which does
not have the character of alienation.   See Coronata, *Institutiones*, I, 693.

[18] As was done in S. C. C., in *Anconitana* (Venditionis) 21 apr. 1792—
Thesaurus, LXI, 63-66; *Fontes,* n. 3876.

[19] E.g., see Formula G. 45ª used by the Sacred Congregation for Religious
in granting such requests.   This formula declares that *pretium ipsum impenda-
tur ad effectum de quo in precibus.*   This formula is quoted in Heston, *The
Alienation of Church Property in the United States,* p. 98, footnote 16.

[20] E.g., the Sacred Congregation of the Council declared that the choice
of the investment was to be made by the bishop in *Nullius Sublacen.,* 16 iun.,
7 iul., 18 aug. 1781; 11 maii, 13 iul. 1782—*Thesaurus*, L, 103-105, 110, 136;
LI, 71, 97; *Fontes,* nn. 3816, 3819, 3822, 3824.

[21] S. C. C., *Asculana,* 21 iun. 1788, ad II—*Thesaurus*, LVII, 102; *Fontes,*
n. 3859; see also canon 1514.

[22] If the Holy See is the superior concerned, it would seem rare that some
such indication would not be given.   See Heston, *The Alienation of Church
Property in the United States,* pp. 97-98.

[23] Coronata, *Institutiones*, II, n. 1071.   Coronata declares that this is so
because such an investment is an act of ordinary administration.   The present
writer views such an investment as an act of extraordinary administration.
(See pp. 35-38.)   Under the terms of canon 1527, § 1, it is nevertheless to be
performed by the administrator, but with the requisite permission.

obtain the written permission of the local ordinary for the validity of his act.[24]

The view appears intrinsically solid that the reinvestment normally is to be made by the administrator subject to the consent of the local ordinary as an act of extraordinary administration under the terms of canon 1527, § 1. This view also appears to be a satisfactory reconciliation of the divergent views of those authors who make some approach to the question. The writer in *Periodica* declares that, by reason of an analogy in the law, canon 1547 provides a norm, and accordingly the investment is to be made by the local ordinary, who must first consult with the diocesan council of administration and other interested parties.[25] The analogy, however, between canon 1547 and canon 1531, § 3, does not appear sufficient to warrant the application of the former of these in every case of reinvestment after alienation. Canon 1547 deals with the investment of endowments pertaining to pious foundations. Canon 1531, § 3, deals with the investment of the proceeds from the alienation of many more kinds of ecclesiastical property. The analogy of law seems to warrant the application of canon 1547 only when the alienation of endowment property which belongs to a pious foundation and its reinvestment is involved, but not for every type of alienation and reinvestment ruled by canon 1531, § 3.

Pistocchi's treatment of this matter is more suggestive than it is analytical.[26] Without giving a general principle for determining who is to make the reinvestment, he suggests that canons 533, §§ 1 and 2, 1539, § 2, and 1547 have a bearing in this matter. This apparently suggests that, when the subject matter of these canons is involved, their norms regarding investment are to be applied also to the reinvestment of the proceeds deriving from an act of alienation.

A satisfactory working principle seems to be had in the conclusion that the reinvestment of the proceeds of the alienation is according to the general principles of administration to be made by the administrator, but with the consent of the local ordinary, for

---

[24] Canon 1527, § 1.
[25] "Quaesita Varia, V, *Periodica*, XI (1922), (24).
[26] *De Bonis Ecclesiae Temporalibus*, p. 401.

the act is an act of extraordinary administration as ruled by canon 1527, § 1.[27]

However, when other laws more specifically indicate who is to make the investment, or establish more specific norms regarding the necessary consent or consultation of others in the investment act,[28] these laws regarding investment seem by analogy to apply also to reinvestment after alienation. When the property involved in alienation is property whose original investment is governed by these other canons, then it seems that these other canons should provide norms for reinvestment after alienation.

For example, canon 1547 declares that the investment of endowment pertaining to a pious foundation is to be made by the local ordinary upon consultation with interested parties and with the diocesan council of administration. Hence, in the event of the alienation of these invested properties, it seems that the reinvestment is to be made in the same manner as the initial investment. Again, by way of example, canon 1415, § 2, provides that a cash endowment of a benefice is to be invested by the local ordinary upon consultation with the diocesan council of administration. The consideration of analogy seems to demand that, if the invested endowment were alienated, its reinvestment should be made under the same rules as the initial investment.

The use of analogy would also pertain to those cases in which some administrator rather than the local ordinary was charged with the selection of the investment. For example, the investment of the dowries of women religious is to be made by the superioress with the consultation of her chapter and the consent of the local ordinary.[29] This same principle appears applicable to the case of reinvestment after alienation on the grounds of analogy even aside from the explicit provision of canon 533, § 2.

In addition to the application of such analogous laws of the Code, other directives affecting investment practices and policies could be established by local ordinaries acting in virtue of their

---

[27] See Berutti, *Institutiones*, IV, n. 184. Berutti reaches this conclusion, but on the basis of slightly different reasoning.

[28] See canons 533; 549; 1415, § 2; 1547.

[29] Canon 549 and canon 533, § 1, 1° and 2°.

legislative power in ecclesiastical temporal matters,[30] and in virtue
of their general supervisory authority over church property in their
jurisdiction.[31]

ARTICLE 2. CONVERSION OF SECURITIES UNDER CANON 1539, § 2

Closely related to alienation is the question of the conversion of
securities. The sale of securities, even for the purpose of repurchase of other securities, is of itself an act having the nature of
alienation. For a sale is an act of alienation.[32] The conversion of
securities was accordingly regarded in a 1906 response of the
Sacred Congregation of the Council as subject to the formalities
required for alienation, including the necessity of the permission of
the Holy See.[33]

This response declared that the same permission of the Holy
See as required for alienation had also to be obtained for the alienation of "bearer securities"; that this permission was needed for the
conversion of these securities into other securities or property, except in a case of urgent necessity in which there was danger in
delay and time was insufficient for recourse to the Holy See. In this
event the consent of the ordinary was required and the conversion
was to be made into very safe securities.

In its response the Congregation gave the reasoning that lay
behind this decision which subjected the conversion of "bearer securities" to the formalities for alienation. This reasoning emphasized
the consideration of "bearer securities" as property subject to alienation formalities, and the consideration of conversion (*permutatio*)
as an act of alienation.

Vermeersch (1858-1936), in annotating this response of the
Congregation,[34] noted that the response marked a departure from

[30] Canon 335, § 1.

[31] Canon 1519, §§ 1, 2. See Comyns, *Papal and Episcopal Administration of Church Property,* The Catholic University of America Canon Law Studies, n. 147 (Washington, D. C.: The Catholic University of America Press,
1942), pp. 102-107.

[32] Coronata, *Institutiones,* II, n. 1070.

[33] S. C. C., *Romana et aliarum,* 17 febr. 1906—*Fontes,* n. 4328; *Thesaurus,*
CLXV, 236-239.

[34] *Periodica,* II (1911), 74-75.

the general practice of administrators, who had accommodated themselves to modern business usages in the matter of sale and conversion of such securities. Furthermore, the "urgent necessity" excusing from the rule existed when the securities could not be held without loss, and also when a profit could be realized from the conversion. This situation existed practically all the time in business affairs dealing with securities. The taking of such a profit, he was quick to point out, could not be regarded as a business practice prohibited to clerics. For when the original purchase was made without the intention of resale, but merely the occasion for profit, as it frequently develops from change in value, was utilized, not even the appearance of *negotiatio* existed.

In his opinion the response applied only to transactions involving units which pertained to ecclesiastical stable capital. The response did not apply to transactions which involved free capital elements even if these were invested.

A more detailed discussion of the response was given by Vermeersch following his annotations.[35] In this treatment several reasons were alleged in the form of a letter of inquiry against the efficacy of the Congregation's response. Among these arguments were noted the great frequency with which the Holy See would have to be approached in these matters in the normal administration of such securities; the great number of such securities in ecclesiastical patrimonies; the great number of these securities in existence, and the consequent inability of even a skilled financier to have a valid judgment regarding most of them; the inability of even a skilled financier at Rome to consider the matter and return a judgment in the short time intervening before some new change in values completely altered the opportunity for a favorable conversion of securities; and the lack of the necessary secrecy and privacy resulting from introducing these matters among subordinate officials at Rome.

In responding to the letter of inquiry which had proposed these arguments, Vermeersch noted that many of these reasons were of some weight. He indicated that the response of the Congregation introduced a new strictness in these matters. He went on to note a rather pertinent distinction between "alienation" and "conversion"

---

[35] "Quaesita Varia," III, *Periodica,* II (1911), 89-93.

(*commutare*). The first was marked by a loss of a source of income; the second was had when money was invested in a different manner. Conversions (*permutationes*), indeed, constituted alienation, but, he insisted, this was not to be understood in too absolute a sense. For then an exchange of silver money for gold or for bank notes would constitute alienation. Rather, the *genus* of the holdings and the manner in which they were held were to be considered. With reference to "bearer securities" the substantial element seemed to be that the sum be preserved intact and that it produce income.

Vermeersch concluded that, in view of these considerations and in view of the fact that the response of the Sacred Congregation was given as a particular response, it did not seem that one should be disquieted who formed his conscience according to the principles alleged in the letter of inquiry, and accordingly directed his action in the converting of securities without seeking the Holy See's permission.

The discussion of this response by Vermeersch has been reviewed herein because of the rather weighty considerations it presented against the policy formulated by the Sacred Congregation in its decision. It is quite evident that great weight is to be accorded to these considerations in view of the fact that canon 1539, § 2, marks a rejection of the policy expressed by the 1906 response of the Sacred Congregation of the Council.

Canon 1539, § 2, permits the conversion of certain securities into other securities without the necessity of obtaining the Holy See's permission regardless of the amount involved.[36] Under canon 1532, § 1, the permission of the Holy See is required for alienations over a stated amount. Hence canon 1539, § 2, is an indication that the conversion of securities does not fall under the rule requiring the Holy See's consent.

The law of the Code in this matter recognizes the frequent necessity of converting securities. In making investments, it is the office of an administrator to obtain the best rate of income commensurate with the necessary safety of the investment and other factors of

---

[36] Canon 1539, § 2: Administratores possunt *titulos ad latorem,* quos vocant, commutare in alios titulos magis aut saltem aeque tutos ac frugiferos, exclusa qualibet commercii vel negotiationis specie, ac de consensu Ordinarii, dioecesani Consilii administrationis aliorumque quorum intersit.

suitability. A reasonably safe investment at the time of its purchase may furnish income at a rate that is good by comparison with the current investment market. At a later date its rate of return may still be the same, but by comparison it may not be as satisfactory as the rate of other available investments. Efficient administration will dictate the liquidation of the first investment and the purchase of a more productive security.

Again, in a time of falling values the most prudent investment for a certain fund might be in the purchase of government securities. Some years later, when in prosperous times greater stability characterizes all investment values, good administration may dictate the sale of the government securities and the repurchase of high grade and secure obligations of private corporations.

Such changes in the investment portfolio of an organization may be required, as in the examples given, to obtain an income reasonably satisfactory in comparison with rates available on the current investment market. Such changes may also be required to protect the organization from loss. If investments are going to be efficiently used, they must be carefully watched, so that proper action may avert loss or secure the benefits offered in changing investment conditions. In the modern economic world this care of investments is a highly technical matter requiring professional knowledge and analysis. Various formulas and techniques have been devised according to which the investment operations of individuals and institutions are managed.[37] Efficient management is the work of professionals. Accordingly, Vermeersch-Creusen declare that there can licitly be given, with the consent of those indicated in canon 1539, § 2, a general mandate which empowers a skilled lay person to make the proper conversion of the securities as long as all appearance of the *negotiatio* prohibited to clerics is similarly prohibited to this lay person acting for the ecclesiastical body.[38] A bank or trust company, so it appears, could also be engaged for that purpose.

[37] The investment plans used in managing the investment of endowments belonging to Kenyon College, Oberlin College, Sheffield Scientific School, Vassar College, and Yale University are examined in Tomlinson, *Successful Investing Formulas* (New York: Barron's, 1947), Part III.

[38] Vermeersch-Creusen, *Epitome*, II, n. 861.

Canon 1539, § 2, declares that in the operations permitted under its terms there is to be no appearance of trade or business. Speculative practices, as they are indicated by the phrase "playing the market," [39] are thereby prohibited [40] as being a form of business forbidden to clerics and religious. Profit resulting from taking advantage of the changes in capital value that frequently occur may legitimately be taken by clerics and religious and their agents, as long as the primary purpose of the original purchase was not that of realizing profit from a resale after anticipated changes in value.[41] Lay persons or professional organizations managing ecclesiastical investments are bound by the same restrictions that apply to clerics or religious themselves.[42] Hence such individuals or organizations cannot be permitted to engage ecclesiastical property in speculative operations.

The canon speaks of "bearer securities" (*titulos ad latorem*). Securities may be either inscribed with the name of the owner or they may not be registered in any name. Ownership of the latter of these—negotiable securities payable to bearer—is generally indicated by possession. Registration of securities insures the payment of interest and principal to the proper owner. Unregistered or "bearer" securities are payable to the bearer. The income from registered securities is normally sent directly to the registered owner. Income from unregistered securities is paid to the bearer, as for example when the bearer presents the interest coupons attached to a coupon bond. Registered coupon bonds are registered as to principal, so that the ownership of the bond is vested in the person whose name appears on the bond or on the books of the issuing company, but the interest coupons are payable to the bearer and may be presented by anyone for payment on the date due.[43]

The canon speaks only of a conversion of negotiable securities payable to the bearer (*tituli ad latorem*) into other securities. Registered securities, however, require the same general kind of admin-

[39] See p. 32.
[40] Berutti, *Institutiones,* IV, n. 189; Vermeersch-Creusen, *Epitome,* II, n. 861; Bouscaren-Ellis, *Canon Law,* p. 783.
[41] *Periodica,* II (1911), 74; Berutti, *Institutiones,* IV, n. 189.
[42] Canons 142 and 592. N. B. In canon 142: ". . . per se vel per alios. . . ."
[43] Taylor, *Investments,* p. 72.

istration as bearer securities. They are equally subject to changes in value, and their conversion into other securities will be required in normal administration just as much as the conversion of bearer securities. Accordingly, it has been expressly concluded that registered securities payable to definite individuals or moral persons can be converted into other securities, under the same terms of canon 1539, § 2, similarly as bearer securities.[44] There do not seem to be any cogent reasons to dispute this conclusion.

The canon uses the word *commutare* to designate the operation permitted with the securities. This has been understood to signify exchange in the strict sense of an innominate contract, wherein one thing is given for another without the use of money as a medium.[45] In view of the reference that has been made to the modification which canon 1539, § 2, effected over the 1906 response of the Sacred Congregation of the Council in order to facilitate administration, it seems that there is permitted also such a conversion of securities to other securities which implies an intermediate sale of the original securities and the repurchase of others. Administration would hardly be facilitated if only exchanges in the strict sense, namely of one group of securities for another, were permitted. Permission to barter in securities would not be much of an advantage. Accordingly it seems reasonable to conclude that the conversion of securities which is permitted refers to the permission to sell and to repurchase other securities.[46]

The conversion of the securities, according to the canon, must be done with the consent of the ordinary, of the diocesan council of administration, and of other interested parties. By analogy, the

---

[44] Vromant, *De Bonis Ecclesiae Temporalibus,* p. 347, nota 1; Bouscaren-Ellis, *Canon Law,* pp. 783-784. See also Cappello, *Summa Iuris Canonici* (3 vols., Vol. II, 4. ed., Romae: apud Aedes Universitatis Gregorianae, 1945), II, 585.

[45] Coronata, *Institutiones,* II, n. 1076.

[46] Bouscaren-Ellis (*Canon Law,* p. 783) declare that a sale may intervene in the conversion. Woywod (*A Practical Commentary on the Code of Canon Law,* 10th printing, 2 vols., New York: Wagner, 1946), II, 189-190) seems to imply that barter is the prime meaning of what is allowed, but that a sale is allowable when barter is not possible.

prescriptions of canon 1532, § 2, are applicable to the bishop's need of acting with the council of administration with the result that he must hear the council when the value of the securities involved is less than 1,000 lire,[47] and must have its consent when the value is above that figure.[48] Although canon 1539, § 2, speaks of the *consent* of the council, the ruling of canon 1532, § 2, seems necessarily applicable in this matter, for if it were not applied, the ordinary would be under an obligation to have the consent of the council for the conversion of securities valued at less than 1,000 lire, while under the general rules for alienation he could completely alienate securities of a similar value without the consent of the council. Furthermore, the chief effect of canon 1539, § 2, seems to be a liberation from the necessity of obtaining the Holy See's permission for the actions involved. Hence the canon is chiefly concerned with transactions involving amounts normally requiring, under canon 1532, § 2, that the Holy See be approached. It therefore seems that, when the smaller amounts of § 2 are involved, the less strict provisions of that paragraph can be regarded as applicable.

The conversion of securities under canon 1539, § 2, is subject to the requirement that the securities obtained in the transaction be of equal or greater safety and productivity. Those making the repurchase of securities must observe this basic principle. Since exact mathematical proportions cannot be established between safety and productivity, a certain measure of discretion is enjoyed by those who are charged with the selection of the proper investments.

Since canon 1539, § 2, has the effect of freeing conversions of securities from the alienation formality of approaching the Holy See, it is evident that only securities pertaining to stable capital are comprehended by the canon. The conversion of securities pertaining to free capital does not come under the restrictions of this canon.[49]

---

[47] $200 according to the former gold content of the dollar; $338 according to present gold content. See p. 55, footnote 54, for the principles involved in this computation.

[48] Berutti, *Institutiones*, IV, n. 189; Coronata, *Institutiones*, II, n. 1076.

[49] Heston, *The Alienation of Church Property in the United States*, p. 179.

Article 3. Annuity Contracts

An encouragement to make dispositions of property in favor of ecclesiastical moral persons is found in the practice of paying annuities to one who confers such property. A gift of money may be made to the ecclesiastical moral person conditioned upon or in return for the agreement to pay an annuity to the donor or someone designated by him. The system of soliciting or accepting funds under the annuity agreement entails the burdening of the ecclesiastical moral person with economic obligations. It has been pointed out in a letter by the Apostolic Delegate in the United States that, since the acceptance of these obligations renders the financial condition of the moral person less secure, the making of the annuity contract is to be regarded as an act of alienation.[50] Because of its character as an act of alienation, the acceptance of annuity obligations is here treated in connection with alienation.

An annuity in its broadest sense signifies a fixed sum, granted or bequeathed, payable periodically, but not necessarily annually; an annuity contract is "a term applied to an obligation to pay to the annuitant a certain sum of money at stated times during life or a specified number of years in consideration for a gross sum paid for such obligation." [51]

The ecclesiastical person accepting the sum of money must invest it if income is to be realized out of which the annuity may be paid. The annuity is not equivalent to income. In a trust fund the income must be paid over according to the terms of the trust. This applies to all the income, less, of course, permitted deductions for certain kinds of expenses. If there is no income, there will normally be no such payment. An annuity need not have any element of a trust.[52] The annuity payment does not necessarily consist of the entire income. It consists of a fixed charge to be paid

---

[50] Letter of November 13, 1936, addressed to all religious superiors in the United States by the Apostolic Delegate in the United States—Bouscaren, *Canon Law Digest* (2 vols., Milwaukee: Bruce, 1934-1943), II, 161-165, at 162.

[51] *Corpus Juris Secundum* (58 vols., Brooklyn, N. Y.: American Law Book Co., 1936-1948), (hereafter cited *C. J. S.*), Vol. III, Annuities, § 1.

[52] 3 *C. J. S.*, Annuities, § 1.

out of income.   If the income is insufficient to meet the annuity,
the charge may be met by payment from the principal.[53]   Upon the
death of the annuitant in the case of a life contract, or upon the
expiration of the time for which annuities were to be paid in other
contracts, the obligation of the annuity payment ceases.   The fund
is then no longer subject to the charge and can freely be used by
the ecclesiastical moral person.

The letter of the Apostolic Delegate, addressed to all the religious superiors in the United States, establishes provisions regarding the making of annuity agreements.   If a religious community desires to obtain money by means of annuity agreements,
there will be no need for recourse to the Holy See for a sum up to
$10,000.[54]   An indult of the Holy See is required when the aggre-
gate of sums committed or to be committed to fulfilling annuity
obligations amounts to more than $10,000.

The contents of the petition to the Holy See required in virtue
of canon 534 are specified by the letter of the Apostolic Delegate.
There must be presented definite and clear statements regarding
the reason for assuming the obligation, the nature of the obligation,
the name of the party with whom the obligation is to be contracted,
the proposed terms of meeting the obligation, and a complete state-
ment of the economic condition of the petitioner.   In the petition
there must also be indicated in detail the amounts involved in the
annuity obligation, the plan of investing the funds and interest arrangement, and plans for meeting the annuity payments.

It is furthermore declared in the Apostolic Delegate's letter that

---

[53] 3 *C. J. S.,* Annuities, § 1 and § 5.

[54] The letter states the figure $6,000, but declares that this figure is to be
understood, in connection with the terms of the Code, as the equivalent of
30,000 lire or francs, and in reference to currency evaluation in terms of gold.
At the time of the Code's promulgation 30,000 lire had a dollar equivalent in
terms of gold of $6,000.   In view of the devaluation of the dollar in 1934 to
59.06 per cent of the previous gold value, the former gold dollar has the value
of 1.69 of the present dollar.   Hence $6,000 under the former standard equals
$10,140 under the present standard, or, in round numbers, $10,000.

there is to be no expenditure whatever of all or any part of the capital annuity fund. This fund must remain intact as long as the annuitant is living.

Although the indicated letter was directed to religious superiors, it is evident that the principle which regards the acceptance of annuity obligations as an act of alienation is applicable to others than religious. As a contract by which the condition of the Church may suffer, the acceptance of annuity obligations is subject to the formalities required for alienation as they are contained in canons 1530-1532.[55]

Under canon 1529 the civil law of the local territory regarding contracts and payments enjoys canonical effect as long as there is no opposition between the civil law and divine law or canon law. This canonical force extends to the effects induced under civil law by contracts.[56] Among such effects of an annuity contract are to be enumerated restrictions established frequently by the civil law over the manner of administering and especially of investing such funds. The statutes and judicial constructions of each state will have to be examined for a notion of these legal restrictions.

By way of example, it may be noted that New York state requires that all assets for payment of annuities by duly organized non-stock corporations or associations conducted without profit, and engaged solely in *bona fide* charitable, religious, missionary, educational, or philanthropic activities, shall be segregated as separate and distinct funds independent of all other funds. These assets shall not be applied for the payment of the debts and obligations of the corporation or association or for any purpose other than the annuity benefits specified. Investment of these assets can be made only in certain described types of securities.[57]

Such civil law requirements, rather than being opposed to the prescriptions of canon law, stand as effective means toward achiev-

[55] Canon 1533.

[56] Vromant, *De Bonis Ecclesiae Temporalibus*, n. 275; Beste, *Introductio in Codicem*, p. 761.

[57] *McKinney's Consolidated Laws of New York, Annotated*, (68 Books, Brooklyn, N. Y.: Edward Thompson Co.), Book 27, *Insurance Law*, 1940, with 1946 Cumulative Annual Pocket Part), § 45.

ing the ends desired under canon law.   The contemporary and local civil prescriptions can furnish legislation of greater specificity than would be possible in these matters in general ecclesiastical law.   It appears that an ecclesiastical administrator in making investment of annuity capital funds is canonically obliged in virtue of canon 1529 to follow the pertinent civil law prescriptions.

CHAPTER IV

INVESTMENT OF SURPLUS FUNDS

INVESTMENT duties devolve upon the administrators of church property with regard to any stable capital elements with whose administration they may be charged. If stable capital elements are to be productive of income, they must be placed in productive uses. Land or buildings must be rented; money must be invested. Property elements belonging to free capital may similarly be invested as a means of using these elements for the advantage of the juristic person holding them. Surplus funds of a church body evidently have the quality of free capital. The mere fact that they are surplus funds does not constitute them as stable capital. For this effect property must be incorporated into the stable capital by the action of competent authority.[1] It is the investment of surplus funds that is ordered by canon 1523, 4°. Herein it is provided that surplus funds are not to remain idle if they can usefully be invested, but are to be invested with the consent of the local ordinary to the advantage of the moral person concerned.[2]

The canon notes that such funds are to be invested if this can usefully be done. Obviously a very small surplus could not be advantageously invested. Hence the obligation of the canon applies only when a notable amount of surplus funds is on hand.[3] It is to be noted that smaller sums than can conveniently be invested in securities can be "invested," in a wide but not canonical understanding of the term,[4] by being placed in bank deposit at interest. It seems that an administrator is thus to dispose of a surplus which cannot be invested according to the strict and proper

[1] Doheny, *Practical Problems in Church Finance*, p. 43.

[2] Canon 1523.—Administratores . . . debent:

4°. Pecuniam ecclesiae, quae de expensis supersit et utiliter collocari potest, de consensu Ordinarii, in emolumentum ipsius ecclesiae occupare.

[3] Cance, *Le Code de Droit Canonique* (7. ed., 3 vols., Paris: Libraire Lecoffre, 1946), III, 255.

[4] See p. 26.

sense of the term. Leaving surplus funds which are not needed in current administration in checking accounts or in safe deposit boxes in such a way that they do not yield interest seems to be contrary to the spirit and purpose of the law, and to point to a defect in administration when safe and insured bank deposit at interest could be made of these funds.

The use of the word *church* in this number of the canon is evidently to be understood as signifying any moral person in the Church in accordance with the rule established by canon 1498. The investment of surplus funds according to canon 1523, 4°, is to be made for the benefit of the moral person which owns the funds.

According to the canon, the consent of the local ordinary is required for the investment. There arises the question whether this requirement for consent affects the validity or merely the permissiveness of the act of investment. Canon 1527, § 1, provides the answer to this question. Since investment constitutes an act of extraordinary administration,[5] the local ordinary's consent is required for the validity of the act; when an act of investment is to be considered as an act of ordinary administration because of the small amount involved, his consent will be required merely for the permissiveness of the act.

Although the surplus funds mentioned in canon 1523, 4°, are themselves free capital elements, it may be asked whether their investment under the terms of the canon establishes them as elements of stable capital subject to the restrictions placed upon alienation. The best answer to this question seems to be that the canon does not order incorporation of the funds into stable capital; it orders their investment. This investment may be made in either of two ways: either *precaria ratione*, so that the property is kept as free capital, expendable at the wish of the administrator acting under the law, or *stabili ratione*, with the result that it becomes stable capital subject to alienation restrictions.[6] This view ap-

[5] See pp. 35-38.

[6] Vermeersch-Creusen, *Epitome*, II, n. 845; De Meester, *Compendium*, III, 397, nota 4; Cocchi, *Commentarium in Codicem Iuris Canonici ad Usum Scholarum* (8 vols., Vol. III, 4. ed., 1937; Vol. IV, 3. ed., 1932; Vol. VI, 3. ed.,

pears quite acceptable in the light of the wording of the canon itself, which refers simply to investment without any distinction between investment which creates stable capital subject to alienation restrictions and investment in which the property is held as freely expendable. The canon is not restricted to one of these types of investment to the exclusion of the other.

There does not appear to be any reason for alleging that every investment made under this canon will automatically constitute the property as stable capital subject to alienation restrictions. The mere investment of funds, even if done with the consent of authority, does not imply that thereby the property becomes constituted as stable capital. Since the status of stable capital imposes restrictions upon administrators, it is evident that this status must be clearly delineated, and that it cannot be rightfully presumed on the basis of investment alone.[7] Property is incorporated into stable capital, or permanent patrimony, by designation as such by competent authority.[8]

There are, however, those who regard this canon as ordering incorporation of the designated funds into stable capital, and who therefore regard every investment made under this canon as constitutive of stable capital subject to all the restrictions applicable to alienation.[9] This conclusion does not seem warranted in the light of what has been considered. Quite acceptable seems the view of those authors who declare, as has been indicated, that investment under this canon may be constitutive either of stable capital

1933, Taurinorum Augustae: Marietti), VI, n. 204 (hereafter cited *Commentarium*). The terms *precaria ratio* and *stabilis ratio* are used by these authors apparently to indicate the intention behind the act of investing and not to indicate different ways of investing. This is particularly evident in Cocchi's treatment, wherein he indicates that an *investment in securities* may be made in either of these two ways. The meanings signified by these two phrases evidently refer to the intention of making a non-permanent investment and of making a permanent and stable investment respectively.

[7] See pp. 27-28, and also Doheny, *Practical Problems in Church Finance,* p. 43.

[8] Doheny, *loc. cit.*

[9] Cance, *Le Code de Droit Canonique,* III, 255; Couly, "Administration des Biens D'Eglise," *Dictionnaire de Droit Canonique* (Fasc. 1-22, Paris: Letouzey et Ané, 1924-1948), Fasc. I, col. 208.

elements subject to alienation restrictions or of freely expendable elements. If the investment is to establish stable capital, designation of this must be made by competent authority. The canon is not to be construed as itself ordering that surplus funds must be established as permanent patrimony.

Vromant offers a further variation by his interpretation of this canon. He declares that the investment may be made in either one of the two ways that have been discussed, but that the requirement for the local ordinary's consent is applicable only when stable capital is constituted, and not when the invested elements retain the quality of free expendability.[10] It is difficult to reconcile this view with the wording of the canon, which without qualification declares that investment is to be made of the surplus funds with the consent of the local ordinary.

There seems to be a point common to both the view of Vromant and the view of Couly and Cance. It lies in the suggestion by each of these views that the only true investment in the sense of this canon is an investment which is constitutive of stable capital subject to alienation restrictions. Vromant implies this when he declares that the consent of the local ordinary is required for only this type of investment. Couly and Cance imply this when they declare that any investment made under the terms of this canon is constitutive of stable capital subject to alienation restrictions. Behind this notion common to both views there seems to be a confusion regarding the relationship between investment and stable capital.

The radical difference between stable and unstable, or free, capital has been declared by Doheny to lie in the fact that stable capital consists of invested funds while unstable or free capital consists of money in its character as a medium of exchange and as something that is perishable.[11] The same author goes on to point out that, canonically considered, money becomes stable capital subject to alienation restrictions only when it has become designated as such by the proper ecclesiastical authority.[12] *Stable capital* thus appears

---

[10] Vromant, *De Bonis Ecclesiae Temporalibus*, n. 204.

[11] Doheny, *Practical Problems in Church Finance*, pp. 42-43.

[12] Doheny, *Practical Problems in Church Finance*, p. 43.

to be used as a term in two different senses. In a financial sense
it is used as indicating a productive source of income; in a canonical
sense it is used as indicating a stable and permanent source of income which is subject to alienation restrictions. Not all stable
capital in the first sense is subject to alienation restrictions.[13]

The proper distinction seems to underlie the view of those
authors [14] according to whom investment *precaria ratione* establishes a source of income, i.e. *capitale,* but in as much as it is effected
precaria ratione it is not *capitale* subject to the rules on alienation.
Although it is not subject to alienation restrictions, it is nevertheless invested capital in financial parlance. Not all invested capital
is necessarily stable capital subject to the restrictions attendant upon
alienation. It is necessary to distinguish between the invested
capital that serves as a capital source of income but nevertheless
remains freely expendable and the invested capital that is established as permanent patrimony which is canonically subject to the
rules for alienation. The law regarding alienation does not apply
to all elements of invested capital. But the law which requires the
consent of the local ordinary for an act of investment does seem
to apply to all investments made under canon 1523, 4°, whether
or not that invested property is subject to the restrictions attendant
upon alienation.

The provisions of law in requiring the consent of superiors give
the advantage of another individual's judgment in an investment
decision made complex by the necessity of considering many factors: safety, rate of income, liquidity, suitable duration, etc. These
factors must be considered in every investment whether or not
the purchased capital elements are subject to alienation restrictions. They must be considered whether the investment is made
permanently or merely for some limited period of time. The question of the requirement of consent for the investment acts does not
seem to be materially changed by the presence or absence of alienation restrictions or by the duration of time for which the investment is to be held. If the investment is to be a temporary
disposition of funds, there is even an increased significance attach-

[13] See pp. 26-30.
[14] See p. 59, note 6.

ing to one of the factors to be considered. This regards the ability to liquidate the investment at the proper desired time if it is indeed to be freely expendable at the wish of the administrator. Accordingly, the added significance of this factor seems to be an additional reason for requiring the consent of another party rather than excusing from it.

This same reasoning is applicable in the case of canon 533. Authors have pointed out in regard to this canon that the local ordinary's consent is necessary only when a definitive and stable investment is made, and not when the investment is to be a merely temporary one. As will be pointed out in the later treatment of this question,[15] reasons for requiring consent seem to be equally present for the making of temporary investments as well as for the making of permanent investments. There may be this one difference, namely, that in the temporary investment the commitment to a rate of return is quantitatively not as important as it is when a long term investment is involved. This difference appears quite negligible, especially in view of the always important factor of safety which must be seriously considered in every investment.

It is difficult to understand the reasonableness of the view of those authors who declare that consent is not needed for the making of a temporary investment, unless by a temporary investment they refer exclusively to a temporary bank deposit at interest. There is some indication that this is what they have in mind when they speak of *collocatio precaria*.[16]

In summary regarding canon 1523, 4°, it appears that the investment to be made of surplus funds under this canon establishes invested capital in the sense that it is an invested source of income. The invested property may be held as permanent ecclesiastical patrimony, or it may be held as a freely expendable element. There is no compulsion from this canon to incorporate the surplus funds or the investments made of them into the permanent patrimony of the ecclesiastical unit. The property will constitute permanent patrimony only when it has been designated as

---

[15] See pp. 114-115, for a discussion of this problem as it applies to canon 533.

[16] See p. 114.

such by the competent ecclesiastical authority.[17] As permanent patrimony it will be subject to the rules regarding alienation. On the other hand, if the property is held as a freely expendable element of church property, it will not be subject to alienation formalities. In both cases the investment must be made with the consent of the local ordinary.

[17] Doheny, *Practical Problems in Church Finance*, p. 43; Heston, *The Alienation of Church Property in the United States*, p. 73.

CHAPTER V

INVESTMENT OF ENDOWMENTS PERTAINING TO BENEFICES AND OTHER NON-COLLEGIATE ECCLESIASTICAL INSTITUTES

I. Benefices

ARTICLE 1. NATURE OF A BENEFICE AND ITS ENDOWMENT

A BENEFICE is a juridical entity constituted or erected in perpetuity by competent ecclesiastical authority, and it consists of a sacred office and the right of receiving the income of its endowment, which income is attached to the office.[1] The juridical entity of a benefice is in the nature of a non-collegiate juridical person.[2] The definition of a benefice as contained in canon 1409 indicates that essential to the notion of a benefice is the right of receiving income from an endowment.

This endowment in the past almost always consisted of real estate, comprising a house and land, but gradually it came to admit of a wider understanding, so that even before the Code it could consist of various rights to money, as, for example, those contained in state bonds or in tithes.[3] The law of the Code establishes even wider bounds within which the notion of an endowment is verified. The endowment of a benefice may consist of property whose ownership rests with the juridical entity itself, of certain and due payments of some family or moral person, of certain and voluntary offerings of the faithful which pertain to the incumbent of the benefice, of stole fees within the legitimate limits, or of choral distributions or a certain part thereof.[4]

It is only in the first of these various classes of endowments,

[1] Canon 1409.—Beneficium ecclesiasticum est ens iuridicum a competente ecclesiastica auctoritate in perpetuum constitutum seu erectum, constans officio sacro et iure percipiendi reditus ex dote officio adnexos.

[2] Canon 99; Coronata, *Institutiones*, II, n. 972.

[3] Vermeersch-Creusen, *Epitome*, II, n. 743.

[4] Canon 1410.

namely, when property is owned by the benefice, that the benefice itself is dealing with productive property. Such property may be immovable, such as agricultural land, woods, or houses, or it may be movable, such as securities.[5] It is obvious from the phrase in canon 1409, *iure percipiendi reditus ex dote,* that this property must be productive, or must be made productive if it is to serve as an endowment. The making of an investment as a means to making such property productive becomes necessary when that property consists of money or is, for any reason, converted into money.

This money must be reinvested if the essential character of the endowment is to be maintained. Property which is not of itself productive must be converted into something productive. This has been accomplished generally, through the medium of sale and reinvestment of the proceeds. It may also happen that endowment property which is already productive may be sold and the proceeds reinvested in another manner for reasons of necessity or utility.[6] Thus investment is necessary when the endowment consists of cash, or when it consists of property that is converted into cash.

ARTICLE 2. INVESTMENT PROVISIONS

A. Endowment in Cash

When the property of the endowment consists of cash, it is the duty of the ordinary to see to it, having first consulted the diocesan council of administration, that the money be invested as soon as possible in safe and productive real estate or securities.[7] Canon 1415, § 2, does not expressly declare that the ordinary himself is to select the investment. However, this seems to be implied by the fact that he must consult with the diocesan council of administration. Since canon 1520, § 3, orders the local ordinary to consult this council in administrative acts of greater importance, it does

---

[5] De Meester, *Compendium,* III, p. 323, n. 1394.

[6] S. C. de Prop. Fide, decr., 27 aug., 1832—*Fontes,* n. 4753; S. C. de Prop. Fide, instr. (ad Patriarch. Armen.), 30 iul. 1867—*Fontes,* n. 4867.

[7] Canon 1415.—§ 2. Si dos in numerata pecunia constituatur, Ordinarius, audito dioecesano administrationis Consilio de quo in can. 1520, curare debet ut quamprimum collocetur in tutis et frugiferis fundis vel nominibus.

not seem unreasonable to conclude that the act for which canon
1415, § 2, orders this consultation is an administrative act rather
than one of mere supervisory vigilance. Thus the selection of the
investment rests with the ordinary.[8]

The requirement that the ordinary consult the council of administration cannot be urged as affecting the validity of his action.
This follows from the *dubium iuris* as to whether canon 105, 1°,
affects validity when a superior is required to consult with others.[9]

According to canon 1415, § 2, the investment is to be made in
safe and productive real estate or securities. The safety of the
principal is of utmost importance in view of the perpetuity of a
benefice as indicated in canon 1409, and the necessity of perpetual
income for the benefice as evidenced in canon 1415, § 1. That the
investment must be productive is obvious in view of the necessary
income which it must supply for the benefice.

In designating the types of investments that may be made,
canon 1415, § 2, uses the terms *fundi* and *nomina. Fundi* in its strict
signification indicates productive agricultural lands; in a wider
signification, it includes other productive stable property, money,
and property that can be converted into money.[10] By the very nature of the situation, *fundi* as used in this canon can signify only
productive property, for it is here used to signify property which
is to be purchased as an investment. Hence its wider signification
of any property that can be converted into money cannot be accepted here. The conclusion that its significance here must be
limited to that of productive property appears quite evident. The
view that an even stricter sense of the term is to be here understood, viz., as signifying productive *real estate,* seems to be warranted by its appearance in this canon in opposition to *nomina.*[11]

---

[8] Vermeersch-Creusen, *Epitome,* II, n. 748; Pistocchi, *De Re Beneficiali*
(Taurini: Marietti, 1928), p. 51; Ayrinhac, *Administrative Legislation in the
New Code of Canon Law* (London, New York, Toronto: Longmans, Green &
Co., 1930), p. 317.

[9] See Bouscaren-Ellis, *Canon Law,* p. 91, for a discussion of this *dubium.*

[10] Coronata, *Institutiones,* I, 694, nota 5; Vermeersch-Creusen, *Epitome,* I,
n. 656; Beste, *Introductio in Codicem,* p. 357.

[11] See Coronata, *Institutiones,* II, 367, where the context indicates such
an understanding of the term. Woywod (*A Practical Commentary on the*

That Pistocchi understands it as referring to real estate seems implied in his declaration that this property may be of either an urban or a rural nature.[12]

The *nomina* of the canon are inclusive of "bearer securities," participations in the public debt, and stocks or bonds of trustworthy corporations.[13]

B. *Endowment Property Alienated—Reinvestment of Proceeds*

Investment also becomes an administrative necessity when the property of an endowment is alienated and the proceeds must be reinvested. In order that the essential character of a perpetual endowment be not lost, reinvestment of the proceeds is necessary. As productive property belonging to an ecclesiastical juridical person, the endowment property of a benefice is ecclesiastical property,[14] and hence is subject to the limitations surrounding the alienation of church property.[15] One of these requirements regarding alienation is that the proceeds of alienation be invested.[16]

The person charged with the duty of making the reinvestment of the proceeds from alienation is discussed in the treatment of canon 1531, § 3.[17] Therein it was seen that if the superior who authorized the alienation did not indicate what reinvestment was to be made [18] or did not designate a person to select the new investment, this duty devolved as an act of extraordinary administration upon the administrator, who needed to have the local ordinary's written

Code of Canon Law, II, 138) and Ayrinhac (*Administrative Legislation*, p. 317) expressly declare that real estate is here signified.

[12] *De Re Beneficiali*, p. 51.

[13] Ferreres, *Institutiones Canonicae* (ed. altera, 2 vols., Barcinone, 1920), II, n. 411; See also Beste, *Introductio in Codicem*, p. 716. Ellis indicates that the term *nomen* signifies a promissory note, a bill of exchange or a security.— "Canonical Terms Dealing with *Bona Temporalia*," *Theological Studies*, I (1940), 171-174.

[14] Canon 1497, § 1; Pistocchi, *De Re Beneficiali*, p. 17.

[15] Heston, *The Alienation of Church Property in the United States*, p. 79.

[16] Canon 1531, § 3.

[17] See pp. 43-47.

[18] It is to be noted that an indication of what reinvestment is to be made will generally be given. See p. 44.

consent for the investment under the terms of canon 1527, § 1. These considerations evidently apply when the endowment of a benefice has been alienated and the proceeds are to be reinvested.

The incumbent in the benefice is the administrator of the goods pertaining to the benefice.[19] Hence, when the superior in allowing the alienation does not provide regarding the reinvestment, the reinvestment as an act of extraordinary administration is to be made by the beneficiary with the written consent of the local ordinary, unless the local ordinary wishes to select the investment himself. The analogy existing between the making of an original investment and the making of a reinvestment after alienation was seen to warrant the application of a law governing the original investment to the situation involving a reinvestment after alienation.[20] Canon 1415, § 2, governs the original investment made of a cash endowment pertaining to a benefice. It appears that the local ordinary should invoke the ruling of canon 1415, § 2, in the analogous situation wherein cash proceeds are to be reinvested after the alienation of the endowment property, and thus take the administrative selection of the investment to himself.

The conversion of securities, even when a sale of old securities and the repurchase of other securities is involved, does not necessitate the permission of the Holy See, regardless of the amount involved. Such conversion of securities is ruled by canon 1539, § 2.[21]

C. *Endowment Investments Reaching Maturity*

In a third instance the making of an investment may become an administrative necessity. This situation arises where the endowment of the benefice consists of any kind of certificates of indebtedness, e.g., bonds or notes, or other securities, which had attained their maturity dates and were paid off. The stable capital represented by such securities is then liquidated, although not by any act of alienation. Thus, if its quality as stable capital is to be preserved, the money received must be reinvested.

[19] Canon 1476.—§ 1. Beneficiarius bona ad suum beneficium pertinentia, ut beneficii curator, administrare debet, ad normam iuris.

[20] See p. 46.

[21] See pp. 47 ff.

This situation seems very similar to the exchange of securities as ruled by canon 1539, § 2. This canon, seen in greater detail elsewhere,[22] permits the exchange of securities without requiring the permission of the Holy See, regardless of the amount involved. The administrator can convert these securities, even through sale and repurchase of other securities, with the consent of the ordinary, the diocesan council of administration, and other interested parties.[23] A parallel situation seems to be had when, instead of a sale, the maturity date of securities is attained and the securities are redeemed. Thus, in such an event, it seems that the administrator must reinvest the money under the terms of canon 1539, § 2, with the consent of the ordinary, of the diocesan council of administration, and other interested parties.

II. Ecclesiastical Institutes for Religious or Charitable Purposes

The administration of the property of a non-collegiate moral person established for religious or charitable purposes is in the hands of the rector of the institute, who has the same rights and obligations as administrators of other ecclesiastical property, and whose administration must be guided by the charter of the institute.[24] The local ordinary can establish such institutes as juridical persons; he is not to approve of them unless, among other requirements, an adequate endowment to achieve the foundation's purpose has been established.[25] If the institute is already in existence as a lay institute, the actual sufficiency of the endowment may be demonstrated from past performance; if the creation of an institute is contemplated, it will be necessary to foresee the sufficiency of endowment.[26]

It is obvious that if the endowment consists of cash or becomes converted into cash, the duties of investment arise if the endowment is to be made productive. In fulfilling these duties, the ad-

---

[22] See pp. 47 ff.

[23] Bouscaren-Ellis, *Canon Law*, p. 783; Woywod, *A Practical Commentary on the Code of Canon Law*, II, 189-190.

[24] Canon 1489, § 3.

[25] Canon 1489, §§ 1, 2.

[26] Vermeersch-Creusen, *Epitome*, II, n. 813.

ministrator must be guided by the general administrative law of the Church and by the charter of the institute, as has been noted, and by any directives established by the local ordinary, acting as the supervisor of ecclesiastical property under canons 335 and 1519. The charter of the institute should provide norms respecting, among other matters, the endowment, the administration and the government of the institute, and the use of the income.[27]

Thus the charter could evidently establish principles of investment policy should more specific directives be desired than those which are furnished by the general law of the Church. Care must be taken in the establishing of such norms that a proper area of discretion be permitted to the administrator, so that the administration of the endowment can readily be adapted to the changing situations encountered in the business world. Certain restrictions established by charter may be advantageous under circumstances prevailing at the time of the charter's creation. At a later date such restrictions could possibly become detrimental to efficient administration in view of changed conditions.

Since investment is an act of extraordinary administration,[28] for the investment of the endowment the consent of the local ordinary will be required.[29]

The supervisory authority of the local ordinary, as is indicated in the canons pertaining to institutes of this kind,[30] constitutes a proper check and control over the management of endowment especially regarding compliance with the norms provided by the general law and by the charter.

[27] Canon 1490, § 1.
[28] See pp. 35-38.
[29] Canon 1527, § 1.
[30] Canons 1489-1494.

CHAPTER VI

INVESTMENT OF DOWRIES OF WOMEN RELIGIOUS [1]

UNDER the law of the Code a dowry is required for nuns in solemn vows.[2] A dowry is not compulsory under the general law for women religious in congregations in which simple vows are taken. In such congregations the matter of dowries is left to the determination of the constitutions of the institute.[3] All dowries for women religious,[4] whether required by the general law or by particular constitutions, are subject to the provisions of the Code respecting dowries.[5] Among these provisions are norms respecting the investment of dowry funds.

It is provided in canon 549 that the dowry is to be invested after the first profession of the religious in safe, licit, and productive securities by the superioress with her council and with the consent of the local ordinary and of the regular superior if the house is subject to one. The dowry may not be expended in any manner prior to the death of the religious, not even for the construction of a house or for the liquidation of a debt.[6]

---

[1] Two Canon Law Studies of the Catholic University of America treat of the dowries of women religious: n. 109, McManus, *The Administration of Temporal Goods in Religious Institutes;* n. 134, Kealy, *Dowry of Women Religious,* (Washington, D. C.: The Catholic University of America Press, 1941). Kealy especially presents a detailed study of the investment of dowries and broader questions regarding their administration. The present study approaches the subject of dowries in their aspect as capital funds to be invested. For considerations of administrative matters not directly related to investment, the two indicated works may be advantageously consulted.

[2] Canon 547, § 1.

[3] Canon 547, § 3.

[4] The law regarding dowries applies only to women religious. See Coronata, *Institutiones,* I, n. 577.

[5] The wording of these canons, viz., canons 548-551, indicates that they apply to dowries of women religious in both kinds of institutes, i.e., whether their members be professed either with solemn or with simple vows.

[6] Canon 549.—Post primam religiosae professionem dos in tutis, licitis ac

72

The principal purpose of the dowry is to provide support for the religious.[7] This is clearly evident in the formulation of the pre-Code law respecting the support of religious.[8] Other purposes also are served by the dowry, especially that of furnishing a religious who leaves the community with some means of support.[9] The prohibition of canon 549 against spending the dowry is a protection against loss of the support given by the dowry, and it is a guarantee that there will be something available to be given to the religious if she leaves the community.

ARTICLE 1. INVESTMENT IN SECURITIES

The type of investment to be made of the dowry was not so specifically designated in the earlier law as it is in the present law of canon 549. One pre-Code provision of law permitted the investment to be made through the purchase either of immovable property or of other claims to income.[10] Although in earlier times investments in immovable property were considered especially desirable because of their safety,[11] this enactment indicates that im-

---

fructiferis nominibus collocetur ab Antistita cum suo Consilio, de consensu Ordinarii loci et Superioris regularis, si domus ab hoc dependeat; omnino autem prohibetur eam quoquo modo ante religiosae obitum impendi, ne ad aedificandam quidem domum aut ad aes alienum exstinguendum.

[7] Cappello, *Summa Iuris Canonici,* II, n. 39; Coronata, *Institutiones,* I, n. 577.

[8] Conc. Trident. sess. XXV, *de regularibus,* c. 3; Clemens VIII. decr., *Nullus omnino,* 25 iul. 1599,—*Fontes,* n. 187; S. C. Ep. et Reg., *Portugallien.,* 6 iun. 1615—*Fontes,* n. 1666.

[9] Coronata, *Institutiones,* I, n. 577; Vermeersch-Creusen, *Epitome,* I, n. 698.

[10] S. C. Ep. et Reg., *Portugallien.,* 6 iun. 1615—*Fontes,* n. 1666. This provision of the Sacred Congregation has been understood as requiring dowry investment in immovable property. See Berutti, *Institutiones Iuris Canonici,* (6 vols., Taurini-Romae: Marietti, Vol. III, 1936), III, 164, text and note 2; Kealy, *Dowry of Women Religious,* p. 84, text and note 11. The words of the Congregation declare that the dowry funds are to be applied "in emptionem bonorum stabilium, aut annuorum redituum. . . ."—*ibid.,* § 3. The second of these designated kinds of investments seems to be clearly indicative that investment was not restricted to the purchase of immovable property.

[11] Larraona, "Commentarium Codicis," *CpR,* XII (1931), 436, nota 502.

movable property was not designated at that time as the only permissible investment for dowries.

The present law of canon 549 specifies that the investment of the dowries must be made through the purchase of securities.[12] The reasons behind this requirement seem to lie in the greater facility in administering securities as opposed to the greater care required in handling investments in real estate, and also in the dangers present in many places to the ecclesiastical tenure of real estate.[13] A further reason for requiring investment in securities may lie in the necessity of returning the endowment to the religious if she leaves the community. In view of this possibility, a suitable investment would be one that could be readily liquidated. Facility of liquidation may be more characteristic of investments consisting of securities than of investments consisting of real estate.[14]

In view of the clear wording of the law, many authors simply accept the requirement that the investment be made in securities without further qualification.[15] Specific declaration has also been made by authors that investments in immovable property are not permitted under the canon.[16] In contrast to this view, other au-

---

[12] The term *nomina* as used in this canon refers to claims to income such as are represented by stocks, bonds, mortgages, and other similar *tituli*. Cf. Beste, *Introductio in Codicem*, p. 372; Schaefer, *De Religiosis*, n. 229. See p. 68, footnote 13, regarding the meaning of *nomina*.

[13] See Schaefer, *De Religiosis*, n. 229; Larraona, *loc. cit.* Dangers of confiscation and civil limitations and other restrictions on the ecclesiastical tenure of real estate appear as considerations against investing in real estate. There is need of considering also any valid economic and social reasons underlying such civil restrictions.

[14] See Oesterle, *Praelectiones Iuris Canonici*, I, 301; McManus, *The Administration of Temporal Goods in Religious Institutes*, pp. 98-99.

[15] Chelodi, *Ius Canonicum de Personis* (3. ed., Vicenza: Società Anonima Tipografica; Trento: Libreria Moderna Editrice, 1942), n. 267; Vromont, *De Bonis Ecclesiae Temporalibus*, n. 255; De Meester, *Compendium* II, p. 437, n. 995; Cocchi, *Commentarium*, IV, n. 67; Berutti, *Institutiones*, III, n. 73, p. 164. Berutti contrasts the present law with the former law, under which investment in immovable property was required.

[16] Schaefer, *De Religiosis*, n. 229; Larraona, "Commentarium Codicis," Commentarium pro Religiosis et Missionariis (henceforth cited *CpRM*), XX (1939), 15, and *CpRM*, XXI (1940), 28.

thors declare that investments need not be limited to securities.[17]

It seems difficult to reconcile with the express wording of the canon the view of those who consider investments in immovable property as permissible. A comparison of the preliminary draft of 1912 of the Code with the present wording of the Code in this matter supports the view that only investments in securities are permissible. In the preliminary draft it was declared that the dowry was to be placed in a safe, licit, and productive *investment*. There was no further specification of the type of investment to be made.[18] The present text of the Code in requiring investment in securities seems to be positively restrictive of the wider signification of the preliminary draft.

That the dowry may be presented to the community either as cash or in certain other forms of property seems to be agreed to by many authors,[19] although there are some who declare that the dowry must be paid in cash.[20] If the property given as a dowry were not characterized by the qualities required by the law for dowry investments, it seems that such property would have to be sold in order that investment in a proper form could be made. If the property were not productive, it obviously would have to be sold.[21] Similarly, if securities were given as a dowry, and they were characterized by a large degree of risk, it seems that they would

[17] Vermeersch-Creusen, *Epitome*, I, n. 699; Wernz-Vidal, *Ius Canonicum* (7 vols., Vol. II, *De Personis*, 3. ed., 1943; Vol. III, *De Religiosis*, 1933, Romae: apud Aedes Universitatis Gregorianae), III, 221, nota 14. Bouscaren-Ellis (*Canon Law*, p. 264) and Creusen-Garesché-Ellis (*Religious Men and Women in the Code*, n. 186) declare that the dowry is to be placed in a safe, licit, and productive "investment."

[18] ". . . in tuto licito et fructifero investimento collocetur. . . ."—*Schema Codicis Iuris Canonici* (Romae, 1912), canon 421, § 2.

[19] Vermeersch-Creusen, *Epitome*, I, n. 698; Bastien, *Directoire Canonique à L'Usage des Congregations à Voeux Simples* (3. ed., Brugis, 1923), n. 101; Coronata, *Institutiones*, I, n. 577 (esp. 5°); Bouscaren-Ellis, *Canon Law*, p. 263; Cappello, *Summa Iuris Canonici*, II, n. 39; Kealy, *Dowry of Women Religious*, p. 63.

[20] See Kealy for a discussion of this question—*Dowry of Women Religious*, pp. 60-63.

[21] See Cappello, *Summa Iuris Canonici*, II, n. 39.

have to be sold and a reinvestment of the proceeds made in safe securities.

Since one of the requirements for the suitability of dowry investments is that the investment be in securities, it seems that when immovable property is given as a dowry it should normally be sold and the proceeds reinvested according to law.[22] Some canonical authors, however, in interpreting the applicability of the law to such a situation declare that the immovable property could be retained as the investment, at least if the property were characterized by the qualities of safety and productivity.[23] The reconciliation of this view with the express wording of the canon seems equally as difficult as the reconciliation of the view which permits investments to be made in immovable property.

There has been alleged as a reason for permitting investments in property other than securities the fact that securities are often unsafe.[24] It is quite true that a lack of safety does characterize many securities. But it is equally true that this danger does not extend to all securities. It seems that in the United States a security of the United States government or a seasoned security of a well-established corporation with assets located widely throughout the nation would normally be an even safer investment than a real estate holding. The value of a particular estate in real property depends not only upon general economic conditions but also upon extremely local conditions. A flood, the construction of a new road or bridge, the erection of a muncipal incinerator and other similar events can substantially affect the value of nearby property. The security of a corporation such as is here described has behind it widespread assets substantially unaffected by conditions peculiar to some one locality.

Furthermore, securities are generally available in relatively smaller units than units of real estate. A $2,000 dowry could be invested in five different units, each consisting of $400 in bonds of

22 Blat, *Commentarium Textus Codicis Iuris Canonici,* Liber II, Partes II et III (3. ed., Romae, 1938), n. 337 (hereafter cited *Commentarium*).

23 Cappello, *Summa Iuris Canonici,* II, n. 39; Bastien, *Directoire Canonique,* n. 101; Creusen-Garesché-Ellis, *Religious Men and Women in the Code,* n. 186.

24 Vermeersch-Creusen, *Epitome,* I, n. 699. See Larraona, "Commentarium Codicis," *CpRM,* XXI (1940), 29.

one company. Even if a suitable investment in real estate were available for $2,000, the entire amount would thus be placed in the one investment. In the previous example of investing in the bonds of five different companies, the risk of loss is spread over these five units. In the real estate investment there is no such division of risk, and hence there is the resulting possibility of a total loss. The greater degree of diversification [25] made possible through investments in securities is an important factor of safety.

If a practical real estate investment could be made only through the combining of several dowries, serious problems in liquidating these investments might be encountered by the community in the event that it became necessary to return the dowry to a departing religious. Such a combining of the dowries for investment in one unit of real estate would also intensify the dangers consequent upon a lack of proper diversification.

In the circumstances that have been indicated, the consideration of safety factors argues for, rather than against, investment in securities.

Except for the indication of the safety factor by Vermeersch-Creusen as a reason for permitting investment otherwise than in securities, no other specific reasons are alleged in support of their view by those authors who have been cited,[26] as permitting immovable property to be held as the dowry investment. It appears that the underlying reason is had in general financial expediency. One specific aspect of this—the safety factor—has already been discussed. Another specific consideration of financial advantage involves the possibility of receiving a higher rate of income from immovable property than from securities.

It seems quite true that the law should not inconsiderately be interpreted as prohibiting a more lucrative form of investment with a consequent loss in prospective net income. However, canon 549 expressly provides that the investment is to be made in securities *(nomina)*. The least that can be admitted is that under some cir-

---

[25] The necessity for proper diversification of investments in order to insure safety of principal is demonstrated in the American civil law which requires diversification in the investment of trust funds. See p. 164.

[26] See p. 75, footnote 17.

cumstances a dispensation from the general law could be sought.[27] Reasons of expediency in matters of property administration seem indeed to call for a certain area of discretion for the exercise of judgment by the immediate administrator. This seems to be true even when the law professes to establish a particular administrative policy. It is not inconceivable that in matters of property administration there may readily arise situations in which an application of the desired policy will not be economically advantageous. Overly specific provisions of property law can make it difficult for the administrator to adapt the affairs of his office to changing and local situations. But these are essentially considerations for the lawmaker; when the law has been established, the normal consequence is simply that of compliance with the law or of a petition for a dispensation from the law.

ARTICLE 2. "SAFE, LICIT, AND PRODUCTIVE SECURITIES"

The securities in which dowry funds are to be invested must possess according to canon 549 the qualities of safety, of licitness, and of productivity. The law makes no determination, indeed it could not make any determination, of the precise proportion between safety and productivity that should exist. Every investment is characterized by some degree of risk, and the rate of income is generally inversely proportioned to the safety of principal.[28] The law can but establish a general framework within which much must be left to the judgment of the administrator.

The administrator of ecclesiastical property is charged through his office with administering the property entrusted to him with the diligence of a "prudent man," [29] and he must protect the property from destruction or loss.[30] Although all investments must accordingly be made with emphasis upon safety, the degree of safety must

[27] See Kealy, *Dowry of Women Religious,* p. 86.

[28] See p. 33.

[29] ". . . diligentia boni patrisfamilias. . . ."—canon 1523. Note the similarity of this with the "prudent man rule" of the American civil law respecting trusts. See pp. 162-166.

[30] Canon 1523, 1°.

be judged by the administrator in view of the nature and destination of the particular property involved.

In view of the nature of a dowry and its purposes, it is evident that dowry investments must be made with a maximum of safety. For the dowry is intended to provide some support for the religious for her lifetime, and must be returned to her if she leaves the community.[31] In view of these purposes, safety in investing takes on an additional importance over and above the general obligation of an administrator to protect ecclesiastical property from loss.

Although the nature of the title by which the community holds and administers the dowry is a disputed point,[32] it is quite evident that the community does not hold an absolute title until the religious dies and the person presenting the dowry retains some kind of right respecting it.[33] Thus the administrator has an additional obligation deriving from this situation to protect the dowry from loss.

Although under American civil law it does not appear that any technical trust is created in the establishment of a dowry with a religious community, the norms established in the American law of trusts for investments by trustees could, apart from any strict obligation to follow them, suggest to the administrator of dowry funds the procedure regarding their safe investment. These norms are aimed at productive use of the property and its preservation. They are marked by variety from one state to another, the most specific provisions being furnished by the establishment of lists of securities legal for trust investments.[34] Such lists could well be consulted by administrators as an indication of the safety of the securities listed thereon.

As to the quality of licitness which must, according to canon 549, characterize the securities which serve for dowry investment, speculative securities would not be licit in view of the general prohibition upon clerics, religious, and their agents to take part in speculative

[31] Coronata, *Institutiones,* I, n. 577; Vermeersch-Creusen, *Epitome,* I, n. 698.

[32] See Kealy, *Dowry of Women Religious,* pp. 127-133, for a discussion of this point.

[33] The words of canon 548 indicate this: "Dos monasterio seu religioni irrevocabiliter acquiritur per obitum religiosae. . . ."

[34] See p. 165.

operations. Speculation is a form of business activity prohibited to clerics, religious, and their agents under canons 142 and 592.[35]

Similarly, the licitness of any investment with a company or a government engaged in morally illicit practices, including actions hostile to the Church, must be judged according to the moral principles regarding co-operation.[36]

ARTICLE 3. THE TIME FOR THE MAKING OF THE DOWRY INVESTMENT

According to canon 549 the dowry is to be invested after the first profession of the religious. The wording of the law does not appear prohibitive of earlier investment. Accordingly, investment prior to profession has been regarded as permissible by some authors.[37] There has also been presented the view which regards such investment as permissible only when consent has been given by the dowered person, or by her parents if she is still subject to them.[38]

The unstable relationship between the person and the community prior to the time of her profession has been suggested by Kealy as a practical reason against committing the funds to investment. He does not regard it as a legal reason, but regards the making of a dowry investment prior to profession as permissible if the permission of the person, or of her parents if she is still subject to them, has been given.[39] There do not appear to be any serious objections to this conclusion of Kealy.

ARTICLE 4. FORMALITIES IN INVESTMENT SELECTION

The investment is to be made by the superioress with her council and with the consent of the local ordinary and of the regular superior if the house is subject to one.[40] The superioress who is to make the

---

[35] See pp. 30-35 for a more detailed study of speculation and its relation to ecclesiastical property administration.

[36] See Kealy, *Dowries of Women Religious,* p. 87.

[37] Vermeersch-Creusen, *Epitome,* I, n. 699; Bastien, *Directoire Canonique,* n. 101.

[38] Schaefer, *De Religiosis,* n. 229.

[39] Kealy, *Dowry of Women Religious,* p. 84.

[40] Canon 549.

investment is the superioress of the monastery if nuns are concerned, and, in the case of congregations, the provincial or general superior who administers the dowry according to canon 550, § 1.[41] The selection of the particular investment is to be made by this superioress. The local ordinary cannot designate the specific securities which are to be purchased. His power is limited to that of granting or withholding approval regarding the selection made by the superioress.[42]

The particular investment made of the dowry must be made by the superioress with her council.[43] The canon does not indicate whether its consent must be had. This more specific determination of the manner in which the council is to take part could be established by the constitutions of the institute.[44] The constitutions must always be regarded in the making of any investments by religious.[45]

In the event that the constitutions make no provision in this matter, the traditional jurisprudence of the Church appears to accord a more favored position to the free administration of property by the superior in relation to the necessity of acting with the council.[46] Thus consultation is to be regarded as satisfying the universal requirement that the superioress act with the council.[47]

Furthermore, requirement for the consent of the council would establish a condition affecting the validity of the act to be performed by the superioress.[48] Such an invalidating condition cannot be presumed. It must be expressly or equivalently declared if the canon is to have an invalidating effect.[49] In the words of canon 549 and of canon 533 there is neither an express nor an equivalent declaration of a requirement for the consent of the council.

---

[41] Coronata, *Institutiones*, I, n. 577.

[42] Bastien, *Directoire Canonique*, n. 101; Coronata, *Institutiones*, I, n. 577.

[43] Canon 549.

[44] Schaefer, *De Religiosis*, n. 229; Coronata, *Institutiones*, I, n. 577; Beste, *Introductio in Codicem*, p. 372.

[45] See canon 533, § 1.

[46] Vermeersch-Creusen, *Epitome*, I, n. 229.

[47] Vromant, *De Bonis Ecclesiae Temporalibus*, n. 255; Oesterle, *Praelectiones Iuris Canonici*, I, 301; Kealy, *Dowry of Women Religious*, pp. 89-90; Schaefer, *De Religiosis*, n. 229.

[48] Canon 105, 1°.

[49] Canon 11.

The requirement of the universal law that the council be consulted is not a condition affecting validity. Under canon 105, 1°, there exists a *dubium iuris* as to whether such a requirement affects the validity or merely the licitness of the act in question.[50] Because of the existence of the *dubium iuris* the requirement that the superioress consult the council cannot be regarded as affecting the validity of her action.[51] This conclusion, based upon the wording of canon 549 and the tangent consideration of canon 11, canon 15 and canon 105, 1°, seems rather well substantiated under the terms of the present law.

In making the dowry investments, the superioress must, under the provisions of the present law, have the consent of the local ordinary.[52] This consent is similarly required for any change made in the dowry investments.[53] Although the Code does not expressly indicate which local ordinary is concerned in this matter of consent and in the matter of vigilance and visitation regarding the dowry administration,[54] the nature of the situation indicates that these controls are to be exercised by the local ordinary of the place where the dowry administration is conducted.[55]

Few authors when treating canon 549 discuss the question whether or not the requirement for the local ordinary's consent, and similarly the regular superior's consent whenever the law calls for it, affects the validity of the administrative act of the superioress. Vromant [56] declares that the consent is necessary only for the per-

---

[50] Vermeersch-Creusen, *Epitome*, I, n. 229; Bouscaren-Ellis, *Canon Law*, p. 91.

[51] Canon 15.

[52] Canon 549 and canon 533, § 1, 1°, 2°. Canon 533, § 1, 1°, requires this consent for all investments made by superioresses of nuns and by superioresses of religious institutes of diocesan approval; 2° requires this consent for dowry investments made by superioresses of religious congregations of pontifical approval. Thus the consent of the local ordinary is required for *all* dowry investments.

[53] Canon 533, § 2.

[54] See canon 550, § 2, regarding the local ordinary's duty to exercise such vigilance.

[55] Berutti, *Institutiones*, III, n. 73; Coronata, *Institutiones*, I, n. 577; Comyns, *Papal and Episcopal Administration of Church Property*, p. 74.

[56] *De Bonis Ecclesiae Temporalibus*, n. 255.

missiveness of the act, and does not affect is validity. Toso
(† 1946) [57] was of the view that this consent is necessary for the
validity of the act.

In the discussion of canon 533 other authors advert to the question in so far as the local ordinary's consent is involved. Canon 533
requires, among other things, that the local ordinary's consent be
had for all dowry investments.[58] This requirement is regarded by
several authors as affecting the permissiveness, and not the validity,
of the act.[59]

Canon 105, 1°, has been regarded as indicating that the local
ordinary's consent is required for the validity of the act of investment.[60] However, the application of canon 105 to the situation ruled
by canons 549 and 533, § 1, 1°, 2°, has been contested. Vromant
declares that canon 105, 1°, refers to the consent of inferiors who
assist a superior, whereas the consent of canon 533 consists of an
authoritative approbation quite different in law from the consent
of counselors or of some chapter, or of other subordinates.[61] The
use of the word "superior" in canon 105 seems to presuppose some
relationship of subordination on the part of those whose consent is
required. This relationship of superior to subordinate quite evidently does not exist between the religious superioress as the superior
and the local ordinary as the subordinate.

It has also been alleged that the sanction of invalidity of canon
1527, § 1, does not apply to the requirement for the local ordinary's
consent. Vromant declares that the entire context of title XXVIII
of the Code indicates that canon 1527, § 1, affects only administrators who properly as subjects of the local ordinary administer the
property of institutions which are completely subject to him. Re-

---

[57] *Ad Codicem Iuris Canonici Commentaria Minora*, Liber II, Pars II
(Romae: Jus Pontificium, 1927), p. 110, n. 2.

[58] See p. 82, footnote 52.

[59] Schaefer, *De Religiosis*, n. 197; Goyeneche, *Iuris Canonici Summa
Principia*, Lib. II, Pars II, (Romae: Tip. Pol. "Cuore di Maria," 1938), p. 67,
nota 7; Vromant, *De Bonis Ecclesiae Temporalibus*, n. 230; McManus, *The
Administration of Temporal Goods in Religious Institutes*, p. 93.

[60] Kealy, *Dowry of Women Religious*, p. 91.

[61] Vromant, *De Bonis Ecclesiae Temporalibus*, n. 230.

ligious of pontifical approval, exempt or non-exempt, are unaffected by the sanction of invalidity attaching to canon 1527, § 1.[62]

It is not inconceivable that this reasoning might fall in the face of other arguments. Nevertheless, the fact that such reasoning has been adduced respecting the relationship of canons 105, 1°, and 1527, § 1, to dowry investment, as also the fact that a number of authors have indicated that the consent of the local ordinary affects permissiveness alone and not validity, makes impossible the practical application of the sanction of invalidity. Canon 11 and canon 15 are critically decisive in establishing the conclusion that the requirement by canons 549 and 533 for the local ordinary's consent cannot be viewed as affecting validity.

ARTICLE 5. CONSOLIDATION OF DOWRY FUNDS

Dowries may be administered either as separate and individual units, or, on the other hand, they may be combined for administrative, and especially investment, purposes in such a way that each dowry consists of a share in the consolidated capital of all the dowries that have been combined.[63]

The technique of combining funds has certain advantages especially in the making of investments. Among these advantages is the possibiliity of a greater degree of diversification of investments and the consequent greater safety of the individual dowries.[64]

There does not appear in the law any suggestion of an obligation to keep separate the investments of the various dowries.[65]

[62] Vromant, *De Bonis Ecclesiae Temporalibus*, n. 230.

[63] See Creusen-Garesché-Ellis, *Religious Men and Women in the Code,* n. 186.

[64] See p. 143 regarding advantages to be derived from combining funds for investment purposes.

[65] The suggestion of such an obligation does appear in the law regarding the endowments of pious foundations, but it is no more than an indication, which is not regarded as forbidding the consolidation of endowment funds. See pp. 141-146 for a discussion of this question in so far as it pertains to pious foundations.

CHAPTER VII

INVESTMENT OF FUNDS GIVEN FOR PIOUS CAUSES (1): GENERAL PROVISIONS AND PROVISIONS REGARDING TRUSTS

I. Pious Disposals of Property in General

THE advantages of property for the uses of the Church may be acquired either by outright donation of property by a benefactor or by a conveyance of the property with the declaration that the property be devoted to some particular designated use or that it be used in a designated manner. The capacity of persons to confer property for pious causes either by act *inter vivos* or by act *mortis causa* is canonically well established independently of the prescriptions or limitations of civil law.[1]

Canon 1514 treats of the wishes of the faithful giving property to *pious causes*. It has been declared that a *pious cause* is had when something is done with the principal end of the work a supernatural end, as the worship of God, the meriting of grace, or satisfaction for sin.[2] This supernatural end may derive from the inherent end of the work or from the intention of the benefactor.[3] Mere supernatural motivation alone does not seem sufficient to draw any disposition of property under the supervisory authority of the Church, although this has been alleged.[4] A supernatural motive on the part of a public-spirited citizen in giving funds for the building of a bridge or for the executing of other thoroughly secular public improvement does not seem to establish his action as done for a pious cause in the canonical sense and therefore subject it to the Church. It seems that in addition to the pious motive which underlies the work, the latter must itself have some inherent "pious" quality,

---

[1] See canon 1513.

[2] Molina, *De Justitia et Jure* (5 vols., Coloniae Allobrogum, 1759), I, 272.

[3] Bouscaren-Ellis, *Canon Law*, p. 755.

[4] Schmalzgrueber, Lib. III, Pars III, tit. XXVI, n. 42.

85

either immediately as in the celebration of masses or, more remotely, as in the care of the sick.

Blat declares that property is to be considered as given to a pious cause only when given to pious institutes at least approved by ecclesiastical authority.[5] This seems to be a rather extreme view, for individual persons undoubtedly can be appointed executors of pious wills and trustees for trusts in benefit of pious causes. A less restricted notion of pious cause seems to be warranted, and would appear to be verified if the work has inherent in itself some rather proximate relation to the supernatural in addition to the supernatural motive that prompted the donation. Such a relation seems to exist when the work consists in the corporal or spiritual works of mercy.

The supernatural motive declared essential in the concept of a pious cause is always to be presumed in the case of Christians; the presumption of course yields to contrary proof.[6]

A further element remains to be considered in the discussion of ecclesiastical supervision over gifts for pious causes. This element is suggested by the example of a gift made under supernatural motivation for a work that does have an inherent reference to the supernatural, but which is conducted by a group which for all practical purposes is not subject to the exercise of the Church's jurisdiction, as, for example, the Red Cross, a secular hospital, or a secular community fund. An adequate solution for this difficulty seems to require that the rule establishing Church supervision of gifts to pious causes be considered applicable only when the property is made over to the trusteeship of a person subject in a practical way to the Church's authority. Hannan points out in this regard that the Church would hardly attempt to control property in the hands of persons not subject to its jurisdiction.[7]

A canonical obligation arises from the expressed wishes of the faithful respecting their gift, and these wishes may be concerned

[5] *Commentarium Textus Codicis Iuris Canonici,* Lib. III, Partes II-VI (Romae, 1923), n. 425 (hereafter cited *Commentarium*).

[6] Coronata, *Institutiones,* II, n. 1053.

[7] *The Canon Law of Wills,* The Catholic University of America Canon Law Studies, n. 86 (Washington, D. C., The Catholic University of America, 1934), p. 73.

with the manner of administration and of expenditure of the property.[8] The indicated wishes of the donor may be concerned with the investment of the money which he gives.[9] Thus the donor could specify that the funds be used as an endowment, the principal to be maintained intact while income alone from the fund was to be spent. He could also indicate his wishes regarding the manner in which investment was to be made of the funds. Thus the donor can establish his own wishes as the law regarding his gift, and canon 1514 gives canonical effect to these wishes.

A historical antecedent of this application of the law to the benefactor's directives regarding investment is furnished by a decision of the Sacred Congregation of the Council given in 1788.[10] The report of the case refers to the legislation of the Council of Trent [11] against changes in last wills. The decision of the Sacred Congregation consists of a refusal to permit the reinvestment of money obtained from necessary alienation of donated property in a manner that contravened the directive of the testator regarding alienation and reinvestment in the event that these became necessary.

The law indicates that some restrictions placed by the donor will have no effect.[12] Such are clauses which if placed in last wills are contrary to the rights of ordinaries over the pious disposals of property.[13] When the establishment of a trust [14] is contemplated by act *inter vivos*, canon 1516, § 1, declares that a cleric or a religious is not to accept a trust when the donor expressly and completely excludes the local ordinary's rights as declared in that same section of the canon. There does not seem to be any provision of law respecting the exclusion by the donor of the local ordinary's supervisory rights over the pious disposals of property made by act *inter vivos* to lay trustees.

Canon 1515 establishes the ordinaries as executors of all pious wills made either in contemplation of death or by act *inter vivos*.

[8] Canon 1514.
[9] Bouscaren-Ellis, *Canon Law,* p. 759.
[10] S. C. C., in *Asculana,* 21 iun. 1788—*Thesaurus,* LVII, 98.
[11] Sess. XXII, de ref., c. 6.
[12] Canon 1514.
[13] Canon 1515, § 3.
[14] A trust is but one specific form of pious disposal of property.

The ordinaries can and must take care that pious wills are properly fulfilled. To that end they are to receive reports from other executors upon the completion of their task, and are called on even to utilize the means of a canonical visitation. It is to be noted that the ordinary is not to take the place of an executor established by law or by the testator, but simply has the right of exercising vigilance over the fulfillment by the executors of the projected pious disposal of the property or funds in question.[15]

Thus the ordinary is charged by virtue of this canon with seeing that all the donor's directives are carried out, including any that may refer to investment. The ordinary is empowered to supervise the carrying out of the obligations placed upon administrators and trustees by a benefactor and sanctioned by the law of canon 1514. Since pious disposals of property obviously include such acts through which the notion of a trust is verified, such trusts are subject to the rule of canons 1514 and 1515. Similarly, a pious foundation as a specific form of pious disposal of property will be governed by canons 1514-1517.[16]

II. Pious disposals of Property in Trust

The instrument of the trust had a prolonged development in Roman law. It had its origin as a device in hereditary succession to pass part of an inheritance on to a third party who was incapable in law of receiving it directly.[17] This device was termed the *fideicommissum*. Prior to the present Code of Canon Law the law of the Church for the administration of its property was the Roman law itself as it was in force in medieval times.[18] This extended to the question of fiduciary relationships. It requires but a cursory

[15] Beste, *Introductio in Codicem,* p. 753; Bouscaren-Ellis, *Canon Law,* p. 760.

[16] See canon 1549, § 1.

[17] *Institutiones Iustiniani,* II, 23, in *Corpus Iuris Civilis,* I (Editio Stereotypa Quinta Decima, Berolini, 1928), 26. Sections 23 and 24 of the *Institutiones,* found on pp. 26-27 of this volume of the *Corpus Iuris Civilis,* trace the development up to that time of the trust in Roman law. See also André-Condis-Wagner, *Dictionnaire de Droit Canonique* (5. ed., 5 vols., Paris, 1901), II, 220-221.

[18] Cappello, *Summa Iuris Canonici,* II, n. 608.

glance at pre-Code commentators to see that the law regarding these trust relationships was substantially drawn from the Roman law. Reiffenstuel (1642-1703)[19] and Schmalzgrueber (1663-1735)[20] in treating this matter quoted extensively from Roman law sources, especially from Gaius and Justinian.

ARTICLE 1. NATURE OF A CANONICAL TRUST

Canonically a trust may be defined as an obligation, incumbent upon a person designated in a disposal of property made in a last will and testament or through an act *inter vivos,* or, in the case of intestacy, by the rule of succession, of conferring to another person or persons or to certain uses the property given to himself, or some part of it or income deriving from it. For this definition Beste, Claeys Bouuaert-Simenon and Coronata furnish several constitutive notions.[21] Bouscaren-Ellis furnish a short but essential description of a trust as "the transfer of ownership of property to one person for the benefit of another."[22]

Four elements are required for a verification of the canonical notion of a trust. First, there must be designated a trustee who may be either a physical or a moral person to whom the title of the trust property is conveyed together with the obligation of administering the property and of spending it in favor of another person or of a pious cause. Secondly, there must be established a beneficiary to whom the benefit of the trust property is to be conferred according to the intention of the benefactor. The beneficiary must be distinct from the trustee if the true notion of a trust is to be verified. Thirdly, there must be property that is to be applied to

---

[19] Lib. III, tit. XXVI, nn. 598 ss.

[20] Lib. III, tit. XXVI, nn. 133 ss.

[21] Beste, *Introductio in Codicem,* p. 750; Coronata, *Institutiones,* II, n. 1056; Claeys Bouuaert-Simenon, *Manuale Juris Canonici* (3 vols., Vols. I et III, 4 ed.; Vol. II, 2 ed., Gandae et Leodii, 1934-1935), III, n. 267. The latter explain that a *trust acceptance* is "ita accipere ut largitio rei acceptae fidei donatarii committatur. Vocatur etiam fidei commissum." De Meester (*Compendium,* III, p. 391, n. 1469) speaks of the concept as especially verified when there is involved "res alicui donata vel legata cum obligatione eam impendendi alicui pio usui vel transmittendi ad institutum pium."

[22] Bouscaren-Ellis, *Canon Law,* p. 757.

the beneficiary. Fourthly, delivery of the property must be effected, the title having passed to the trustee.[23]

A trust in the canonical sense does not exist when no administration of property is involved, as for example when a person is the mere instrument for the procurement of some specified articles for a church.[24] Vromant makes an observation [25] suggestive of the necessary exercise of the administration of property if the notion of a trust is to be had. In order that a trust exist, he says, the property itself must be actually burdened with the obligations of the trust (*bona gravantur*). Thus, when a sum of money was given for the celebration of but one mass, and the money was to be spent immediately but the mass was to be celebrated only after the donor's death, a trust did not exist because *"bona non proprie gravantur."* Rather, there was imposed upon the community no more than the obligation of carrying out the donor's intention, safeguarded by the provisions of law regarding the acceptance of mass stipends. Thus property if vested with some obligation must be held with the duty of administering it if the notion of a trust is to be verified. This element is essential to the notion of a canonical trust. It is, obviously, not found in all pious disposals of property.

ARTICLE 2. COMPARISON WITH ANGLO-AMERICAN CONCEPT OF TRUST

By way of comparison, the concept of a trust as understood in the civil law of the United States may be examined. A trust is a fiduciary relationship in which one person is the holder of the title to property, subject to an equitable obligation to keep or use the property for the benefit of another." [26] It has also been defined as

---

[23] Beste, *Introductio in Codicem*, p. 750; Bouscaren-Ellis, *Canon Law*, pp. 757-758.

[24] Beste, *Introductio in Codicem*, p. 750; Vromant, *De Bonis Ecclesiae Temporalibus*, n. 152; Coronata, *Institutiones*, II, n. 1056; Bouscaren-Ellis, *Canon Law*, p. 758.

[25] *De Bonis Ecclesiae Temporalibus*, n. 152.

[26] Bogert, *Handbook of the Law of Trusts* (2. ed., St. Paul: West Publishing Co., 1942), p. 1.

"a fiduciary relationship with respect to property, subjecting the person by whom the property is held to equitable duties to deal with the property for the benefit of another person, which arises as a result of a manifestation of an intention to create it." [27]

A charitable trust in the civil law has been defined as "a fiduciary relationship with respect to property arising as a result of the manifestation of an intention to create it, and subjecting the person by whom the property is held to equitable duties to deal with the property for a charitable purpose." [28]

The analogies which exist between the qualities of a trust in Roman and canon law and the qualities of a trust in Anglo-American law are not indicative of an evolution of the notion from Roman law into the common law. Indeed, the origin of the common law trust has been ascribed by early writers such as Gilbert, Spence, and Blackstone to Roman law influences.[29] This conclusion was evidently encouraged by the analogy existing between the position created by the testamentary *fideicommissum* or the *inter vivos* grant of *usus* or *ususfructus* as distinguished from full *dominium* and the position created at common law by *feoffment* to one person for the use of another. It is now quite clear that the English notion did not grow out of the Roman concept.[30]

The assertion has also been made that the English concept had its roots in the law of the Germanic tribes, specifically in the *Salman,* or *Treuhand,* a person to whom property was transferred for certain purposes which were to be carried out either within the lifetime or after the death of the person conveying it.[31] Through this device the Germanic law was familiar with the idea that a person who held property for the use of another was bound to fulfill his trust.

[27] *Restatement of the Law of Trusts* (2 vols., St. Paul: American Law Institute Publishers, 1935), I, 6.

[28] *Restatement of the Law of Trusts,* II, 1095.

[29] Holdsworth, *A History of English Law* (12 vols., Boston: Little, Brown & Co., 1924-1938), IV, 410.

[30] Pollock and Maitland, *The History of English Law* (2 vols., Cambridge, 1895), II, 235-236; *Corpus Juris* (72 vols., New York: American Law Book Co., 1914-1937), LXV, 219; Scott, "Fifty Years of Trusts," 50 *Harvard Law Review,* 60, 75 (1936).

[31] Holdsworth, *A History of English Law,* IV, 411.

It has also been alleged that the origin of the trust was a development as equally independent of the *Salman* of Germanic law as of the Roman testamentary trust, the *fideicommissum,* and the Roman servitude of *usus.*[32]

Because of the lack of dependence of the common law notion of the trust upon the similar Roman law concepts and the lack of identity between them, it is important that the term be understood in the sense in which it is used, as indicating either the canonical concept or the common law notion. The canon law notion of *fiducia* is not the same as the common law concept of the *trust,* although it is difficult to translate *fiducia* with any word other than *trust.* It is also true that the *fideicommissum* because of its similarity with the *use* or *trust* can best be translated as *testamentary trust.*[33] Although quite similar in effect they do not represent the same concept. This point of difference between canon law and the common law has been declared to be one of two essential differences between the two systems respecting modes of holding property.[34]

The chief difference appears to lie in the fact that the Roman or canonical notion of a trust is concerned with an obligation to transfer to another the title to the property involved or to spend it for some pious cause,[35] while the Anglo-American concept of trust involves the trustee's continued holding of the title to the trust property while conferring the benefit of that property upon another or for the accomplishment of some charitable purpose. Thus the Anglo-American concept of a trust is a specific mode of holding property which does not have a canonical counterpart.[36]

The canonical notion of *fiducia* reflects a broader and more

---

[32] Radin, *A Handbook of Anglo-American Legal History* (St. Paul: West Publishing Co., 1936), pp. 430-433.

[33] Radin, *A Handbook of Anglo-American Legal History,* p. 431. Beste translates *fideicommissum* as *trust bequest.—Introductio in Codicem,* p. 750.

[34] "Memorandum by Dean Motry and Dr. Brown," *The Jurist,* II (1942), 77-78. The other point of difference is the existence of the incorporated *res* without incorporators, found in Roman and in canon law, but not in the common law.

[35] See p. 89 supra for the definition of the canonical trust and pp. 90-91 for the definition of the common law trust.

[36] "Memorandum by Dean Motry and Dr. Brown," *loc. cit.*

generic notion of obligation.   Indication of this is also had in the
fact that the *fiducia* comes into existence as a result of the donor's
intent manifested even by merely *precatory* words. The more specific
and technical nature of the common law trust is indicated by the
fact that it comes into existence only through *mandatory* words of
the settlor.   Precatory words of themselves are not constitutive
of the technical trust in common law, while in canon law the notion
of precatory words as legally invalid is not known.[37]

In so far as the Anglo-American trust requires the conferring
of the trust property's benefits to another person or to a charitable
purpose, this trust appears to fall within the broader canonical notion of a fiduciary obligation.   Hence the Anglo-American trust
would be governed in ecclesiastical matters by canonical provisions
respecting donations to pious causes [38] and respecting the *fiducia* [39]
in so far as the benefits of the trust property are to be conveyed to
pious causes.

It is also to be noted that civil law provisions respecting the management of property held under a technical civil trust, especially
in its investment aspects, may be given canonical effect by canon
1529.[40]

Article 3. The Trust In Canonical Legislation

A pious trust, canonically, is one form of the pious disposal of
property and will accordingly be governed by the law regarding
such pious disposals.   In such provisions of the law, as they are
contained in canons 1513, 1514, 1515, and 1517, there is no specific
mention of the trust relationship.   Mention of this appears in canon
1516, but then regarding only one class of pious trusts, namely,
those in which the trustees are religious or clerics.[41]

[37] See "Memorandum of Dean Motry and Dr. Brown," *The Jurist*, II
(1942), 79.

[38] Canons 1514 and 1515.

[39] Canon 1516.

[40] See pp. 156-160.

[41] Further provisions of law are established in canons 1544-1551 for pious
foundations, which frequently exist in the form of a trust. There are also
pious foundations which do not possess all the essential qualities of a trust.

Canon 1516 [42] is of more limited application than the two immediately preceding canons in two respects. First, as is evident from the words of the canon,[43] it applies only to those disposals of property for pious causes in which the property is received in trust. Secondly, it applies only to those trust disposals for pious causes in which the designated trustee is a cleric or a religious. Canons 1514 and 1515 apply certain general provisions to all pious disposals of property. Canon 1516 makes certain specific provisions applicable only to those trusts in which the trustees are clerics or religious. These provisions require that the clerical or religious trustee report the fiduciary obligation to the ordinary and indicate the property given in trust together with the attached obligations. It is also required that the ordinary demand that a safe disposition be made of the property pending the execution of the trust, and that he see to it that the intentions of the settlor of the trust be carried out according to the provision made in canon 1515, viz., by means of the canonical visitation and the exaction of a report on the execution of the trust.[44]

Thus trusts to clerics and religious are made subject to four supervisory controls, viz., that an initial report of the trust relationship be made by the trustee to the ordinary, that the ordinary demand that a safe disposition be made of the trust property, that the ordinary can use his right of visitation regarding the trust, and that an accounting be rendered to the ordinary upon execution of the trust. The first two of these controls are had in virtue of canon 1516, and so apply to clerical and religious trustees alone. The last

---

[42] Canon 1516.—§ 1. Clericus vel religiosus qui bona ad pias causas sive per actum inter vivos, sive ex testamento fiduciarie accepit, debet de sua fiducia Ordinarium certiorem reddere, eique omnia istiusmodi bona seu mobilia seu immobilia cum oneribus adiunctis indicare; quod si donator id expresse et omnino prohibuerit, fiduciam ne acceptet.

§ 2. Ordinarius debet exigere ut bona fiduciaria in tuto collocentur et vigilare pro exsecutione piae voluntatis ad normam can. 1515.

§ 3. Bonis fiduciariis alicui religioso commissis, si quidem bona sint attributa loci seu dioecesis ecclesiis, incolis aut piis causis iuvandis, Ordinarius de quo in §§ 1, 2, est loci Ordinarius; secus, est Ordinarius eiusdem religiosi proprius

[43] . . . *fiduciarie accepit.* . . .

[44] Canon 1515, § 2.

two controls are had in virtue of canon 1515, and accordingly apply to all pious trusts, those whose trustees are lay persons [45] as well as those whose trustees are clerics or religious.[46]

The succeeding articles of the present chapter will treat in detail the elements in and implications of the canonical trust relationship.

ARTICLE 4. THE TRUSTEE

When property is given in trust for pious causes, the trustee is held to carry out the intentions of the donor even regarding the manner of administering and expending the property.[47]   As has been seen,[48] the intentions of the donor which must be carried out extend to any directives given regarding investment. So, too, if it is of the very nature of the trust that the income alone is to be expended, the trustee must invest the trust property in order to realize income. In carrying out the intentions of the settlor of the trust, the trustee is subject to the vigilance of the ordinary by virtue of canon 1515, and accordingly must report to the ordinary upon the completion of his task and remains subject in the meantime to the ordinary's visitation. What has so far been said about the trustee applies to all trustees of pious trusts: lay, clerical or religious.

Canon 1516 makes certain further requirements for the trustees of pious trusts who are clerics and religious. As has been seen, they must, in virtue of this canon, make an initial report of their trust and submit to the ordinary's supervision over the placing of the property in a safe and secure status.

It may be asked whether lay trustees are subject to the provisions of canon 1516. Possibly because trusts are explicitly mentioned only in this canon and not in the two preceding canons, it may have been felt by some that all trustees are to be governed by canon 1516. If the pre-Code law furnished the interpretation

[45] Beste, *Introductio in Codicem,* p. 753.

[46] Canon 1516, § 2.

[47] This is the general obligation, expressed in canon 1514, incumbent upon all administrators of property given with some intention of the donor to be carried out.

[48] See p. 87.

for the present law, these lay trustees would here be included. A response of the Sacred Congregation of the Council in 1909, whence the present law is drawn, subjected lay trustees as well as priests to its provisions.[49] Coronata alleges this response in support of his view that lay trustees are subject to the ruling contained in canon 1516.[50] He views this canon as a corollary of the immediately preceding one. The express mention of clerics and religious in canon 1516 is understood by him as indicating for them a special obligation, the while a less intensive obligation exists for lay trustees as well.

Contrary to the view which would subject lay trustees to the ruling of canon 1516 is the explicit wording of the law. The canon clearly indicates that only religious and clerical trustees are governed by its provisions. From the general principle of law expressed in canon 19, a law which restricts the free exercise of rights, as canon 1516 does, should receive a strict interpretation. Bouscaren-Ellis declare that lay trustees are not ruled by canon 1516.[51] They regard the 1909 response of the Sacred Congregation, which has been mentioned above, as indicative of the pre-Code law on the subject in virtue of which lay trustees were subject to these obligations. The Code in their opinion changed the law. Vromant similarly declares that lay trustees are not ruled by this canon. His reason for rejecting the response of the Sacred Congregation as interpretative of the present law is, however, different. Vromant declares that this response was a particular rescript and therefore obligatory only upon those persons for whom it was issued.[52]

Accordingly, lay persons who are named trustees in a pious disposal of property in trust are not ruled by canon 1516. They are obliged only under the provisions of canon 1515 to give a report to the ordinary on the completion of their task and to submit to his visitation.[53]

---

[49] S. C. C., *Bellovacen*, 9 aug. 1909—*Fontes*, n. 4355.

[50] *Institutiones*, II, n. 1056.

[51] *Canon Law*, p. 761.

[52] *De Bonis Ecclesiae Temporalibus*, n. 161.

[53] Beste, *Introductio in Codicem*, p. 753; Bouscaren-Ellis, *Canon Law*, p. 761; Vermeersch-Creusen, *Epitome*, II, n. 836.

Although lay trustees of pious trusts are not obliged in consequence of the ruling of canon 1516 to make an initial report of their trust to the ordinary, they may be invited to inform the ordinary of their own accord concerning their trust.[54]   They could thus secure the benefits of the ordinary's supervision.

It is of interest to note that canon 1516 implies that religious, even those in solemn vows, can be trustees in trust dispositions for pious purposes.[55]   This interestingly exemplifies the chief difference between the canonical *fiducia* and the Anglo-American trust.   The latter, as has been seen,[56] is, unlike the former, a specific mode of holding title to property.   Thus the religious in solemn vows could be a trustee under the canonical obligation of *fiducia,* while he could not, because of his canonical incapacity for taking title of ownership,[57] take the legal title to property such as the trustee in the Anglo-American trust must take.

ARTICLE 5. DUTIES OF THE ORDINARY UNDER CANON 1516

The first paragraph of canon 1516 is quite clear in its provision that clerical and religious trustees must notify the ordinary of their trust, its property, and its attached obligation.   The second paragraph [58] is not so clear in its provisions in view of the difficulty of understanding the precise meaning of the word *collocentur.*   The terms *collocatio* and *collocare* appear elsewhere in the Code as referring to investment.[59]   In its appearance in this canon the term has been unequivocally understood by some authors as signifying investment.[60]   As will be seen, there are serious difficulties attendant upon the acceptance of this meaning.

[54] Vromant, *De Bonis Ecclesiae Temporalibus,* n. 161; Beste, *Introductio in Codicem,* p. 753.

[55] Cf. Coronata, *Institutiones,* II, n. 1056.

[56] See p. 92.

[57] Bouscaren-Ellis, *Canon Law,* p. 275.

[58] Canon 1516.—§ 2. Ordinarius debet exigere ut bona fiduciaria in tuto collocentur et vigilare pro exsecutione piae voluntatis ad normam can. 1515.

[59] *Collocare*: Canons 549; 1415, § 2; 1523, 4°; 1531, § 3; 1547; *Collocatio;* Canon 533, §§ 1 and 2.

[60] Cappello, *Summa Iuris Canonici,* II, n. 599; Woywod, *A Practical Commentary on the Code of Canon Law,* II, 176; Augustine, *A Commentary*

In looking to the sources of the law indicated by the footnote to this paragraph of the canon, the references to the Decretals of Gregory IX [61] are of no assistance in determining the intended meaning of the troublesome phrase. These two *capita* are concerned merely with expressing the bishop's right to oversee the execution of pious intentions expressed in last wills. There is no mention in either of any specific disposition of property which the bishop is to enforce prior to the carrying out of the intentions of the testator. Thus there is in these *capita* no provision parallel to the provision of the canon containing the word *collocentur*.

The response of the Sacred Congregation of the Council indicated in the same footnote to paragraph two of the canon is a less specific provision than the present law, and it is of no assistance in determining the meaning of *collocentur*.[62]

A dictionary of legal terms, the *Vocabularium Juris Utriusque*,[63] lists five meanings for the word *collocare*. Three of these have no possible application in the context of the canon.[64] The other two meanings are suggestive for the present discussion. Both of these are characterized by the notion of placing something in productive use. *Collocare* is said to denote the giving of a loan at interest (*mutuum dare*). The other signification listed for *collocare* is *to spend* (*impendere*). An example given under this meaning is indicative of a disposition of something to productive use: viz., *collocare pecuniam in emptionem praediorum*.

Although all these considerations point to an understanding of the term as meaning *to invest,* the difficulties attendant upon such an understanding appear to make this acceptance of the word im-

---

on the New Code of Canon Law, (8 vols., Vol. VI, 3. ed., St. Louis: Herder, 1931), VI, 573; Cance, *Le Code de Droit Canonique,* III, 244-245.

[61] C. 17, 19, X, *de testamentis et ultimis voluntatibus,* III, 26.

[62] S. C. C. *Bellovacen.,* 9 aug. 1909: "Omnes sive sacerdotes sive laicos, quorum fidei concredita sunt legata ad pias causas, teneri de hoc quamprimum certiorem reddere Episcopum, qui ius habet vigilandi super administrationem et consulendi securitati eorumdem legatorum."—*Fontes,* n. 4355.

[63] Scotus-Kahl-Brissonius-Heineccius (2. ed., 4 vols., Neapoli, 1760), I, 283-284.

[64] These three meanings are as follows: a condition is said *to be placed* in another, *to place* a son in marriage, *to institute and confer* a benefice.

possible. These difficulties are readily apparent from the fact that a trust disposition need not involve any investment of the trust property.[65] It is of the nature of some trusts that the expenditures for the purposes of the trust be made only from income that is derived from the property. It is of the nature of other trusts that the principal itself be expended by the trustee, either all at one time or progressively over a period of time. Thus, when the principal itself is to be expended, it may very well be that its investment would not be practicable under the terms of the trust. In such a situation it would not be practicable or perhaps even possible to make any investment. For example, if the principal of a trust fund were to be expended over a period of one year, a suitable investment for such a period could hardly be found. It would be strange indeed if the law were to insist upon such a short term investment at the cost of time, energy, and risk to the principal. And yet if *collocentur* is to be understood as referring to investment, the law would indeed be making such an unqualified demand for investment. If, however, the term in context with *in tuto* is to be understood in the more radical sense of signifying a *placement in some safe disposition,* this unqualified requirement is easily applied to all trust properties which are to be held for a time by the trustee.

Bouscaren-Ellis seem to be aware of the difficulty, for in their explanation of the canon they use a parenthetical phrase to qualify the notion of investment. They declare that "the Ordinary must oblige the trustee to deposit the trust fund in a safe place and to invest it (if necessary)." [66] The very use of the two notions of deposit and investment in explaining the one word *collocentur* together with the parenthetical qualification of investment are indicative of the difficulty of the interpretation.

Other authors are of little help in ascertaining the proper signification, for they merely quote the difficult words without making any attempt to explain them or even to furnish a context in which the meaning would be evident.[67]

---

[65] Vromant, *De Bonis Ecclesiae Temporalibus,* n. 347.

[66] *Canon Law,* p. 761.

[67] Among these authors are: Cocchi, *Commentarium,* VI, 380; Coronata,

In view of these considerations, the phrase *in tuto collocentur* seems to be best understood as signifying that the ordinary must see that a safe disposition is made of the property, rather than that it must specifically be invested. This safe disposition may consist simply in placing the property or the funds in safe custody. Blat, and he alone among the authors consulted, unequivocally accepts this signification. He writes: ". . . *ut bona fiduciaria . . . in tuto collocentur,* tum bona mobilia, tum pecuniam et syngrapha, ne furentur aut quocumque modo pereant. . . ." [68] However, the *safe disposition* does not preclude the making of a safe investment if this were required or even only useful. It seems proper to conclude, however, that investment is not absolutely required by this paragraph of the canon.

Canon 1516, § 2, with reference to trusts held by clerics and religious, also gives to the ordinary the same supervisory rights which he has over all pious disposals of property by virtue of canon 1515, viz., the rights of vigilance, of visitation, and of requiring accountings.

ARTICLE 6. DUTIES OF THE ORDINARY REGARDING TRUST INVESTMENTS

Having taken the phrase *in tuto collocentur* of canon 1516 as referring to the more general designation of a safe disposition rather than to the more specific demand for investment, no special provision regarding investment can be understood of canon 1516, except in so far as paragraph two of this canon refers back to canon 1515. Canon 1516 simply sets up the requirement of two additional solemnities for trusts held by clerics and religious, viz., the

---

Institutiones, II, n. 1056; Vermeersch-Creusen, *Epitome,* II, n. 836. Beste completely abstracts from paragraph two of canon 1516 (*Introductio in Codicem,* pp. 753-754). Vromant merely qualifies somewhat the wording of the canon when he declares that, if the property is to be preserved (*bona asservari debent*) for some time, *in tuto sunt collocanda* under the direction of the ordinary (*De Bonis Ecclesiae Temporalibus,* n. 162).

[68] *Commentarium,* Lib. III, Partes II-VI, n. 428. The final clause is indicative that this author takes the phrase to refer to safe custody and not to investment.

making of an initial report of the trust to the ordinary, and the ordinary's duty to demand that some safe disposition be made of the trust property. The supervisory authority of the ordinary over the investment of trusts derives from canon 1515 and extends to any investment made of trust property, whether the trustees are lay persons, clerics, or religious. Canon 1515 must, then, be looked to regarding this supervisory authority over investment. Canon 1516 makes no specific addition to the ordinary's authority over the investment of any trust property except in so far as his concern for the safety of the disposition is emphasized.

The question is indeed complicated by the fact that canonical writers give little space to any discussion of the investment of trust properties and the ordinary's supervision over them. The greater number of the authors whom the writer could consult regarding the general provisions of canons 1514 and 1515 as applicable to pious disposals of property do not advert to the question of investing this property.[69] Other authors indicate briefly the possibility that such property may be placed in investment, but they make no specific comment concerning the ordinary's supervision in investment matters.[70] Those authors who understand canon 1516, § 2, as requiring the investment of trust property—which view, let it again be noted, runs counter to the conclusion of the present writer— simply declare that the ordinary is to demand the safe investment of the property.[71] No details of how the ordinary is to carry out this duty are discussed by them.

Although neither the law nor those who comment upon the law give any specific directives regarding the supervision of trusts, it seems to be within the supervisory powers of the ordinary, as vindicated for him in canon 1515, that he can supervise the investment

---

[69] See e.g. Coronata, *Institutiones,* II, nn. 1053 et 1055; Beste, *Introductio in Codicem,* pp. 752-753; Vermeersch-Creusen, *Epitome,* II, n. 836; Cocchi, *Commentarium,* VI, 377-379; Cance, *Le Code de Droit Canonique,* III, 243-245.

[70] Vromant, *De Bonis Ecclesiae Temporalibus,* n. 157; Bouscaren-Ellis, *Canon Law,* pp. 759-760.

[71] See p. 97, footnote 60.

of the property of a trust to insure its safety and suitability. Upon these factors depend the execution of the settlor's purpose.

If investment directives have been given by the settlor of a trust, these must be carried out by the administrators in virtue of canon 1514,[72] which declares that the intentions of the benefactor must be carried out most diligently even regarding the manner of administration and the expenditure of the property. If no specific directives have been given regarding investment, the administrator, in order to fulfill the terms of those trusts whose funds are to constitute endowment, will be obliged by the very nature of those trusts to invest the funds given. In both cases the ordinary has supervisory authority over such trusts in virtue of canon 1515. The first paragraph of this canon indicates that the ordinary is the executor of all pious disposals of property. The second paragraph further specifies the ordinary's authority and indicates that he is to exercise vigilance, and this even by means of a canonical visitation, and that other executors,[73] if in the case of trusts, they are made the trustees, must submit an accounting to him on the execution of their task.

This exercise of vigilance, especially when it includes the right of visitation, seems to extend especially to matters of investment. For upon the safety and productivity of the investment will depend the satisfactory execution of the trust. The accountings to be made to the ordinary, normally on the completion of the executor's task, may be demanded whenever the ordinary thinks it expedient in the event that the execution of the benefactor's mandate has a prolonged duration, as, for example, when over some period of time certain obligations must be fulfilled annually.[74] This would be the case whenever trust property is to be invested for the purpose of producing income that is to be expended, or when-

---

[72] Vromant, *De Bonis Ecclesiae Temporalibus,* n. 157; Bouscaren-Ellis, *Canon Law,* p. 759.

[73] *Exsecutores delegati* of canon 1515, § 2: i.e., designated by the donor, testator, or the ordinary (Vermeersch-Creusen, *Epitome,* II, n. 836). It is to be noted that the ordinary's power is one of supervision. He cannot encroach upon the rightful administration undertaken by the executors whom the donor or testator has appointed (Beste, *Introductio in Codicem,* p. 753).

[74] Berutti, *Institutiones,* IV, 488.

ever the trust property itself is to be expended over a period of time.

In conclusion to the remarks regarding the duties of ordinaries relative to trusts, it is to be noted that by virtue of canon 1515, the administration is in the hands of the trustee, the supervision only being in the hands of the ordinary.[75] The ordinary could not demand that the property be sent to himself in order that he might administer it.[76] Accordingly the selection of the investments belongs to the trustee. The local ordinary could of course register his disapproval if the investment chosen by the trustee were unsafe or otherwise unsuitable.

ARTICLE 7. PROPER ORDINARY FOR SUPERVISION

In virtue of canon 1515 ordinaries possess supervisory authority over pious disposals of property, including trusts. Among these *ordinaries* are to be included according to canon 198, § 1, local ordinaries and the major superiors of clerical exempt religious.[77] The particular ordinary who is to exercise this authority is determined by the nature and destination of the property given.[78] The proper ordinary for supervision will therefore be, not the proper ordinary of the trustee, but the ordinary in whose jurisdiction an interest is acquired from the gift in trust, in short, the ordinary of the beneficiary.

This notion is further elucidated in canon 1516, § 3. This paragraph declares that when property is given in trust to a religious for the benefit of the churches, inhabitants, or pious causes of the place or the diocese, the ordinary indicated in §§ 1 and 2 is the local ordinary, that is, the ordinary of the place in which is located the pious cause that is to benefit from the trust.[79] This

---

[75] Beste, *Introductio in Codicem*, p. 753.

[76] Cance, *Le Code de Droit Canonique*, III, 244.

[77] Vermeersch-Creusen, *Epitome*, II, n. 836; Beste, *Introductio in Codicem*, p. 753.

[78] Coronata, *Institutiones*, II, n. 1055.

[79] Beste, *Introductio in Codicem*, p. 754.

applies even when a religious trustee is an exempt religious.[80]   In other cases, viz., when there is no designation of place in the trust, it is the proper ordinary of the religious.[81]   The only religious who can have a proper ordinary other than the local ordinary is a clerical exempt religious.[82]

Canon 1516 makes no explicit provision regarding what ordinary is concerned when property is given in trust to a secular cleric. The authors who treat of the matter seem to apply the same principle underlying § 3, viz., that when trust properties are to benefit the churches, inhabitants, or pious causes of an ecclesiastical jurisdiction, the ordinary for the performance of the due solemnities and the exercise of supervision is the ordinary of the place, persons, or causes benefitted by the trust.[83]

When the trust is intended to benefit churches, paupers, missions, or pious causes, and these are designated merely in general, no specific determination of place having been made, the ordinary in such an event will be the proper ordinary of the trustee.[84]   Thus a secular cleric submits his trust to his proper local ordinary; an exempt clerical religious, to his major superior; any other religious, to the local ordinary of the place in which is situated the house to which he is attached.[85]

---

[80] Nebreda, "Quaestiones Selectae de Iure Administrativo Ecclesiastico," *CpR,* VII (1926), 326; Berutti, *Institutiones,* IV, 489.

[81] Canon 1516, § 3. See Bouscaren-Ellis, *Canon Law,* p. 761; Beste, *Introductio in Codicem,* p. 754.

[82] See canon 198, § 1.

[83] Vromant, *De Bonis Ecclesiae Temporalibus,* n. 163; Beste, *Introductio in Codicem,* p. 754; Vermeersch-Creusen, *Epitome,* II, n. 836.

[84] Beste, *Introductio in Codicem,* p. 754.

[85] Vromant, *De Bonis Ecclesiae Temporalibus,* n. 163. Vromant here expresses the principle that, when no determination of place is made, the ordinary of this canon is the proper ordinary of the trustee. However, in enumerating the specific conclusions that flow from this principle, Vromant declares that an exempt religious must submit his trust only to his own major superior; a non-exempt religious to the local ordinary of the house to which he is assigned. A further distinction, however, must be made, viz., between exempt clerical institutes and exempt lay institutes. Only the major superiors of the former are termed "ordinaries" under canon 198, § 1. The only ordinaries for exempt lay institutes are local ordinaries. (See Vermeersch-Creusen, *Epitome,* II, n. 836). Hence, only a member of an exempt *clerical* institute

ARTICLE 8. SUPERVISION OF TRUSTS IN BENEFIT OF A RELIGIOUS
INSTITUTE

When it is intended that the trust should benefit a religious institute or its own proper activities and the constituted trustee is a
member of that institute, who is charged with its supervision? The
canon itself by its terminology provides for a certain diversity of
supervision. The term *ordinary* is inclusive of local ordinaries and
certain major religious superiors, viz., those of clerical exempt institutes. Certain specified kinds of trusts must be submitted to the
local ordinary. Other kinds of trusts are to be submitted to the
proper ordinary of the religious. This is a very explicit provision of
the canon. The concept of the proper ordinary of a religious is,
unlike many concepts in the law respecting religious, quite definite
and precise. The proper ordinary for a member of an exempt clerical institute is his major superior.[86] If, as has been seen, the trust
is to benefit churches, persons, or pious causes of a place or a diocese,
it must be submitted to the local ordinary regardless of any exempt
status enjoyed by a religious trustee. If it is not such a trust,
the proper ordinary of the religious is the ordinary concerned,
being for exempt clerical religious, the major superior; for all other
religious, the local ordinary of the religious. Thus the law itself
contains precise norms for establishing the supervisory authority.

Berutti follows the law closely in regard to trusts for the benefit
of the religious institute. In his view, when a trust is destined for
the good of a clerical exempt institute or its own proper activities,
the trustee who is a member of that institute submits the trust to
his major superior.[87] If, however, the trust is to benefit churches,
persons, or pious causes of a place or a diocese not proper to his
institute, the trustee who is a member of an exempt clerical institute must submit his trust to the local ordinary. Berutti then

could, in certain cases, submit his trust to his major superior. Other religious,
exempt lay and all non-exempt, can submit their trusts only to a local ordinary,
for this is the only *ordinary* they can have. Nebreda's exposition is characterized by the same lack of this distinction as Vromant's. ("Quaestiones
Selectae de Iure Administrativo Ecclesiastico," *CpR*, VII (1926), 326).

[86] Bouscaren-Ellis, *Canon Law,* p. 136.

[87] *Institutiones,* IV, 489.

goes on to treat of trusts held by members of exempt lay institutes or of non-exempt institutes. He declares without further distinction that these must be submitted to the local ordinary. Thus it seems that pious trusts for the benefit of the institute or for its own proper works must be submitted to the local ordinary by religious trustees who are not members of an exempt clerical institute.

Other authors, however, hold a different view, permissive of greater exemption of trusts from the authority of the local ordinary. Nebreda declares that no religious must notify the local ordinary if property is given in trust for the utility of his institute.[88] He simply makes this assertion without indicating any reasons for it. Lacking cogent reasons, this view appears untenable in view of the clear provisions of the law of canon 1516.

Vromant similarly declares that no local ordinary need be notified by a religious of an institute of pontifical approval when the property is given for the utility of that institute. His reasons for this declaration lie in the alleged fact that an essential element of the trust is lacking.[89] He declares that the element lacking is the requirement that the trustee confer the property not to himself but to another. He thus hints at a lack of distinction between trustee and beneficiary. This reasoning does not appear conclusive. For the religious trustee as a physical person is distinct from his institute which is to benefit by the trust. Hence the requisite distinction between trustee and beneficiary is verified, and a trust formally exists. And, as a pious trust held by a religious trustee, it is ruled by canon 1516 with the result that it must be submitted to the proper *ordinary* of the religious, viz., the major superior of an exempt clerical religious, and the local ordinary in the case of all other religious. The law makes no further distinction.

Goyeneche holds the same view as Vromant and his arguments are similar. He declares that property given to a religious for the benefit of his institute can indeed in a wide sense be termed trust property, but that such property has rather the complexion of a

---

[88] "Quaestiones Selectae de Iure Administrativo Ecclesiastico," *CpR*, VII (1926), 326.

[89] Vromant, *De Bonis Ecclesiae Temporalibus*, n. 164.

donation or legacy made directly to the institute to be spent by the institute for its proper work.[90]

In reply to both Vromant and Goyeneche it should be noted that if the property is given to a religious institute to be used for its benefit then no trust exists. The religious moral person can receive and possess property, even property productive of regular income.[91] Use of such property for the benefit of the institute does not involve a trust in the formal sense, for the trustee and the beneficiary are identified. Thus such donations or bequests to a religious *moral* person for the benefit of that person are not trusts,[92] even though an individual religious may be the instrument in receiving the donation or the bequest and in transmitting it to the institute. Such conveyances therefore are not ruled by canon 1516. On the other hand, if the property is given not to a religious moral person, but to an individual religious in trust for the benefit of his institute, a trust does exist, and accordingly is governed by canon 1516. There may be reasons of congruity why such a trust should be subject wholly to the institute. Such reasons, however, hardly outweigh the provisions of canon 1516.

It does not seem that such reasons will obtain in any considerable measure of frequency. For it appears that a transfer of property to a religious for the benefit or for the purposes of his institute normally indicates a transfer of title to the institute with a designation of the purposes for which the donated property is intended. Such a conveyance appears at least presumptively to be made to the institute. The more complex arrangement whereby the donor transfers property to the individual religious with a trust obligation to use it for the institute should hardly be presumed. For such an effect an express declaration seems necessary.

Vromant adduces a further exemption of religious trustees from the authority of the local ordinary. As has been seen, he declares that a trust to a religious for the benefit of his institute is not subject to the local ordinary. He draws the further corollary that a non-exempt religious of an institute of pontifical approval need not

[90] "Consultationes," *CpR*, III (1922), 267.
[91] Canon 531.
[92] Beste, *Introductio in Codicem*, p. 750.

submit to the local ordinary a trust made for some pious work in general (i. e., without any designation of place) when that pious work is by the approbation of the Holy See an official work of the institute.[93] He declares that such a donation is not to be considered as a trust properly so called.

Quite evidently he has in mind here, as before, the lack of distinction between trustee and beneficiary. However, the same objection that was made to his previous conclusion regarding the exemption of a trust committed to a religious for his institute may be lodged against this further corollary. If, indeed, property is given to the institute for its own purposes, no trust exists,[94] and canon 1516 is not applicable. If, however, the property is given to a religious formally in trust for the purposes of the institute, a trust does exist and accordingly must be submitted to the *ordinary* of the religious in virtue of canon 1516, § 1.

Pertinent to the study of the proper ordinary for the solemnities of canon 1516, a comparison with can 533, § 1, 3°,[95] is in order. For this latter refers to certain property given for local benefit, and requires the local ordinary's consent for its investment. Among such property elements are obviously included property given in trust for local charity or worship. Canon 1516 and canon 533, § 1, 3°, are similar in this that under each of these canons trusts for local purposes are made subject to the supervision of the local ordinary, although in slightly different ways. The investment of the trusts under canon 533, § 1, 3°, requires the local ordinary's consent; furthermore he has a right to keep informed about them.[96] Canon 1516, however, extends to all trusts, including those for local as well as those for other than local purposes. It requires controls similar to but not identical with those which are required by canon 533, § 1, 3°, and canon 535, § 3, 2°. The major difference appears to lie in the fact that canon 1516 applies to trusts made to any clerics or religious, while canon 533, § 1, 3°, applies to trusts made to the *house* of a religious congregation.

---

[93] Vromant, *De Bonis Ecclesiae Temporalibus*, n. 164.

[94] Beste, *Introductio in Codicem*, p. 750.

[95] For a full discussion of canon 533, § 1, 3° and 4°, and § 2, see Chapter VIII.

[96] Canon 535, § 3, 2°.

A comparison must be made between canon 1516 and canon 533, § 1, 4°. Each of these has a variety of situations subject to its rule. Canon 533, § 1, 4°, governs absolute donations of money to the parish or mission, and donations to a religious for the benefit of the parish or the mission. An absolute donation is one that is free of conditions or trust provisions. Donations to religious for the benefit of the parish or the mission may be gifts in trust or just simply gifts with an attached obligation.[97] Canon 1516 governs all pious trusts in which individual clerics or religious are the trustees, including those which are made for the benefit of a parish or a mission as well as other pious trusts. Thus common to both canons and ruled by each is that class of pious trusts which are held by religious for the benefit of a parish or a mission.

There is no conflict in this application of both canons to the same situation. Canon 533 requires the consent of the *local ordinary* for investment; canon 1516 charges the *ordinary* with certain supervisory duties. And when a determined parish or mission is designated as the beneficiary, it is the *local ordinary* who has this authority.[98]

When no specific designation of a parish or a mission is made, no *local ordinary* need be approached in virtue of canon 533, § 1, 4°.[99] However, if a formal trust is made to a religious as the trustee—and such a trust is not to be confused with a gift to a religious institute for the purposes of that institute—such a trust will be subject to the *ordinary* by virtue of canon 1516 even when the trust is to benefit undesignated parishes or missions. Thus no trust is left without some supervision by some ordinary. This clearly seems to be the purpose of canon 1516.

Fiduciary obligations upon ecclesiastical moral persons involving the management and investment of the endowments of pious foundations and the expenditure of income will be governed by the laws provided for and regulative of pious foundations.[100]

[97] The concept of a trust would not be verified if no administration of property were involved. Such would be the case if a religious were simply the agent or instrument for the purchase of something for a parish or a mission. See p. 127.

[98] Canon 1516, § 3.

[99] See p. 127.

[100] See Chapter IX.

CHAPTER VIII

INVESTMENT OF FUNDS GIVEN FOR PIOUS CAUSES (2): PROPERTY SUBJECT TO THE PROVISION OF CANON 533

SIMILAR to the trust properties indicated in canon 1516 is the property ruled by canon 533, § 1, 3°, 4°. This canon requires the consent of the local ordinary for the investment of certain types of funds.[1] The entire canon, as is obvious, refers to investments made by religious. Numbers 3 and 4 of the first paragraph of this canon specifically refer to property that has been given for certain ecclesiastical purposes. Number three refers to property given for local worship or charity; number four refers to property given to a parish or a mission, or to religious for a parish or a mission.

The first and second numbers of the paragraph are not treated here, for the funds indicated by these numbers of the canon are not specifically of the class of funds under discussion here. The first number is a blanket requirement for the local ordinary's consent, and also for the regular superior's consent when such a superior is involved, for all investments made by the superioress of nuns and by the superioress of institutes of merely diocesan approval. Inasmuch as the provision applies to all investments, no distinction is to be made between the various types of funds, nor is there any

[1] Canon 533, § 1.—Pro pecuniae quoque collocatione servetur praescriptum can. 532, § 1; sed praevium consensum Ordinarii loci obtinere tenentur:

1° Antistita monialium et religionis iuris dioecesani pro cuiusvis pecuniae collocatione; imo, si monialium monasterium sit Superiori regulari subiectum, ipsius quoque consensus est necessarius;

2° Antistita in Congregatione religiosa iuris pontificii, si pecunia dotem professarum constituat, ad normam can. 549.

3° Superior vel Antistita domus Congregationis religiosae, si qui fundi domui tributi legative sint ad Dei cultum beneficentiamve eo ipso loco impendendam;

4° Religiosus quilibet, etsi Ordinis regularis alumnus, si pecunia data sit parochiae vel missioni, aut religiosis intuitu paroeciae vel missionis.

necessity of analyzing the nature of the funds involved, as there is in numbers three and four. The second number of the paragraph pertains to dowry investments. It has already been discussed in its proper place.[2]

The third number of the paragraph requires the local ordinary's consent for the investment of certain property which was given to houses of religious congregations with the obligation of expending it locally for the worship of God or for other charitable purposes. This local designation is apparently viewed as establishing equitable interests in the place designated with the consequent subjection of the matter to the local ordinary. The fourth number of that same paragraph requires this consent for the investment of money to which a parish or a mission has the beneficial, or equitable, interests either by reason of the fact that the money has been given directly to the parish or the mission, or directly to religious but for the benefit of the parish or the mission. It was felt that these two numbers of the canon's first paragraph should be treated following the treatment of trusts in the previous chapter, both because the previous treatment of trusts has thrown some light upon them, and also because the study of these two numbers seems to illustrate even more fully the previously developed notions regarding the protection of the beneficial, or equitable, interests attached to trusts.

ARTICLE 1. CANON 533, § 1

Before an approach is made to the third and fourth numbers of canon 533, § 1, it is apropos first to set out certain considerations related to the entire first paragraph of the canon. This paragraph requires that for any investment of money the constitutions of the respective religious institutes be followed. In addition it requires the consent of the local ordinary for investment in certain situations specified in nn. 1-4. It has been declared that the local ordinary's consent is required only for the permissiveness of the act and not for its validity.[3]

[2] See Chapter VI.

[3] Schaefer, *De Religiosis*, n. 197; Larraona, *"Commentarium Codicis," CpR*, XII (1931), 439-440, nota 518; Goyeneche, *Iuris Canonici Summa Principia,*

Vromant declares that the requirement for the local ordinary's consent affects permissiveness, and not validity, except in the event that money is given directly to a parish or a mission over which a religious is in charge. When money is given directly to the parish or the mission, as can occur under the terms of canon 533, § 1, 4°, its investment can be *validly* made only with the consent of the local ordinary. Vromant's reason for this distinction lies in the applicability of canon 1527, § 1, and its sanction of invalidity in only that case wherein money is given to the parish or the mission. Only in this event, he declares, does canon 1527, § 1, apply to religious. The whole context of its title in the Code, Vromant asserts, indicates that canon 1527, § 1, is to be regarded as applying to only those administrators who as subjects of the local ordinary administer property of secular institutes subject in every way to his jurisdiction; the canon does not apply to religious of pontifical approval.[4] Thus, even though the act of investment constitutes an act of extraordinary administration, the invalidating effect of canon 1527, § 1, would not be applicable.

The reasoning indicated by Vromant together with the conclusion of those authors who view the need for the local ordinary's consent as affecting only permissiveness makes their view mandatory. For in the light of canons 11 and 15, sanctions of invalidity must be express and not open to doubt if they are to have effect. It is therefore to be concluded that the local ordinary's consent, as required by canon 533, affects the permissivness and not the validity of the act of investment. There is an exception to this conclusion in the case of money given directly to the parish or the mission. Such money is thoroughly subject to the local ordinary because of his jurisdiction over the parish or the mission. Accordingly the sanction of invalidity of canon 1527, § 1, has application when the ordinary's consent is required for the extraordinary administrative act of investment.[5]

There appears to be some disagreement among canonical au-

Lib. II, Pars II, p. 67, nota 7; McManus, *The Administration of Temporal Goods in Religious Institutes,* p. 93.

[4] Vromant, *De Bonis Ecclesiae Temporalibus,* n. 230.

[5] Vromant, *De Bonis Ecclesiae Temporalibus,* n. 230.

thors on the point whether a bank deposit of funds at interest is to be considered an act of investment and therefore subject to canon 533. Some declare that such a bank deposit does not constitute an investment and that therefore the local ordinary's consent under canon 533 is not required.[6]

A contrary opinion holds that a bank deposit at interest juridically does constitute an investment and is, therefore, subject to canon 533 in its requirement for the local ordinary's consent for investment.[7]

McManus satisfactorily clarifies the situation by means of his distinction between deposit at interest as an administrative routine for insuring the safety of money and for achieving a greater facility in paying bills and deposit at interest in a quasi-permanent way in order primarily to render the property productive.[8] He points out that the first type of bank deposit does not constitute an investment and that accordingly the consent of the local ordinary would not be required for such a disposition of funds. Deposit in the second manner is to be considered juridically as an investment, and the plan should be submitted to the local ordinary for his judgment regarding the utility and fruitfulness of such a disposition of funds. He further implies that the facility with which the money may be withdrawn from a productive disposition is not the critical difference between bank deposit at interest and investment in its more strict and proper sense,[9] since most investments can be converted into cash in a relatively short time.[10]

Thus, a bank deposit at interest when made for purposes of administrative convenience is not to be considered as an investment. When made as a productive disposition of funds in preference to other modes of investing it is to be considered as an in-

---

[6] Coronata, *Institutiones,* I, n. 559; Vermeersch-Creusen, *Epitome,* I, n. 652; O'Brien, *The Exemption of Religious in Church Law,* p. 254; Larraona, "Commentarium Codicis," CpR, XII (1931), 437. See also Bouscaren-Ellis, *Canon Law,* p. 251.

[7] Oesterle, *Praelectiones Iuris Canonici,* I, 277.

[8] *The Administration of Temporal Goods in Religious Institute,* p. 94.

[9] See pp. 23 ff. regarding the senses of the term "investment."

[10] McManus, *loc. cit.*

vestment and therefore as subject to norms established regarding investment.

Several authors make a similar, but a confusing, distinction regarding what investment practices are subject to the ruling of canon 533. They limit the canon's applicability to investments that are stable and permanent as opposed to those that are temporary.[11] The reasonableness of this restriction of the canon's scope is difficult to appreciate if by the temporary investments allegedly not subject to the ruling of the canon are to be understood investments properly so called, as, for example, short term bonds or other readily marketable securities to be held for a short time. For in these temporary investments, as in all investments, there is present the element of risk and the necessity of considering many investment factors. It seems that the law, in view of its purpose of protecting the property, should in their regard be no less applicable.[12]

There does not appear to be any basis in the canon for distinguishing between permanent and temporary investment. Investment is there mentioned without any qualification. Thus if an act constitutes a true investment it appears to be ruled by the provision contained in canon 533.

The difficulty disappears if what the indicated authors mean by a temporary investment is a temporary bank deposit at interest. For such a deposit with a reliable banking institution is generally marked by safety and the almost immediate availability of the funds upon demand. That such is the meaning of temporary investment in this regard seems to be indicated by the fact that a bank deposit at interest has been given as an example of temporary investment,[13] and by the fact that other authors who do not make any distinction between temporary and permanent investment do

---

[11] Vromant, *De Bonis Ecclesiae Temporalibus*, p. 246, nota 2; Prümmer, *Manuale Iuris Canonici*, p. 260; Schaefer, *De Religiosis*, n. 197; Nebreda, "Quaestiones Selectae de Iure Administrativo Ecclesiastico," *CpR*, VII (1926), 265.

[12] A somewhat similar problem arises regarding temporary and permanent investment of surplus funds under canon 1523, 4°. See pp. 59-64 for a discussion of this problem.

[13] Prümmer, *Manuale Iuris Canonici*, pp. 260-261.

make a distinction between investment properly so called, deposit at interest, and deposit simply for safe-keeping, and understand only the first of these as ruled by the provision in the canon.[14]

The distinction between investment and deposit at interest for administrative convenience seems to be more accurate and pertinent than that between permanent and temporary investment in the matter of establishing what acts are ruled by the provision of canon 533. It must be kept in mind that deposit at interest can under some circumstances juridically constitute investment, as is the case when such deposit is made in a rather permanent way for the yielding of income in preference to other modes of rendering the money productive. In summary, all investment properly so called is governed by canon 533 as is also deposit at interest when it may be said to constitute investment. Deposit at interest made for security and convenience in administration is not so governed. Similarly, such deposit if made for the yielding of interest would not be governed by the canon when made temporarily, as, for example, pending the purchase of a regular investment.

ARTICLE 2. NUMBER 3 OF CANON 533, § 1
A. Persons Subject to This Provision

This section of the canon indicates as subjects of its provision the superior or the superioress of a house of a religious congregation. Thus communities of men and those of women are indicated, although this specific mention would not be necessary.[15] It is the superior of a house who is concerned, viz., of the house to which the indicated property is given. Thus this canon does not apply

[14] Vermeersch-Creusen, *Epitome,* I, nn. 652, 656; Beste, *Introductio in Codicem,* p. 356. Claeys Bouuaert-Simenon declare that the canon applies to investment. They describe investment as something that is "de se stabile, ita ut pecunia prompta seu liquida rursus haberi nequeat nisi mediante quadam alienatione," and contrast such an investment with deposit of money even at interest. (*Manuale Juris Canonici,* I, n. 632).

[15] Canon 490 provides that what is established concerning religious, although expressed in the masculine gender, applies also for women, unless non-applicability is evident from the context or from the nature of the matter.

to provincial superiors,[16] or, as it is put perhaps more accurately by Vermeersch-Creusen, it does not apply to property given to the congregation itself, but it is applicable only when the property is given to the house.[17] This manner of expressing the limits of the canon seems more accurate, for a provincial superior could be the superior of a house as well as of the province. In this case the wording of the law seems to lend itself better to Vermeersch-Creusen's expression. For property given to the house would be subject to the provisions of number three even though the provincial superior were the superior of the house. Property given to the province would not be so subject.

The house indicated in the canon is the house of a religious congregation. Thus superiors of regulars are not subject to this provision.[18] This exemption of regulars is also readily seen in the original source of this section of the canon. This number three is taken from the Constitution of Leo XIII, *Conditae a Christo*.[19] The opening sentence of this constitution indicated that its provisions were to apply to institutes whose members took simple vows.[20]

The law of the Code is drawn from the second part of the constitution which treats *de Sodalitatibus . . . quarum Apostolica Sedes vel leges recognovit vel institutum commendavit aut approbavit*.[21] In the language of the Code these are institutes of pontifical approval. Thus Congregations of pontifical approval which do not have the privilege of exemption from the local ordinary's jurisdiction were formerly and are presently unquestionably subject to the provision of the law now expressed in canon 533, § 1, 3°.[22]

---

[16] Coronata, *Institutiones*, I, 694, nota 4.

[17] *Epitome*, I, n. 656.

[18] Vermeersch-Creusen, *Epitome*, I, n. 656; Coronata, *Institutiones*, I, 694, nota 4; Schaefer, *De Religiosis*, n. 197.

[19] Leo XIII, const. *Conditae a Christo*, 8 dec. 1900—*Fontes*, n. 644.

[20] An *order* is an institute whose members make profession of solemn vows. Although some religious of an order may take only simple vows, this does not destroy the institute's quality of being an order. (Creusen-Gareschè-Ellis, *Religious Men and Women in the Code*, p. 9).

[21] *Loc. cit.*

[22] See also canon 618, § 2, 1°.

The first part of the Constitution *Conditae a Christo,* which treated of institutes of diocesan approval, gave to the local ordinary a much broader control over these than over congregations of pontifical approval. This broader control is contained in the Code law of canon 533, § 1, 1°, for institutes of diocesan approval. Thus the situation in 3° is already adequately provided for in 1° regarding institutes of merely diocesan approval. The status of exempt congregations under canon 533, § 1, 3°, is however a matter of great dispute. Schaefer († 1948) was of the opinion that a religious superior of a house belonging to an exempt religious congregation must have the consent of the local ordinary for the investment of money of the kind indicated.[23] A considerable number of authors are in agreement with this view.[24]

But there is an impressive array of canonists who support the view that houses of exempt congregations are not subject to the provisions of canon 533, § 1, 3°.[25] Vermeersch-Creusen presented the opinion that this section of the law does not apply to exempt clerical congregations,[26] implying that it does apply to lay congregations although exempt. This view is based on the fact, in their opinion, evident from canon 1550, that exempt religious are no more dependent upon the local ordinary for worship in their own churches than are regulars. It is difficult to see the basis for

---

[23] *De Religiosis,* n. 197.

[24] Chelodi, *Ius Canonicum de Personis,* n. 260; Pejška, *Ius Canonicum Religiosorum* (3 ed., Friburgi Brisgoviae, 1927), p. 64; Wernz-Vidal, *Ius Canonicum,* III, 176; Larraona, "Commentarium Codicis," *CpR,* XIII (1932), 25; Claeys Bouuaert-Simenon, *Manuale Juris Canonici,* I, n. 632.

[25] Nebreda, "Quaestiones Selectae de Iure Administrativo Ecclesiastico," *CpR,* VII (1926), 321 ss.; De Meester, *Compendium,* II, p. 425, nota 4; Vromant, *De Bonis Ecclesiae Temporalibus,* p. 249, nota 1; Bastien, *Directoire Canonique,* n. 316; McManus, *The Administration of Temporal Goods in Religious Institutes,* pp. 110-111; O'Brien, *The Exemption of Religious in Church Law,* p. 254; Cappello, *Summa Iuris Canonici,* II, n. 29; Melo, *De Exemptione Regularium,* The Catholic University of America Canon Law Studies, n. 12 (Washington, D. C.: The Catholic University of America, 1921), pp. 158-159; Blat, *Commentarium,* Liber II, Partes II et III, n. 259; Regatillo, *Institutiones Iuris Canonici* (2 vols., Vol. I, 2. ed., Santander: Sal Terrae, 1946), I, n. 680.

[26] *Epitome,* I, n. 656.

declaring that clerical exempt religious are not bound by this provision, but that lay exempt religious are bound. Coronata, although apparently inclining to the view that all religious congregations are subject even though they may be exempt, nevertheless indicates the doubtful status of the question.[27] Such a suspension of judgment seems to be an extremely sensible attitude, in view of the arguments and authorities ranged on each side, until an authentic interpretation of the law is had.

B. Funds Subject to This Provision

The local ordinary's consent is required by canon 533, § 1, 3°, for the investment of money which is given to a house of a religious congregation to be expended locally for the worship of God or for charitable purposes. His consent is also required for the investment of money received from the sale of property given for the same purposes. The canon uses the word *fundi* in designating this property. But the canon applies only to the investment of money, as is evidenced by its first words, *pro pecuniae quoque collocatione.* Thus the *fundi*[28] of the canon can be governed by the canon only when the property signified by this term is converted into money.[29] If income-producing real estate or securities were given to the house of a religious congregation, and the income was to be used for local worship or charity, canon 533 would not be applicable, for then the making of an investment would not be involved. If such property were sold, canon 533 would apply to the reinvestment to be made of the proceeds.

The signification of the word *fundi* in its context in the canon comprehends all property given to the house of the religious congregation for local worship or charity, and the canon evidently becomes operative when that property consists of money or is con-

---

[27] Coronata, *Institutiones,* I, 694, nota 4.

[28] Although the term *fundus* properly signifies productive real estate, it is also to be understood as comprehensive of any productive immovable property, other property including securities, and money itself. See Larraona, "Commentarium Codicis," *CpR,* XIII (1932), 31; Coronata, *Institutiones,* I, 694, nota 5; Schaefer, *De Religiosis,* n. 197.

[29] Larraona, "Commentarium Codicis," *CpR,* XIII (1932), 31, nota 554.

verted into money and its investment is planned. It appears that
the canon is applicable to the investment of all money given to
the house for the purposes indicated in the canon,[30] whether that
money is to be held as an endowment [31] or whether the money has
no such restriction placed upon its use.

The applicability of the canon has been limited by McManus
to the investment of funds which have been established as an
endowment whose principal must be preserved.[32] He argues to
this restriction of the canon's applicability from the fact that the
money is to be invested, and from the reason underlying the local
ordinary's supervision, which, he says, is the desire to keep the
principal intact.[33] However, these considerations appear to have
the same validity in any investment, regardless of whether or not
the funds constitute endowment which must be invested. Even
funds which were given to be themselves expended, i. e., if the
principal itself is to be consumed, may be invested pending their
ultimate consumption.

If, for example, funds were given to the house of a religious
congregation for the purpose of building a hospital locally, the immediate expenditure of the funds in this project would perhaps
have to wait because of shortages in labor or in materials. Pending
the ultimate expenditure, the funds could well be profitably invested. Canon 533, § 1, 3°, appears to be applicable to such a
contemplated investment. There does not appear in the canon any
basis for the distinction between investment of money given as an
endowment and investment of money given for outright expendi-

----

[30] Also to be included, obviously, is money received from the sale of
other forms of property which were given for the purposes indicated in the
canon.

[31] It is the nature of an endowment that the principal be preserved and
the income alone be expended. See p. 170, note 66.

[32] McManus, *The Administration of Temporal Goods in Religious Institutes*, p. 103.

[33] McManus (*loc. cit.*) refers to the words of the Constitution *Conditae a
Christo* from which the present law is drawn: "[Episcopus] ne sortes minuantur,
redditus ne perperam erogentur, curabit." Cf. Leo XIII, const. *Conditae a
Christo*, 8 dec. 1900, § 2, n. IX—*Fontes*, n. 644.

ture for the purposes indicated in 3°. This section of the canon refers simply to the investment of money given for certain purposes.

The words of the Constitution *Conditae a Christo* as quoted above indeed refer to the preservation of principal, as McManus has been seen to point out. However, both this provision of the pre-Code law and the provision of the present law undoubtedly have for their purpose the preservation of the principal, but not in the absolute sense of permanent preservation as endowment, but rather preservation relative to the accomplishment of the purposes for which the donation was made. Hence it is to be concluded that the superior must have the local ordinary's consent for the investment of the money that is given, or of the money that is derived from the sale of property which was given, for the purposes indicated in the canon, regardless of whether that money possesses or lacks the nature of endowment. The canon does not appear to indicate any basis for the distinction made by McManus between endowment property which must be invested and other property. The investment of endowment funds or of other funds given for the purposes described in the ruling of canon 533, § 1, 3° appears to be equally subject to the law. It seems immaterial whether the funds exist as endowment or as donations for direct and complete expenditure. The investment of each requires the consent of the local ordinary.

Similarly there does not appear to be any basis for the distinction between endowment funds and other funds in the pre-Code provisions of the *Normae* of June 28, 1901,[34] and of the section of the constitution *Conditae a Christo* [35] whence this number of the *Normae* was drawn.

The only other author consulted who demonstrated a view similar to that of McManus is Blat. He considers the canon applicable only when property is involved which is destined for a

---

[34] "Ad rem oeconomicam quod attinet, episcopus non cognoscat, nisi de fundorum legatorumve administratione, quae sacris sint attributa, vel loci aut dioecesis incolis iuvandis."—*Normae Secundum quas S. Cong. Episcoporum et Regularium procedere solet in Approbandis Novis Institutis votorum Simplicium* (Romae: S. C. de Prop. Fide, 1901), n. 261.

[35] § 2, XI—*Fontes*, n. 644.

foundation.[36] The considerations that have been alleged against the restriction placed by McManus apply *a fortiori* against that placed by Blat. Other authors do not make the distinction between funds which as endowment are to be kept intact absolutely and invested and those funds which are not constituted as endowment. The very absence of any such distinction in the law itself is an argument against the applicability of this distinction.

A further specification regarding the type of property contemplated in this section of the canon is indicated by the words *tributi legative sint*. These words point to property given by act *inter vivos* or by act *mortis causa*.[37] Thus not everything that constitutes income for the house is to be included under the rule of the canon.[38]

The property contemplated in the canon is property that has been given for the purposes indicated by the words of the canon, *ad Dei cultum beneficentiamve eo ipso loco impendendum*. The *worship of God* comprehends the celebration of masses, the exercise of other church functions, maintenance of the church and the repair of its furnishings.[39]

Beneficentia is understood as connoting the works mentioned in canon 1544, § 1,[40] which speaks of works of piety and of charity. More specifically, it is considered as comprising the corporal and the spiritual works of mercy.[41]

When the object of the donation of the property is the sustenance of the community or the upkeep of their houses, churches, novitiates, etc., canon 533, § 1, 3°, is not applicable.[42] Schaefer disagreed with this view. He declared that the consent of the local ordinary

---

[36] *Commentarium,* Liber II, Partes II et III, n. 258.

[37] Schaefer, *De Religiosis,* n. 197; Larraona, "Commentarium Codicis," *CpR,* XIII (1932), 33.

[38] McManus, *The Administration of Temporal Goods in Religious Institutes,* p. 103.

[39] Larraona, "Commentarium Codicis," *CpR,* XIII (1932), 33.

[40] Larraona, "art. cit.," *ibid.,* pp. 33-34.

[41] Schaefer, *De Religiosis,* n. 197.

[42] Coronata, *Institutiones,* I, 694, nota 6; McManus, *The Administration of Temporal Goods of Religious Institutes,* p. 104; Blat, *Commentarium,* Liber II, Partes II et III, n. 258.

is required even when the property is given for the sustenance of the community, since this purpose is still comprehended under the term *beneficentia*.[43] Blat takes specific issue with the opinion represented by Schaefer, and declares that when property is given in aid of the community the notion of *beneficentia* does indeed obtain, but the property is given, not to be spent through the community, but for the community. Hence the local ordinary's consent is not required by reason of canon 533, § 1, 3°, in such a case.[44] This view seems to be the more reasonable of the two. The local ordinary's interests in local charitable projects and in local worship do not seem to extend to the internal support of the religious institutes.

The property contemplated in this section of the canon is property which when given for the indicated ends is to be expended *eo ipso loco*. Authors variously discuss the extent of the area designated by this phrase. Coronata understands it as referring to the town or the city as the place for the expenditures.[45] He indicates, however, that other authors understand it as referring also to the larger area of the entire diocese. Vermeersch-Creusen,[46] De Meester [47] and Schaefer [48] understand it as of the diocese in which the religious house is located. Since the question relates to the authority of a local ordinary, their view seems to be the more reasonable one. It is the designation of the place in which the house is located that brings the matter under the authority of the local ordinary. It seems quite logical to conclude that the designation of any place within the jurisdiction of that local ordinary will have the effect of bringing the matter under his supervisory authority when the other conditions are verified.

It is clear from the words of the canon that, if no designation of place is made, the matter does not come under the jurisdiction of the local ordinary by virtue of this canon. Similarly, if the

---

[43] *De Religiosis*, n. 197.

[44] Blat, *Commentarium*, Liber II, Partes II et III, n. 258.

[45] *Institutiones*, I, 694, nota 7.

[46] *Epitome*, I, n. 656.

[47] *Compendium*, II, p. 425, n. 980.

[48] *De Religiosis*, n. 197.

place designated is in the jurisdiction of a local ordinary different from the one for the religious house, the canon does not apply, for the words *eo ipso loco* are not verified.[49]

ARTICLE 3. NUMBER 4 OF CANON 533, § 1

A. Persons Subject to This Provision

Any religious must have the consent of the local ordinary for the investment of money given to the parish or the mission, or to the religious for the benefit of the parish or the mission. The express inclusion of regulars by the very words of 4° of canon 533, § 1, precludes any difficulty as to exemption, such as arose regarding the inclusion of exempt congregations under the terms of 3°. Since even regulars are included, obviously members of exempt congregations of pontifical approval will be included. Any religious is ruled by this provision whether he be a superior or an inferior.[50]

B. Funds Comprehended Under This Provision

Comprehended under the provision of this section of the canon is the money which is given to a parish or a mission or to religious for the benefit of a parish or a mission. The authors consulted do not place emphasis upon the term *religiosus,* but place it rather upon the money which is given and the fact that it is given for the parish or the mission.[51] Yet, because of the stress which the indicated authors place upon the money in so far as it is given for the parish or the mission, it seems that the canon aims at establishing control over the investment of such funds regardless of what religious holds them or in what capacity he holds them. It seems proper therefore to conclude that *religiosus* is to be understood of

---

[49] Blat, *Commentarium,* Liber II, Partes II et III, n. 258.

[50] Vermeersch-Creusen, *Epitome,* I, n. 656; Beste, *Introductio in Codicem,* p. 357.

[51] This emphasis is especially noticeable in Vromant, *De Bonis Ecclesiae Temporalibus,* n. 232, and Nebreda, "Quaestiones Selectae de Iure Administrativo Ecclesiastico," *CpR,* VII (1926), 262. These authors put their expression in the passive voice by making the phrase, *money given for the parish or the mission,* the subject of the sentence.

a physical person acting either as a private person or as an official or agent of a religious moral person. Thus any money given to the religious in either capacity with the designation that it is meant for a parish or a mission seems to be comprehended under the law here in question. This conclusion is borne out by McManus, who pointedly declares that all donations and offerings are comprehended under this law if they were made for the benefit of the parish or the mission, whether they were made directly or indirectly to the religious house or church, or to the individual religious for the parish or the mission.[52]

Vromant also declares that, if property is given to the institute itself or to a province of the institute but for the benefit of the parish or the mission, such property is subject to the vigilance of the ordinary of the place which acquires an interest from the donation, and this local ordinary's consent is required when investment is made of money so given.[53]

The determination of what donations are to be considered as made for the parish or the mission in the lack of an express designation is helped by the application of the presumption contained in canon 1536, § 1.[54] The presumption herein established is that, unless the contrary be proved, donations made to the rectors of churches, even the churches of religious, are to be considered as made to the church.[55] This provision very obviously applies to pastors and their parish churches.

The primary determinant as to whether an offering is for the rector or for the church is had in the intent of the donor as expressed explicitly or implicitly in the circumstances surrounding the donation, and only in the absence of any express intention so indicated is the presumption operative.[56] A presumption of law

[52] McManus, *The Administration of Temporal Goods in Religious Institutes,* p. 113.

[53] Vromant, *De Bonis Ecclesiae Temporalibus,* nn. 231, 234.

[54] Beste, *Introductio in Codicem,* p. 357, nota 8; Schaefer, *De Religiosis,* n. 197.

[55] Canon 1536, § 1. See also, for the origins of this, Leo XIII, const. *Romanos Pontifices,* 8 mai 1881, § 26—*Fontes,* n. 582.

[56] Coronata, *Institutiones,* II, n. 1073; Vromant, *De Bonis Ecclesiae Temporalibus,* n. 324; Bouscaren-Ellis, *Canon Law,* p. 781.

yields to contrary proof—not only the indirect proof which successfully impugns the very basis upon which the presumption rests, but also the direct proof which effectively challenges the presumption itself.[57]

For establishing other presumptions regarding the person for whom the property was given, there are certain factors which if present would support a presumption in favor of the religious or his institute. Such factors could obtain when the donor is a parent, a relative, or a friend of the religious, or a benefactor of the house or of the institute.[58]

There are other situations in which, according to some authors, the presumption should be made in favor of the religious institute. Cocchi, in commenting on canon 1536, § 1, observes that frequently alms given for the missions pertain to the institute which cares for the missions rather than to the churches established in the missions. This is true, he continues, in so far as the donors intend to aid these churches, stations, and quasi-parishes through the agency of the religious institute which they know.[59] Similarly Vermeersch-Creusen declare that although the constitution *Romanos Pontifices* was extended to the far distant missions, the presumption established therein as favoring the mission is frequently not verified regarding these distant places. The reason lies in the presumption that the benefactors intend to favor the religious congregations which they know and trust, rather than the missions themselves which are unknown to them.[60] It seems that the presumptions thus indicated by these authors are reasonable and can be applied when the circumstances warrant, with the result of removing such donations from the rule of canon 533, § 1, 4°.

The word *parish* as it appears in this section of the canon is sufficiently clear, designating as it does a precise moral person in the Church. The word *mission,* however, is not so clear in its signification. It is to be taken to include a variety of units, including

[57] See canon 1826.

[58] Schaefer, *De Religiosis,* n. 197; Creusen-Garesché-Ellis, *Religious Men and Women in the Code,* p. 120.

[59] Cocchi, *Commentarium,* VI, n. 219.

[60] Vermeersch-Creusen, *Epitome,* II, n. 857.

dioceses, vicariates, prefectures apostolic, quasi-parishes [61] and other territorial subdivisions of vicariates and prefectures.[62]

The fact that a parish is incorporated with a religious community does not remove the necessity for the local ordinary's consent as required in canon 533, § 1, 4°. This is evident from a study of canon 631, § 3, and from a response of the Commission for the Interpretation of the Code. Canon 631, § 3, expressly subjects a religious pastor or vicar to the rule of canon 533, § 1, 4°.[63]

The response of the Commission [64] indicates that the ordinary's rights in virtue of canons 631, § 3; 533, § 1, nn. 3 et 4; 535, § 3, n. 2, obtain even with regard to a parish incorporated *pleno iure* with a religious community, without prejudice to the prescriptions of canon 630, § 4, and canon 1550.[65] Thus the religious pastor or vicar is still subject to the supervision of the local ordinary regarding parish property, and must have the local ordinary's consent for investing the money which belongs to the parish.[66] The full incorporation of the parish with even an exempt institute does not remove it from the rule of the ordinary in this matter.[67]

C. Proper Ordinary for Consent

The local ordinary whose consent must be had in virtue of canon 533, § 1, 4° is the ordinary of the place in which is situated the

[61] Coronata, *Institutiones*, I, n. 559.

[62] Beste, *Introductio in Codicem*, p. 357. Cf. also Blat, *Commentarium*, Liber II, Partes II et III, n. 258.

[63] Canon 631, § 3—Quod attinet ad parochi vel vicarii religiosi remotionem e paroecia, servetur praescriptum can. 454, § 5; et quod ad bona temporalia, praescriptum can. 533, § 1, n. 4, et can. 535, § 3, n. 2.

[64] Comm. ad Interp. Cod. Iuris Canonici, resp. 25 iul. 1926, ad IV—*Acta Apostolicae Sedis*, XVIII (1926), 393; Bouscaren, *Canon Law Digest*, I, 699.

[65] Canon 1550 provides that the local ordinary's rôle regarding pious foundations is to be fulfilled by the major superior when the foundations are made in the churches, even parochial, of exempt religious. Canon 630, § 4, empowers a religious pastor regarding the administration of property in general.

[66] Bouscaren-Ellis, *Canon Law*, p. 299; Coronata, *Institutiones Iuris Canonici*, I, n. 635.

[67] Coronata, *Institutiones*, I, n. 559.

parish or the mission for which the benefit is intended.[68] Vermeersch-Creusen add that the canon presupposes that the ordinary of the religious house is also the ordinary of the parish or the mission. No further conclusion is explicitly drawn by them which would exempt the situation from the requirement for the local ordinary's consent when two different local ordinaries are concerned.

Regarding canon 533, § 1, 3°, it was noted that when the phrase *eo ipso loco* was not verified, i.e., when property was given for worship or charity in another local ordinary's jurisdiction, then the rule contained in n. 3 of the canon does not apply.[69] But canon 533, § 1, 4°, does not have any phrase restricting its effect to the situation in which only one ordinary is involved. Number 4 is therefore not parallel to n. 3 in this respect. Hence, when the local ordinary of the parish or the mission is different from the ordinary of the place where the donation was made, the consent of the former, and not of the latter, is required.[70]

D. Unspecified Donations for the Missions in General

If donations are made for parishes or missions in general, or for the parishes or missions which pertain to some religious institute, and there is no designation more specific than this, the administration of such property and any investment that is to be made of it pertains exclusively to the administrators appointed for this purpose subordinately to the superiors of their institute.[71]

[68] Beste, *Introductio in Codicem,* p. 357; Vermeersch-Creusen, *Epitome,* I, n. 656.

[69] See pp. 122-123.

[70] Coronata, *Institutiones,* I, n. 559; Schaefer, *De Religiosis,* n. 197. These authors specifically advert to the question of different local ordinaries. Nebreda's expression of the view that the ordinary of the parish or the mission must be informed, and his consent given, readily applies to the situation wherein different ordinaries are concerned. "Quaestiones Selectae de Iure Administrativo Ecclesiastico," *CpR,* VII (1926), 266-267.

[71] Coronata, *Institutiones,* I, n. 559; Schaefer, *De Religiosis,* n. 197; Fanfani, *De Iure Religiosorum, ad Normam Codicis Iuris Canonici* (ed. altera, Taurini-Romae: Marietti, 1925), n. 155; Beste, *Introductio in Codicem,* p. 357; Cocchi, *Commentarium,* IV, n. 54; De Meester, *Compendium,* II, p. 425, n. 980.

ARTICLE 4. CANON 533, § 2

In virtue of canon 533, § 2, the provisions of paragraph 1 regarding investment apply likewise to any change of investment.[72] Accordingly for such a change the constitutions are to be followed and the consent of the local ordinary and sometimes of the regular superior is to be obtained. The canon uses the phrase *pro qualibet collocationis mutatione.* Thus any change of investment seems to be ruled by this provision. Not only would a change require the consent of the local ordinary when the new investment was of a different type, as for example when a mortgage was sold and bonds purchased, but also when the change involved investments of the same type, as when one set of bonds would be replaced with another set of bonds.[73] Schaefer made the same declaration, but then he invoked a further distinction which permitted reinvestment in the very same kind of bonds apart from any newly accorded consent.[74] This, he maintained, would require only a notification of the local ordinary and not his consent. This distinction does not seem to be warranted in the case wherein bonds are sold or redeemed at maturity and new bonds even of the same company are bought. For the changes that characterize the investment market, for example in the interest rate, and in the conditions of stability and of safety, would normally warrant, so it seems, the intended protection that hinges on the local ordinary's consent. Even the judgment about whether the situation is the same as when the old investment was made, so that a similar reinvestment seems warranted, belongs properly to the local ordinary.

McManus, apparently, following Schaefer, would allow a change without new consent, but only when the original investment was withdrawn and reinvestment was made under the same conditions that attended the first investment.[75] To the present writer it seems

---

[72] Canon 533, § 2.—Haec item servanda sunt pro qualibet collocationis mutatione.

[73] Blat, *Commentarium,* Liber II, Partes II et III, n. 258.

[74] "Si e contrario obligationes vendantur et aliae eiusdem speciei emantur, certioratio quidem, non vero consensus requiri videtur, cum talis mutatio evitari non possit."—*De Religiosis,* n. 198.

[75] *The Administration of Temporal Goods in Religious Institutes,* p. 117.

that even the change involved in the withdrawal of the investment and a subsequent new reinvestment would come under the signification of the phrase *"pro qualibet collocationis mutatione."*

The example given by McManus, wherein a reinvestment in government bonds is allowed without a new consent when the earlier purchased bonds have been redeemed at maturity, does not however appear to be marked by any *"mutatio"* in the sense of the canon, for in such a case the bonds were not in fact withdrawn. The arrival of the maturity date alone was responsible for the liquidation. It may here be remarked that the great stability of United States Government bonds, which stability is responsible for the fact that the conditions of safety remain unaltered, is not enjoyed by the bonds of all other governments, nor generally by the bonds of commercial corporations.

A reason for subjecting all changes of investment, even those which Schaefer allowed to be made without the obtaining of a new consent, to the decision of the local ordinary lies in a further consideration. The price paid for a bond sometimes will be different from the price returned at maturity. This difference of the purchase price from the redemption value is due to the fluctuations of the bond market, the demands for money, and the demands for investments. It can occur that the redemption value is less than the price originally paid. Thus, when a reinvestment is made, the amount of the original purchase price should be fully reintegrated. If this is not done, there occurs a form of alienation in that some part of the income-producing property has been dissipated. To prevent this and to insure a full reintegration of the original amount invested, it is necessary to consider some part of the income as a return of principal and to set it aside as restoring the principal. Thus, when an investment is changed for another investment, care must be taken that the proper reintegration is made of the capital sum. This is an excellent reason for subjecting the change to the authority of the local ordinary.

Article 5. Accountings to the Local Ordinary

The local ordinary has the right to demand an accounting at any time regarding the funds indicated in canon 533, § 1, 3°, and the funds whose beneficial interests rest with a parish or a mission as indicated in n. 4 of the same paragraph of the canon.[76] Thus his authority is not limited to approving the investment decisions that involve such property, but it consists in full supervisory authority. The local ordinary is empowered to demand reports of the administration of the property whose investment is subject to his consent.[77]

Canon 535, § 3, 2°, applies to all the property indicated by the canon, whether or not any conversion into money and the investment of this money has followed.[78] Thus pious donations for local worship or charity when made to religious houses are subject to the supervision of the local ordinary even when no investment is involved.

[76] Canon 535, § 3, 2°. Cf. also Bouscaren-Ellis, *Canon Law*, pp. 252-253.
[77] Vermeersch-Creusen, *Epitome*, I, n. 660.
[78] McManus, *The Administration of Temporal Goods in Religious Institutes*, p. 103.

CHAPTER IX

INVESTMENT OF FUNDS GIVEN FOR PIOUS CAUSES (3); ENDOWMENTS OF PIOUS FOUNDATIONS

ARTICLE 1. NATURE OF A PIOUS FOUNDATION

THE notion of a pious foundation is to be found in the Code itself.[1] A pious foundation consists of property given in any manner to some moral person in the Church, with the obligation perpetually or for a long period of time of celebrating masses, of carrying out other defined ecclesiastical functions, or of performing certain pious or charitable works,[2] from the annual income from the property. There are four elements essential to the notion of a pious foundation.[3]

First, there must be property that is to be kept. It is not to be spent at once, but is to be kept and invested if not already productive. Income deriving from it is to be used in support of the pious works indicated. The property is termed the endowment of the foundation. It may consist of any kind of property: immovable property such as farm land, and houses, or movable property such as money and securities.[4]

Secondly, the property must be given to a moral person in the Church. Benefactors who wish to dispose charitably or piously of property through the establishment of a revenue-producing endow-

---

[1] Canon 1544, § 1.—Nomine piarum fundationum significantur bona temporalia alicui personae morali in Ecclesia quoquo modo data, cum onere in perpetuum vel in diuturnum tempus ex reditibus annuis aliquas Missas celebrandi, vel alias praefinitas functiones ecclesiasticas explendi, aut nonnulla pietatis et caritatis opera peragendi.

[2] Among the charitable works for which pious foundations may be established is the care and upkeep of the burial places and graves of the deceased. "Perpetual care funds" are a prominent type of endowment which may pertain to a pious foundation.

[3] Bouscaren-Ellis, *Canon Law*, p. 788.

[4] Coronata, *Institutiones*, II, n. 1079.

ment may accomplish their purpose in any one of three ways. The property may itself be erected as a moral person whose nature is defined in the general law of the Church as for example in the case of benefices and seminaries. A second way consists in constituting the property as an independent juridical person whose individual nature is defined in the establishment of the new corporation. Both of these types of non-collegiate juridical persons exist independently of the membership of any physical persons. Investment provisions regarding property pertaining to these are treated in their place.[5] A third way consists in establishing the endowment with an already existing ecclesiastical moral person, by which arrangement the endowment itself does not become constituted as a juridical person. Only in this last manner does a pious foundation in the technical sense of canon 1544, § 1, come into existence.[6] It is only a foundation of this type that is here under discussion.

The moral person receiving the endowment must be a moral person erected or acknowledged by the Church, so that it exists canonically as a juridic person.[7] If this is not verified, the endowment is not governed by the canons for pious foundations. An endowment for pious causes that is not technically a foundation is nevertheless ruled by the general law regarding the pious disposals of property, and is subject to the supervision of the ordinary in virtue of canon 1515.[8] The ordinary must see that any investment provisions established by the donor are carried out.[9] The investment provisions of canon 1547 that apply to pious foundations obviously do not apply to these other endowments which are given to non-ecclesiastical moral persons.

It is to be noted that the endowment on being legitimately accepted by an ecclesiastical moral person becomes technically ecclesiastical property,[10] and accordingly becomes subject to all the

---

[5] See Chapter V.

[6] Coronata, *Institutiones,* II, n. 1079.

[7] Pistocchi, *De Bonis Ecclesiae Temporalibus,* p. 472.

[8] See Coronata, *Institutiones,* II, n. 1079.

[9] See pp. 87-88.

[10] Pistocchi, *De Bonis Ecclesiae Temporalibus,* p. 471. Cf. also canon 1497.

legislation affecting such property including in their administrative significance the rules regarding alienation. These endowments of pious foundations are considered as stable capital, and they are subject to all the canonical restrictions on alienation.[11]

The third essential quality that characterizes a pious foundation is the fact that it involves an obligation in justice for the performance of the attached works. The fact that a foundation, when legitimately accepted, implies the existence of a contract [12] indicates that the obligation is one of commutative justice.

The fourth essential element of a pious foundation is the fact that the obligation is to be carried out perpetually or over a long period of time by means of the income which derives from the endowment. The minimum time period that suffices to fulfill this requirement is variously described by different authors. Pistocchi establishes it as a period of from forty to fifty years.[13] Coronata declares that a twenty-year period is the minimum.[14] Beste declares that ten years suffice, and alleges in support of this view the fact that the authors who wrote before the Code considered ten years as sufficient both for the operation of legal prescription and for the establishment of legally effective custom.[15] Claeys Bouuaert-Simenon,[16] Vermeersch-Creusen,[17] Cance [18] and De Meester [19] declare that ten years suffice to establish the *diuturnum tempus* to which the canon adverts. Vromant declares that if the civil law establishes a requirement in this matter, it must be followed.[20] As a contract, the arrangement comes under the pertinent provisions of the civil law of contracts by virtue of canon 1529. In Belgium, where Vromant was writing, a period of six years sufficed under the civil law.[21]

[11] Heston, *The Alienation of Church Property*, p. 76.
[12] Canon 1544, § 2.
[13] *De Bonis Ecclesiae Temporalibus*, p. 472.
[14] *Institutiones*, II, n. 1079.
[15] *Introductio in Codicem*, p. 769.
[16] *Manuale Juris Canonici*, III, n. 296.
[17] *Epitome*, II, n. 865.
[18] *Le Code de Droit Canonique*, III, 279.
[19] *Compendium*, III, p. 417, n. 1499.
[20] *De Bonis Ecclesiae Temporalibus*, n. 346.
[21] Vromant, *loc. cit.*

Is it the canonical notion or is it the civil law provision that is to be applied in appraising the duration of the *diuturnum tempus* requisite for the concept of a pious foundation? The correct answer seems to be that neither one furnishes an exclusive norm. The Code does not define what is meant by *diuturnum tempus*. The commentators, as has been seen, give a variety of opinions. From among these the view which establishes ten years as the minimum period for *diuturnum tempus* seems to be best substantiated and quite acceptable among recognized authors.

If this view be accepted, then the *diuturnum tempus* is had when a period of at least ten years is involved. This notion should prevail over any civil law provision that required a longer duration of time. Although the contract involved in a foundation is ruled by the civil law in virtue of canon 1529, it appears that a canonical foundation is had when the necessary canonical elements are present. The lack of some civil law requisite would not vitiate the canonical notion of a foundation, just as the complete legal invalidity under civil law of such foundations would not imply any canonical invalidity.

On the other hand, it appears that the canonical element of the *diuturnum tempus* could be verified in a period shorter than ten years when the civil law has established a shorter period as a constitutive element of a foundation. The time period could thus be considered *diuturnum* not only in virtue of the canonical notion but also in consequence of the civil law concept.[22] As long as it may be considered *diuturnum* under either canon law or civil law, the time period will fulfill this necessary constitutive element of a foundation.

If the time requirement for the establishment of a foundation, as strictly understood, were not verified, the arrangement would constitute a "pious trust"[23] and would be ruled by the provisions for trusts according to the manner in which these have already been discussed.

The notion of a foundation may be understood more precisely by the examination of the points of difference that exist between a

---

[22] Vermeersch-Creusen, *Epitome*, II, n. 865; Vromant, *De Bonis Ecclesiae Temporalibus*, n. 346.

[23] Bouscaren-Ellis, *Canon Law*, p. 788.

foundation and a canonical trust. A foundation is committed to a moral person; a trust may be committed to a moral or also to a physical person. The distinctive quality and formal element of a foundation is that the obligations are to be carried out over a long period of time; there is no necessary time consideration in the notion of a trust. A foundation requires the investment of its endowment so that the specified works may be supported from the income; a trust does not necessarily involve investment. A trust may be concerned simply with the expenditure of the principal.[24] It is evident from this comparison that a foundation is one species of the larger *genus* of property dispositions which are designated and denominated as trusts.

ARTICLE 2. ACCEPTANCE OF A FOUNDATION

In order that a foundation come into existence and accordingly that the provisions of canon 1547 regarding the investment of the endowment become applicable, the foundation must be accepted by the moral person. For this acceptance the written consent of the local ordinary must be obtained.[25] Authors are in disagreement regarding whether this consent is required for the validity or merely for the permissiveness of the acceptance. Beste, for example, declares that it is necessary for the validity.[26] Coronata[27] and Bouscaren-Ellis[28] declare that the requirement affects only the permissiveness of the acceptance. Vromant seems to have the correct explanation.[29] He states that the requirement affects the validity of the acceptance and cites canon 1527, § 1, as the basis of his conclusion. This canon declares that administrators act invalidly when they place an act exceeding the bounds and the mode of ordinary administration, unless they first shall have obtained the consent of the local ordinary, which consent is to be given in writing. The ac-

[24] See Vromant on these differences—*De Bonis Ecclesiae Temporalibus*, n. 347.
[25] Canon 1546, § 1.
[26] *Introductio in Codicem*, p. 770.
[27] *Institutiones*, II, n. 1080.
[28] *Canon Law*, p. 789.
[29] *De Bonis Ecclesiae Temporalibus*, n. 349

ceptance of a foundation is unquestionably an act of extraordinary administration.[30]

Vromant, however, indicates that this sanction of nullity is in effect only for foundations of secular institutes which are properly subject in every way to the jurisdiction of the local ordinary. In another section of his work [31] he points out that canon 1527 is applicable only to those administrators who as subjects of the local ordinary administer the property of secular institutes which are in every way subject to the jurisdiction of the local ordinary as distinguished from similar institutes belonging to religious. He alleges that this is evident from the context of the whole title. Thus his conclusion implies that the consent of the local ordinary is necessary for the validity of the acceptance of pious foundations if these be entrusted to moral persons over which he has full jurisdiction, but simply for the licitness of the acceptance of those foundations which are entrusted to religious moral persons. In view of the applicability of canon 1527 in one instance, but of its non-applicability to religious moral persons, Vromant's distinctions and conclusions seem warranted.

It could be argued that, since under the earlier law the consent was necessary only for the permissiveness of the acceptance, the same interpretation should be applied to the law of the Code. The earlier law was contained substantially in the Constitution *Nuper* of Innocent XII (1691-1700),[32] and the pertinent passages spoke only of a strict prohibition against acceptance without the consent of the local ordinary rather than of any stricture affecting validity. There was no clause that could be construed as having an invalidating effect. P. Gasparri (1852-1934) held that under that law no invalidity was involved in the requirement for consent.[33] Pignatellus (ca. 1620-ca. 1695) had earlier declared that mass foundations if accepted without the proper consent nevertheless stood contractually

---

[30] S. C. de Prop. Fide, 21 iul. 1856—*Collectanea*, I, n. 1127; *Fontes*, n. 4841.

[31] *De Bonis Ecclesiae Temporalibus*, n. 230.

[32] Innocentius XII, const. *Nuper*, 23 dec. 1697, § 7—*Fontes*, n. 260.

[33] *Tractatus Canonicus de Sanctissima Eucharistia* (2 vols., Parisiis et Lugduni, 1897), I, n. 561.

valid.[34] He declared in support of this view that he had seen a decision of the Sacred Congregation of the Council, viz., *in Romana,* 16 ian. 1644, which made such a declaration.

However, the interpretations that were applicable to the pre-Code law do not find application to the present law. This conclusion seems to be warranted because of the change in the wording that was made when the present law was drawn up. The words of the Constitution *Nuper* evidently indicate no more than a simple prohibition.[35] The wording of canon 1546, § 1, while not necessarily indicating any invalidating effects, does however allow for such an interpretation if other reasons warrant it.[36]

The presence of such reasons appears to exist in view of the fact that the whole scope of the law has been widened. The Constitution *Nuper* applied only to mass foundations; the scope of the canon under consideration extends to pious foundations of all types. The applicability of the present general law for administrators in canon 1527 argues conclusively for the new interpretation given by Vromant and others who have been seen above to view the requirement as affecting validity.

That the consent required in canon 1527 be written is a condition that affects simply the lawfulness of the act.[37]

The authority of the local ordinary as deriving from the canons concerning pious foundations extends to several aspects of such foundations. He is to prescribe norms which establish the minimum endowment sum below which foundations cannot be accepted and rules for the proper distribution of the income of the endowment.[38] This proper distribution of income will be the local ordinary's concern when a variety of obligations are attached to the foundation.[39]

His written consent is required, as has been seen, for the acceptance by a moral person of a pious foundation. He is not to give this

[34] *Consultationes Canonicae* (10 vols., Coloniae Allobrogum, 1700), IV, 370.

[35] *Nuper,* § 7—*Fontes,* n. 260.

[36] *Ut . . . fundationes . . . acceptari possint, requiritur consensus Ordinarii loci. . . .*

[37] Vermeersch-Creusen, *Epitome,* II, n. 848.

[38] Canon 1545.

[39] Pistocchi, *De Bonis Ecclesiae Temporalibus,* p. 474.

consent unless he shall first have ascertained that the moral person
is able to carry out both the new obligations and others that are already incumbent upon it, and the ordinary must see to it that in
accordance with the traditional and established financial standards
in the diocese the income is sufficient for the pious work involved.[40]

The acceptance of a pious foundation should be made as quickly
as possible. Prior to its acceptance a pious foundation is revocable
if made by act *inter vivos*. It becomes void if the owner dies prior
to its acceptance.[41]

By way of exclusion regarding the acceptance, establishment,
and administration of a foundation, it is to be noted that the patron
of a church has no rights whatsoever.[42]

ARTICLE 3. THE ENDOWMENT AND ITS ADMINISTRATION

A. Deposit and Investment of the Endowment

Regarding money or movable goods assigned to the endowment
of a foundation, a twofold duty devolves upon the same local ordinary whose consent was requested for the acceptance of the foundation. This twofold duty is the designation of a safe place for the
immediate deposit of the money or the movable goods, and then the
selection of the investment to be made of the property. Canon 1547
itself indicates these duties and notes the details pertaining to each.[43]

The endowment of a pious foundation pertains to the moral
person by whom it has been accepted. It therefore becomes *"bona
ecclesiastica"* in the sense of canon 1497, § 1.[44] Any alienation of
the endowment property even for the purpose of reinvestment be-

---

[40] Canon 1546, § 1.

[41] Cocchi, *Commentarium*, VI, n. 228; Bargilliat, *Praelectiones Juris
Canonici* (37. ed., 2 vols., Parisiis, 1923), II, n. 1515.

[42] Canon 1546, § 2.

[43] Canon 1547. Pecunia et bona mobilia, dotationis nomine assignata, statim
in loco tuto, ab eodem Ordinario designando, deponantur ad eum finem ut
eadem pecunia vel bonorum mobilium pretium custodiantur et quamprimum
caute et utiliter secundum prudens eiusdem Ordinarii arbitrium, auditis et iis
quorum interest et dioecesano administrationis Consilio, collocentur in commodum eiusdem fundationis cum expressa et individua mentione oneris.

[44] See p. 132 above.

comes subject to the rules for alienation of church property.[45] The conversion of securities as indicated in canon 1539, § 2, may be made under the terms of that canon.[46] Such conversions are not left unprotected in consequence of the fact that they are free of any requirement for the Holy See's permission. Canon 1539, § 2, requires for such conversions the consent of the ordinary, of the diocesan council of administration, and of others who have legal interests in the matter. A fuller study of this canon was made elsewhere.[47]

A further distinction in this matter, however, appears to be indicated. The wording of canon 1547 [48] and the very nature of the contract involved in a foundation indicate that movable property must be sold and the price received be invested.[49] Accordingly this property may be sold for the purpose of investing the proceeds without any reference of the act to the Holy See, even when the movable goods consist of precious articles as defined in canon 1497, § 2.[50] This sale may be deferred for a time in order to insure sale at a fair price.[51]

Immovable property may constitute the endowment, and this obviously may be kept as the investment. If such an endowment or investments in securities given as the endowment were characterized by a lack of safety or other considerations which made them unsuitable as investments for a pious foundation, it seems that the ordinary should require the liquidation of these investments and a reinvestment of the proceeds in a suitable manner. If any intention of the founder in this matter was manifested, canon 1514 orders that such an intention must be respected and carried out. The administration of pious foundations by the proper administrators and the supervision of the ordinary are governed also by the general

---

[45] Heston, *The Alienation of Church Property*, pp. 75-76.

[46] Beste, *Introductio in Codicem*, p. 770.

[47] See pp. 47-53.

[48] . . . *bonorum mobilium pretium*. . . .

[49] Coronata, *Institutiones*, II, n. 1081; Miller, *Founded Masses According to the Code of Canon Law*, The Catholic University of America Canon Law Studies, n. 34, Washington, D. C.: The Catholic University of America, 1926, p. 36.

[50] Bouscaren-Ellis, *Canon Law*, p. 790.

[51] Bouscaren-Ellis, *loc. cit.*

law for all pious disposals of property as these are contained in canons 1514-1517.[52]

Regarding the investment of the money constituting the endowment, canon 1547 orders that the investment be made as soon as possible. Since an important consideration of any investment choice involves the condition of either the real estate or the securities market, it seems that an alert and efficient administration could properly defer the purchase of an investment for a time for the purpose of obtaining a lower price. The lapse of time should not be unduly prolonged, for then obviously any possible price advantage would be offset by the lack of revenue from the idle funds. This relationship can be estimated and a decision can be made accordingly. The point of this discussion is that the *quamprimum* of the law is to be understood, not in an absolute sense, but in reference to the financial benefit of the foundation. The indication of the price factor is certainly not to be taken as an emphasis in any way upon the speculative aspect of the investment. The utmost conservatism is mandatory for church investments.[53] However, practically every investment has some speculative aspect.[54] Although church investments necessarily will be those which reflect a minimum of speculative qualities, nevertheless that minimum is a factor to be considered.

The selection of the investment rests, according to canon 1547, with the local ordinary, but he must consult first with certain other parties. Throughout the canon law on property administration there appears the constant demand for multiple judgment in matters wherein judgment and discretion are of great importance. The monarchical government of the Church does unquestionably leave decisions ultimately to the ruling authority of the unit involved. There is, however, an attempt to temper and diminish the risks inherent in this situation by requiring variously either the consent of other individuals or groups or their counsel. Before making his se-

---

[52] Canon 1549, § 1; Coronata, *Institutiones,* II, n. 1082; De Meester, *Compendium,* III, p. 421, n. 1502. It is to be noted that a pious foundation constitutes one particular species of pious disposals of property.

[53] See pp. 30-35 above for the canonical status of speculative practices.

[54] Taylor, *Investment,* pp. 6-7. See also p. 33 above.

lection of the investment for the endowment of a pious foundation, the local ordinary must first, according to the canon, consult interested parties and the diocesan council of administration.

Although the local ordinary is not bound to follow the expressed opinions of those whom he must consult, he must nevertheless consult them.[55] Whether this requirement affects the validity of the ordinary's action remains a *dubium iuris*. According to canon 15, invalidity therefore could not be urged against the ordinary's action if taken without consulting the indicated persons.[56] Among the interested parties are the rector of a church where a foundation has been established,[57] the founder or his heirs, and the moral person to whom the foundation was granted.[58]

B. Consolidation of Endowments

By virtue of canon 1547 the investment of the endowment is to serve for the benefit of the same foundation and there is to be an express and individual mention of the obligation attached. Beste points out that the foundation's endowment is not to be used for the purposes of the moral person, as for example the building of a house or the payment of debts, but is to remain distinct, and is to be invested in such a manner that the attached obligation may be supported from the income.[59] As for the express mention of the obligation, Vromant declares that this can be advantageously done in the instrument of investment.[60] This obviously will depend upon

[55] Canon 105, 1°.

[56] A *dubium iuris* exists as to the invalidating effect of the clause regarding consultation in canon 105, 1°. The canon declares *satis est ad valide agendum ut superior illas personas audiat. . . .* It does not say that *it is required*. Some authors declare that this clause affects validity; others that it affects merely the permissiveness of the act. Canon 11 adds weight to the view of these latter. Bouscaren-Ellis (*Canon Law,* p. 91) indicate the dispute and the opposed authors and reach the conclusion that here a *dubium iuris* exists and that until a definite authentic interpretation is made the effect of invalidity cannot be urged against the act of a superior undertaken without the counsel required by law.

[57] Cappello, *Summa Iuris Canonici,* II, n. 631.

[58] Bouscaren-Ellis, *Canon Law,* p. 790.

[59] Beste, *Introductio in Codicem,* p. 770.

[60] *De Bonis Ecclesiae Temporalibus,* n. 350.

the manner in which title is held to different types of investment properties under the prevailing civil law techniques.

The last words of canon 1547, *cum expressa et individua mentione oneris,* insinuate that the endowment properties of different foundations should remain separate and distinct.[61] The words "in commodum *eiusdem* fundationis" carry the same notion. Thus, if a church had three mass foundations, each would apparently be required to have its invested endowment property distinct and segregated from that of the others. Some of the commentators, however, as will be seen, agree that a commingling, or consolidation,[62] of foundation funds is permissible for the investment of foundation endowments. This situation can be best understood after a consideration of the legal sources which underlie canon 1547 as they are indicated in the footnotes appended to this canon.

The indicated sources of the law are the Constitution *Nuper* of Innocent XII[63] and two decrees of the Sacred Congregation of the Council.[64] One of these decrees dates from 1625 and the other together with the constitution dates from 1697. These three sources contain practically identical provisions. The present law expressed in canon 1547 is taken in part from the Constitution *Nuper.* The constitution speaks of deposit being made of the money or movable goods given as the endowment of mass foundations "ad effectum illa, seu illorum pretium quamprimum investiendi in bonis immobilibus fructiferis *cum expressa et individua mentione oneris,* quod illis annexum reperitur."[65] The italized words are found verbatim in the present law. The segregation of the separate endowment properties as indicated in the words of the Constitution *Nuper* is seen to apply in that document only to immovable productive property which was the only type of investment property permissible. Such segregation, as opposed to any consolidation of the

[61] Coronata, *Institutiones,* II, n. 1081.

[62] Consolidation signifies the combining of endowment funds for investment purposes. Each endowment then consists of a share in the pool.

[63] Innocentius XII, const. *Nuper,* 23 dec. 1697—*Fontes,* n. 260.

[64] S. C. C., decr. 21 iun. 1625; decr. 23 nov. 1697—*Fontes,* nn. 2460 et 2958.

[65] *Ibid.,* § 7—*Fontes,* n. 260.

holdings especially with property owned outright by the moral person, would be instrumental in preventing the attached mass obligations from becoming confused. Segregation was convenient and effective in keeping mass obligations clear and definite when real estate was the only permissible investment. Real estate by its nature readily lent itself to segregation for the purpose of keeping attached mass obligations quite definite. The same convenience and effectiveness could not be had when investments in securities would be involved in view of the more mobile nature of these.

In the law contained in canon 1547, permissible investments are not limited to investments in productive real estate. Another point of difference lies in the fact that the Constitution *Nuper* was concerned solely with mass foundations; canon 1547, as well as the entire title on pious foundations, treats of foundations of types other than those involving mass obligations. This is evident from canon 1544, § 1. The notion of mutual segregation of endowments is, however, kept in the wording of the law. Investment needs today can frequently be met most effectively by investments other than real estate. The one very obvious difficulty in real estate invest-ments is the great care and attention that must be given to such a type of investment. In an investment program in which securities are purchased, as for example government bonds, bonds of religious corporations, or very high grade obligations of other types, the segre-gation of the different endowment properties can prove less efficient than their consolidation.

Among the advantages that have been enumerated relative to the combining of investment funds,[66] two appear particularly perti-nent to pious foundations, viz., the diversification for each unit in the combination and the less expensive administration of the funds. Regarding the former of these, it is to be noted that if one endow-ment were invested in one security, the diversification that is a safety factor would be lacking. If the obligation were defaulted upon, either the income or the entire endowment could be wiped out. If, on the other hand, the endowment consisted of a share in a consolidation, the failure of one investment in the group would

[66] *First National Bank of Birmingham* v. *Basham,* 238 Ala. 500, 191 S. 873 (1939).

not cause the complete destruction of any one endowment. The loss suffered would be spread over all the endowments in the consolidation. So, too, diminution of income from one security would be similarly compensated for by the regular returns from the others.

Some authors who comment on this matter of consolidation versus segregation [67] insist on the meaning implied in the words of the canon. Claeys Bouuaert-Simenon [68] and De Meester [69] insist that consolidation for foundations is not permitted under the provisions of this canon. Beste declares that the endowment must be kept distinct from the moral person, and seems to imply that it must be kept distinct absolutely.[70]

On the other hand, Coronata,[71] while declaring that segregation must always be the rule when the endowment consists of immovable property, nevertheless is of the opinion that the Code does not seem to demand strictly and absolutely the segregation of endowments together with their obligations when the investment is made in securities. He goes on to say that at least for foundations already in existence, the technique of consolidation, where it has been strengthened by custom, can be retained. He points out the advantages of consolidation which have already been indicated here, and declares that where consolidation obtains there is an implicit contract of insurance.

Vermeersch-Creusen declare that segregation not only of the obligations but also of the property is presupposed.[72] They go on to note, however, that in their opinion a better manner of investing, viz., through consolidation of endowments, is not prohibited by this canon. In their description of consolidation [73] they emphasize the insurance that such a practice affords to the different endowments, and consequently the greater guarantee of the execution of the attached obligation.

[67] The canonical terms used for these notions are *"generalizatio"* and *"specializatio"* respectively.

[68] *Manuale Juris Canonici,* III, n. 297.

[69] *Compendium,* III, 419, nota 1.

[70] *Introductio in Codicem,* p. 770.

[71] *Institutiones,* II, n. 1081.

[72] *Epitome,* II, n. 867.

[73] *Epitome,* II, n. 837.

Vromant [74] states that, although the canon presupposes special and individual mention of the obligations and of the endowment property, nevertheless the canon does not inherently seem to prohibit a better investment through the consolidation of the securities of several foundations. This is especially the case, he states, when the endowment consists of securities payable to the bearer. He excepts from such consolidation those endowments which by their nature, or through the intention of the founder, are to be kept distinct and separate.

From the fact that accepted authors approve the consolidation of foundation endowments for investment purposes, and especially from the considerations of the relationship between the present law and the pre-Code law which applied the requirement of segregation to immovable property alone, this consolidation does not appear to be prohibited by canon 1547. What does seem to be required is that such endowments be kept distinct and separated from the property of the moral person to which the foundation is attached.[75] Apparently supporting this notion is question n. 60 appearing in the formula for the quinquennial report to be made to the Holy See by generals of institutes whose members profess simple vows.[76] This question asks whether money by which foundations were made for the celebration of masses or the performance of works of charity was duly invested and administered separately from all other funds. The question apparently indicates concern that foundation endowments be kept segregated from the property of the institute, and not necessarily that the individual endowments be kept segregated among themselves.

While consolidation of endowments does not seem to be absolutely prohibited, it must be noted that when a founder gave as an endowment an excellent and extraordinarily safe investment, as for example certain real estate or very high grade securities, it would not seem right in justice to weaken the endowment of his foundation by consolidating it with other weaker and less safe investments of other endowments. None of the authors consulted regarding founda-

---

[74] *De Bonis Ecclesiae Temporalibus,* n. 351.
[75] See Beste, *Introductio in Codicem,* p. 770.
[76] S. C. de Religiosis, instr., 25 mart. 1923—*AAS,* XV (1923), 463.

tions mention such a situation, although it may well be in the minds of those who have been seen to view segregation of endowments as mandatory. Vromant apparently adverts to this situation when he does not allow a consolidation of those endowments which *by their nature or by the intention of the founder* are to be kept separate.

Similarly, insecure and weak investments which are given as endowment should not be permitted to weaken an investment pool consisting of other endowments. In such a case commingling could be accomplished with equity to all who have established foundations by sale of the weak investments and the reinvestment of the proceeds according to the investment formula or plan which is being followed in managing the commingled funds.

Thus it seems to be necessary to qualify the permissiveness of consolidation as obtaining only in the situations in which the founder has given money, or movable goods to be converted into money, so that an investment remains to be made. In such cases there is no weakening of the founders' endowments. Rather the technique of consolidation is a protection to the individual endowments in that it affords them mutual insurance, as this has already been described.[77]

Article 4. Official for the Formalities Concerning Pious Foundations

A. General Principle

The official who is charged with the various rights and duties relating to pious foundations is the local ordinary. These various rights and duties extend to the establishing of conditions for admitting pious foundations (canon 1545), consent for their acceptance (canon 1546), the investment of their endowment (canon 1547), the possession of a copy of the instrument establishing the foundation (canon 1548), vigilance, inspection, and accountings (canon 1549).[78] The indicated canons expressly designate the local ordinary. The phrase "formalities concerning pious foundations" as

---

[77] See pp. 143-144.

[78] De Meester, *Compendium*, III, p. 421, n. 1502.

used in the following discussion is to be understood as referring to
these rights and duties as indicated in canons 1545-1549.

B. Foundations Entrusted to Non-Exempt Religious

It is well established that for foundations entrusted to non-
exempt religious, the official for the requisite formalities can be only
the local ordinary.[79]

C. Foundations Entrusted to Exempt Religious

As to the question of determining the proper official for the
formalities concerned with foundations entrusted to exempt religious, the matter becomes complex by reason of the pertinency of
the canons on foundations themselves,[80] of the element of exemption on the part of religious from the local ordinary's jurisdiction,
and of the applicability of canons 533, § 1, 3° and 4°, and 1550.
The interpretation of canon 1550 appears as the center of the problem as to who is the proper official for the formalities concerning
pious foundations held by exempt religious. This canon is critical,
for it indicates that the local ordinary does not carry out these
formalities in every pious foundation. The approaches made by
different authors to an interpretation of this canon are remarkable
for a rather complete lack of agreement regarding the different elements necessary to arrive at an adequate interpretation.

Regarding the phrase "pious foundations in churches . . ." as it
appears in canon 1550, there is little indication as to whether the
meaning relates to those pious foundations which are established
with a church as the receiving unit, or rather to those pious foundations whose obligations are to be carried out in the church. Vromant
understands the phrase as referring to pious foundations whose
obligations are to be carried out in a church.[81] This understanding

---

[79] Vromant, *De Bonis Ecclesiae Temporalibus*, n. 356; Reilly, *The Visitation of Religious*, The Catholic University of America Canon Law Studies, n.
112 (Washington, D. C.: The Catholic University of America, 1938), p. 110.

[80] The phrase "the canons on foundations" is used here and will be used
in the following discussion to indicate canons 1544-1549.

[81] Vromant, *De Bonis Ecclesiae Temporalibus*, n. 354.

seems warranted in view of the immediate context in which the word *churches* appears best understood if taken in its literal signification [82] rather than in its wider signification of any ecclesiastical moral person as indicated in canon 1498. If the word *church* is understood in its literal sense, and not as signifying a moral person, a pious foundation could not be given to it. Only an ecclesiastical moral person can accept a pious foundation.[83] Hence a "pious foundation in a church" could only be a foundation whose obligations were to be carried out in a church. The acceptance of this meaning seems warranted also because of the fact that it offers a basis for a coherent explanation of canon 1550 which is consistent with canon 533, § 1, 3° and 4°.

Before further discussion, it is necessary to establish precisely what churches are designated in the phrase, "the churches, even parochial, of exempt religious," as it appears in canon 1550. A church belongs to religious when the religious institute has full ownership of the church, or, at least, when the institute has its *dominium utile* perpetually.[84] When the church is a parish church, the determination as to whether the church may be designated as belonging to the religious will depend upon the type of union that exists between the parish and the religious moral person.

A parish may be joined to a religious house or institute in a variety of ways. The Code treats of the incorporation of a parish with a religious house in canon 1425, §§ 1 and 2. The first paragraph treats of a union which is effected *ad temporalia tantum quod attinet;* the second, of a union which is effected *pleno iure.*

In discussing the union of benefices, Wernz (1842-1914)-Vidal (1868-1939) treated of the two types of incorporation of a benefice with a religious house.[85] They declared that the less complete type of union consists in the transfer of the temporal goods of the benefice to the religious house to which the incorporation was made.

---

[82] Especially the phrase, *etiam paroecialibus,* suggests this signification.

[83] Canon 1544, § 1.

[84] Beste, *Introductio in Codicem,* p. 770. See also Miller, *Founded Masses,* p. 51.

[85] *Ius Canonicum* (7 vols. in 8, Vol. II, *De Personis,* 3. ed., Romae: apud Aedes Universitatis Gregorianae, 1943), II, 234.

This transfer of the temporalities to the house is described as being made to the true and properly so-called subject of ownership, so that there solely remain reserved, in the manner of a servitude upon the incorporated goods, the burdens for the sustenance of the vicar or for meeting similar expenses. The spiritual office remains separate, and has its own independent existence. The vicar of the incorporated benefice must be taken from the secular clergy. The *pleno iure* effected incorporation passes to the incorporating subject not only the temporal rights but also the spiritual rights of the office.

In view of the effect regarding the temporalities in both of these types of incorporation, the conclusion appears warranted that the churches belonging to the parish are to be considered as belonging to the religious when either type of incorporation takes place.[86]

On the other hand, when parishes are merely entrusted to religious, there is no change in the status of the parish itself, and the only significance of such an arrangement is that a secular parish has been conferred upon a religious cleric rather than upon a secular.[87] In these circumstances it does not seem that the church could be said to belong to religious or to be a church of religious.

The designation implied in the words of canon 1550, "churches

---

[86] See O'Brien, *The Exemption of Religious in Church Law*, p. 266. A quite contrary view has been presented in the article, "A Contract Determining the Status of a Religious Parish,"—*The Jurist*, IX (1949), 65-86, esp. 73-74. The writer of this article insists that neither the union effected *quoad temporalia tantum* nor the union effected *pleno iure* between a religious institute and a parish confers ownership of parish property upon the religious institute. It is declared that only the *usus* and the *ususfructus* of parish property passes to the religious house by these types of incorporation. Even in this view the churches could be termed "churches of religious" because, as has been seen above, a church may be said to belong to religious when the religious institute has full ownership of the church or, at least, when it holds perpetually the *dominium utile* of the church.

[87] Mundy, *The Union of Parishes*, The Catholic University of America Canon Law Studies, n. 204 (Washington, D. C.: The Catholic University of America Press, 1945), p. 74.

of exempt religious," obviously extends to churches of all exempt institutes, both clerical and lay.[88]

On the basis of what has been considered up to this point, it is to be concluded that the phrase "pious foundations in churches, even parochial, of exempt religious" signifies those foundations whose obligations are to be carried out in churches of exempt religious, and that among these churches are to be included parish churches when the parish has been incorporated with a religious house either in a union negotiated *pleno iure* or in a union effected *ad temporalia tantum*. This interpretation thus establishes definite limits for the operation of canon 1550.

Since canon 1550 deals with exempt religious, the notion of exemption as it relates to this matter must be examined. The endowment of pious foundations when given to an ecclesiastical moral person is owned by the ecclesiastical moral person concerned, and because of this is termed "ecclesiastical property." [89] But this ownership is held by a particular moral person. When this moral person is exempt from the jurisdiction of the local ordinary, its property is also exempt from his jurisdiction, including the property pertaining to pious foundations.[90] Hence there does not appear to be any reason for regarding the designation of the local ordinary in canons 1545-1549 as applicable when exempt institutes are concerned, just as there is no reason to regard canon 1527, § 1, and its requirement for the local ordinary's consent as applicable to exempt religious institutes.

The investment of endowment as ruled by canon 1547, aside from any question of exemption, is to be made by the local ordinary under the terms of the canon. When property of an exempt institute is concerned, including endowments of pious foundations, there does not appear to be any reason to deny the privilege of exemption in this regard. The investment accordingly would be in the hands of the personnel of the exempt institute to be carried out according to its constitutions.[91]

[88] Vermeersch-Creusen, *Epitome*, II, n. 869; Miller, *Founded Masses*, p. 51.
[89] Canon 1497, § 1; Pistocchi, *De Bonis Ecclesiae Temporalibus*, p. 471.
[90] O'Brien, *The Exemption of Religious in Church Law*, p. 265. See canons 1519, § 1; 615; 500.
[91] Canon 533, § 1.

If the privilege of exemption has this effect regarding the management and investment of the endowment of pious foundations held by exempt religious institutes, what reason necessitates the exemptive provisions of canon 1550? The answer is to be found in considering the nature of exemption. Both the law establishing regulars as exempt from the jurisdiction of the local ordinary,[92] and the law respecting the privilege of exemption as conferred on some religious institutes,[93] indicate that this exemption from the local ordinary's jurisdiction is not absolute, and that the local ordinary retains certain rights under the general law.

Canon 533, § 1, 3° and 4°, furnishes an example of the expression of such rights as enjoyed by the local ordinary over exempt religious.[94] Numbers 3 and 4 of § 1 of canon 533 require the consent of the local ordinary for the making of an investment which involves certain types of property, viz., money given to or for the benefit of a parish or a mission (n. 4) and property given for local charity or worship (n. 3). Pious foundations may be established for such purposes, and consequently the investment of their endowments would be ruled by canon 533. There is no inconsistency involved in the formalities concerning foundations, especially the investment of endowment, being handled by an official of the exempt institute the while there is a requirement also for the local ordinary's consent for the act of investment. The application of canon 533, § 1, 3° and 4°, does not appear to warrant further inroads upon the exempt status of an institute than is specifically declared in the canon.

Thus the exempt religious institute will control the formalities concerning foundations, including—and this precisely is the significant matter here—the making of the investment of endowment.

[92] Canon 615.

[93] Canon 500, § 1.

[94] Number four of the first paragraph of this canon certainly applies to exempt religious; the application of number three of the same paragraph to houses of exempt religious is a matter of dispute. See pp. 117-118. In the present discussion the view is hypothetically accepted that exempt religious are subject to number three. It is accepted as a hypothesis which makes possible the interpretation of canon 1550 given below. It is not, however, accepted absolutely because of reasons which will appear in the discussion of the problem.

When the endowment is established for the benefit of a parish or a mission, or for local charity or worship, there will also be required the consent of the local ordinary for the investment under the terms of canon 533, § 1, 3° and 4°.[95]

It is with regard to situations involving the last named purpose, viz. worship, that canon 1550 has its applicability. When the obligations of the foundation are to be carried out in the churches of exempt religious, the formalities concerning the foundation are to be carried out exclusively by the major superior.[96] The effect of this provision seems to be that this exclusive competence, especially regarding the investment of the endowment, frees the religious from the obligation of obtaining the local ordinary's consent such as would otherwise be required under the terms of canon 533, § 1, 3°.[97]

This interpretation of canon 1550 is offered as a hypothetical approach which may be indicative of the elements involved in the problem. It is not offered as a thoroughly satisfactory interpretation, but as an interpretation made of the legislation as it exists and on the hypothesis that canon 533 § 1, 3°, governs exempt religious congregations. Inasmuch as this hypothesis makes possible the instant interpretation, it has been accepted, but only as a hypothesis. This help which it offers does not appear to warrant its absolute acceptance because of many other uncertain and disputed points which have prevented the formulation of a thoroughly satisfactory interpretation.[98]

These uncertain and disputed factors, which prevent a proper

---

[95] See Larraona, "Commentarium Codicis," *CpR,* XIII (1932), 28-29.

[96] Canon 1550.

[97] This exclusive competence of the major superior seems also to exempt him from the necessity of making accountings to the local ordinary regarding pious foundations ruled by canon 1550. See Comm. ad Interp. Cod. Iuris Canonici, resp. 25 iul. 1926—*AAS,* XVIII (1926), 393; Bouscaren, *Canon Law Digest* I, 699.

[98] Some of the disputed points encountered in a study of the authors consulted on this question are here presented:

1. The term "churches" in canon 1550 is to be understood in its literal signification according to McManus, *The Administration of Temporal Goods in Religious Institutes,* p. 107. Bouscaren-Ellis declare that it is to be understood as signifying any ecclesiastical moral person.—*Canon Law,* p. 791.

understanding of the canon, indicate that for a satisfactory solution of the problems raised by canon 1550 there is necessary some legal creation by way of legislative action, or through an authentic interpretation, or by the establishment of custom respecting the modes of administering pious foundations. On the basis of the analyses presented by various authors, and on the basis of the possible legal comparisons and inferences, a satisfactory conclusion has not been reached.

D. Foundations Given to Religious Institutes for Their Own Benefit

Agreement is general that, when a foundation is conveyed to a religious institute of pontifical approval for its own benefit or for a pious cause not distinct from the approved purposes of that institute, the foundation does not come under the supervisory authority of the local ordinary.[99]

2. "Pious foundations in churches . . ." is apparently understood by Larraona as referring to foundations made to a church as the moral person receiving it.—"Commentarium Codicis," *CpR*, XIII (1932), 28-29. The phrase is understood by Vromant as referring only to those foundations whose obligations are to be carried out in a church.—*De Bonis Ecclesiae Temporalibus,* n. 354.

3. McManus declares that pious foundations made to houses of religious congregations are governed by canon 533, § 1, 3°, and are not governed by the canons on foundations.—*Op. cit.,* pp. 105-108. Larraona declares that these foundations are governed by both canon 533, §1, 3°, and the canons on foundations.—"Commentarium Codicis," *CpR*, XIII (1932), 28-29. Miller declares that it is probable that no foundations at all are ruled by canon 533, § 1, 3°.—*Founded Masses,* p. 55. Blat declares that only property which is destined for a foundation is ruled by canon 533, § 1, 3°.—*Commentarium,* Liber II, Partes II et III, n. 258.

4. Authors are well divided on whether canon 533, § 1, 3° is applicable to exempt religious. See p. 117.

5. Canon 1550 speaks of the *major superior* of exempt religious. In discussing this person indicated by the canon there are authors who use the term *religious ordinary.*—Larraona, "Commentarium Codicis," *CpR*, XIII (1932), 28; Blat, *Commentarium,* Liber III, Partes II-VI, n. 468. Only the major superior of exempt clerical religious is a religious ordinary. See canon 198, § 1. Canon 1550 does not exclude exempt lay religious.

[99] Vromant, *De Bonis Ecclesiae Temporalibus,* n. 356; Goyeneche, "Consultationes," *CpR*, III (1922), 269; Hannan, *The Canon Law of Wills,* n. 771; Reilly, *Visitation of Religious,* p. 110.

CHAPTER X

AMERICAN CIVIL LAW [1] AFFECTING THE INVESTMENT OF ECCLESIASTICALLY ADMINISTERED FUNDS

ARTICLE 1. CANONICAL APPLICABILITY OF THE CIVIL LAW OF CONTRACTS IN GENERAL

FORMERLY the Church in its own forum followed the prescriptions of the Roman law, as it was almost universally received in the Middle Ages regarding matters pertaining to contracts dealing with property.[2] Now in such matters the Church canonizes the provisions of the civil law in effect locally regarding contracts and payments in ecclesiastical matters, unless these provisions are contrary to the divine law or unless the canon law provides otherwise.[3] Accordingly, in the United States the laws of the states pertaining to contracts and to payments are so canonized.

An investment is made through the medium of a contract. If funds are to be used in the purchase of real estate as an investment, the contract of sale intervenes.

Every acquisition of investment securities involves a contract with the person issuing the securities, and this is true whether one acquires the securities directly from the maker, through a banker at the time of the flotation, from a third party either for a consideration or by gift, or if he comes into possession of them by as-

---

[1] The expression "civil law" is frequently used in legal writings to signify a legal system, and in this sense it is used in contradistinction to the legal system of the "common law." This is not its signification in the present study. Herein it is used in contradistinction to "canon law," and thus signifies the law of the secular jurisdiction.

[2] Cappello, *Summa Iuris Canonici*, II, n. 612.

[3] Canon 1529.—Quae ius civile in territorio statuit de contractibus tam in genere, quam in specie, sive nominatis sive innominatis, et de solutionibus, eadem iure canonico in materia ecclesiastica iisdem cum effectibus serventur, nisi iure divino contraria sint aut aliud iure canonico caveatur.

signment for the security of a debt or otherwise.[4] It is obvious that in the acquisition of investment securities there may be, in addition to the essential contract between the maker and the acquirer, other incidental contracts arising from the mode of acquisition, as for example the contract of purchase and sale between the acquirer and a third party.

Productive disposition of ecclesiastical funds may be made through a deposit of these funds at interest in a bank. Such deposit at interest obviously constitutes a contract.[5] Accordingly the civil law relating to contracts will be applicable by virtue of canon 1529 in ecclesiastical matters involving the contractual elements of investment, whether the investment is made by purchase of real estate or securities or by deposit at interest.

The canonization of civil law by canon 1529 applies, unless divine law or canon law rule otherwise, to the form of contracts, contractual consent, their effects, presupposed clauses, prohibited clauses, time, place, and manner of payments, substantial conditions in contracts, hidden defects in things bought and sold, and the time of transfer of ownership.[6]

The civil provisions regarding the time of actual assumption of ownership with all the inherent advantages and risks involved in such ownership have canonical validity,[7] and have a particular applicability in the purchase and sale of investments. In American law a sale is a present transfer of property, while a contract to sell is a contractual understanding to make and accept such a transfer in the future.[8] Thus the consequences of theft or loss of unregis-

---

[4] Kirschman, *Principles of Investment*, p. 156. See Chapter VII of Kirschman's work for an extensive treatment of the contract element of investments.

[5] Noldin, *Summa Theologiae Moralis* (3 vols., Vol. II, 27. ed., Oeniponte Lipsiae: Rauch, 1941), II, n. 564. Regarding the civil law understanding of deposit as a contract: "The relation created by a voluntary deposit is one of contract. . . ." 26 C. J. S., *Depositaries*, § 2.

[6] Vermeersch-Creusen, *Epitome*, II, n. 850; Vromant, *De Bonis Ecclesiae Temporalibus*, n. 275; Beste, *Introductio in Codicem*, p. 761.

[7] Vermeersch-Creusen, *Epitome*, II, n. 850.

[8] Vold, *Handbook of the Law of Sales* (St. Paul: West Publishing Co., 1931), p. 6.

tered securities before their delivery are borne by the seller when
a contract to sell has been made; by the buyer, when a contract of
sale has intervened. So also the ownership of income or profit accruing will be similarly determined. Also of canonical significance
will be the civil law provisions regarding the *pro rata* payment made
to creditors on the insolvency of a debtor.[9] This would be of concern to ecclesiastical administrators holding investment securities
of an insolvent corporation. Each type of security has its own particular degree of priority of claim upon the assets of a corporation.[10]

ARTICLE 2. CANONICAL APPLICABILITY OF THE CIVIL LAW
OF TRUSTS

When the disposal of property to pious causes has the technical
nature of a trust at civil law, then there arises the question regarding
the canonical status of civil law provisions affecting trusts. Is the
civil law of trusts canonized by canon 1529?

Should the civil law declare donations by act *inter vivos* or by act
mortis causa in trust for pious causes invalid, canon 1513, § 1, which
establishes the capacity of persons to dispose of property for pious
causes, prevails and the civil prescriptions are devoid of canonical or
moral effect.[11] When the civil law establishes certain solemnities
for the validity of testamentary conveyances, these should be kept
if possible, but are devoid of canonical or moral force as to invalidating effects.[12]

Respecting gifts *inter vivos* in favor of pious causes, it is con-
troverted whether solemnities established by the civil law must be
regarded as affecting their validity.[13] Certainly it is true that
solemnities necessary in civil law for the creation of the trust in
its technical civil sense must be complied with if a trust in this
sense is to exist. Even if it is concluded that the civilly required
solemnities are not to be regarded as affecting validity, and that

---

[9] Vromant, *De Bonis Ecclesiae Temporalibus,* n. 278.

[10] Kirschman, *Principles of Investment,* p. 171.

[11] Vromant, *De Bonis Ecclesiae Temporalibus,* n. 276; Cappello, *Summa
Iuris Canonici,* II, n. 608.

[12] Canon 1513, § 2.

[13] Cappello, *Summa Iuris Canonici,* II, n. 596.

therefore the donation to pious causes is valid regardless of the observance or the non-observance of such solemnities, it is obvious that no technical trust in the civil sense can exist when the necessary formalities are absent. The trust in this sense is exclusively a creation of the settlor operating under the definite rules established by civil law. There is no canonical counterpart to the Anglo-American trust. If the civil rules are not carried out, a civil law trust does not exist, regardless of any moral or canonical obligation to carry out the intention of the benefactor.

The implication of this consideration is that the civil law respecting trusts and the various obligations of trustees is civilly effective only when the technical trust exists. There then arises the question whether these civil prescriptions regarding trusts are given canonical effect by canon 1529 when the technical trust does in fact exist.

It must be noted that canon 1529 applies *"in materia ecclesiastica."* A purely private trust for the benefit of a private individual does not seem to have any ecclesiastical quality that would make canon 1529 applicable. If the trust were to confer the benefits of property upon some group in the Church, or were to support some work of the Church, this ecclesiastical interest would seem to be sufficient to make canon 1529 operative.

Can the civil law of trusts be considered as constituting provisions *de contractibus?* The chief difficulty in seeking an answer to this question lies in the fact that the trust in its Anglo-American technical sense is unknown in canon law. It would be surprising to find canonical commentators analyzing the concept in its relationship to the canonical notion of contract. Yet this analysis must be made if the canonical efficacy or inefficacy of the civil law of trusts is to be determined.

A contract, also termed in a wide understanding of the term an agreement (*pactum*), is defined as the consent of two or more persons centering in the same thing, manifested by a sensible sign, and giving rise to an obligation in at least one of the parties.[14] The notions of a common consent of at least two persons, and of the creation thereby of an obligation in at least one, characterizes the

---

[14] Beste, *Introductio in Codicem*, p. 761.

definitions of contract given by canonical authors, especially in describing unilateral contracts.[15] In the creation of a trust the legal title to property is conveyed to one person for the benefit of another or of others or for the accomplishment of charitable purposes. By the acceptance of the trusteeship there appears to be present a common consent on the parts of the settlor of the trust and of the trustee that title be passed to the trustee with the consequent obligation upon the trustee that the property be used for the benefit of another, or in the case of charitable trusts, for the accomplishment of certain charitable purposes.

When a trust has been established according to civil law, certain obligations under civil law are incumbent upon the trustee as arising out of his acceptance of the trust. Canonical authorities have declared that the canonization of civil law by canon 1529 extends to the effects of a contract [16] and to the manner of carrying out an obligation assumed.[17] In view of the agreement between settlor and trustee and the consequent legal obligations of the trustee, it seems indisputable that the civil law of trusts in so far as it determines the manner of carrying out the trustee's obligations will be subject to the canonization of canon 1529.

This conclusion is based upon an understanding of the phrase *de contractibus* of canon 1529 in a canonical sense. It appears that the phrase is to be so understood in this sense rather than in the sense which it has in American civil law. Similarity between the Latin word *contractus* and, in its technical legal sense, the English word *contract* does not indicate an identity of concept. In American law the *contract* is marked by certain characteristics which need not necessarily be present in order that the canonical notion of *contract* be verified. This canonical notion has been described above. The broader canonical sense behind the word *contractus* appears to be indicated in canon 1529. For this provision of law is a canonical provision and its terms are to be understood in their

---

[15] Coronata, *Institutiones*, II, n. 1069; Cappello, *Summa Iuris Canonici*, II, n. 608; Vromant, *De Bonis Ecclesiae Temporalibus*, nn. 269, 270.

[16] Vromant, *De Bonis Ecclesiae Temporalibus*, n. 275; Beste, *Introductio in Codicem*, p. 761; Cocchi, *Commentarium*, VI, n. 211.

[17] Bouscaren-Ellis, *Canon Law*, p. 772.

canonical signification. That the canonical sense of contract is to be here understood rather than the technical legal sense in use in the secular jurisdiction appears further evidenced by the modifying phrase *sive nominatis sive innominatis,* which is an essentially canonical classification of contracts.

Considered from another aspect, the conclusion that the civil law of trusts respecting investment is canonized by canon 1529 seems to be equally valid. This aspect refers to the proper matter for contracts. It is declared by canonical authorities that canon 1529 canonizes those provisions of civil law which determine the proper matter for contracts.[18] Regarding trusts, the civil law variously provides [19] norms as to what investment contracts may be made by the trustee relative to the funds which pertain to the trust. This is evidently a determination of what is permissible subject matter for contracts involving trust property. The civil law also in providing rules respecting the manner of administering trust property, e. g., the prohibition against mingling trust funds without proper authorization, similarly seems to be setting up rules that intimately affect the contracts entered upon in relation to trust properties.

Thus, both from the viewpoint of the legal obligation arising from the acceptance of a trusteeship, which acceptance appears to constitute a canonical contract between trustee and settlor, and from the viewpoint of the trust property as involved in contracts in the normal administration of a trust fund, the conclusion appears valid that the civil law of trusts is to be considered as canonized by canon 1529.

It is to be noted that this civil law of trusts is canonically applicable only where it is civilly applicable. The canon law follows upon the civil law in this matter. Thus, when a technical trust under civil law does not exist, the civil law of trusts will not be applicable either civilly or canonically. It may be of value, even if not strictly applicable, in guiding administrators in the administra-

[18] Beste, *Introductio in Codicem,* p. 761; Bouscaren-Ellis, *Canon Law,* p. 772. Although not all the authors specify the designation by the civil law of the proper matter for contracts as one type of provision canonized by 1529, it appears that their more general statements admit of this more specific principle.

[19] See pp. 162-166.

tion of property even when a technical civil trust does not exist. By way of example, a list of securities legal for trusts may well be consulted by administrators desirous of securing safe investments.

There does not appear to be any conflict between either the divine or canon law and the civil law of trusts, except when trusts for charitable or religious purposes are declared invalid by the civil law.[20] The freedom of administrators is indeed curtailed by the civil law of trusts, but this limitation appears canonically not so much as deriving from the civil law but rather as deriving from the intention of the benefactor who establishes a technical trust. And canonically, by virtue of canon 1514, the intention of the donor is a most important norm in regard to his disposition of property for pious causes.

Furthermore, the civil law of trusts has the same purpose as the canon law, viz., the carrying out of the wishes of the settlor of the trust. No conflict can be found in the general principles of purpose in the two systems. It can rightfully be said that the civil law may furnish an even surer protection than the canon law, since it is a law developed specifically in and for the economic milieu in which the administration of trusts must be carried on. On the other hand, it must be pointed out that the lesser degree of specificity of norms that characterizes the canon law gives a greater measure of freedom, which could be profitably used to advantage by competent and efficient administrators.[21]

[20] Charitable trusts were once invalid in New York, Virginia, Maryland, Michigan, Wisconsin, Minnesota, and West Virginia, but today all the states recognize them. Scott, *The Law of Trusts* (4 vols., Boston: Little Brown & Co., 1939), III, § 348.3.

[21] Further judgments of value regarding the advantages and disadvantages of various legal factors and administrative techniques in trust administration are beyond the scope of the present study. A study of these factors as they pertain to charitable trusts is contained in an unpublished dissertation by Guilfoyle: *Charitable Trusts: an attitude and a consideration of administrative patterns and policies,* Thesis (LL. M.), Columbia University, New York, 1946.

It is also beyond the scope of the present study to examine the most advantageous legal manner of taking title to donated property to which the donor has attached certain obligations. The present study deals with the investment implications of the technical trust as it can, and frequently does, exist, without entering upon a consideration of the advantages and disadvantages involved in the legal

ARTICLE 3. CHARITABLE TRUSTS IN CIVIL LAW

American civil law furnishes special protection to funds established in trust. It has been shown that the civil law of trusts is to be considered as canonically applicable in virtue of canon 1529. It is the purpose of the present section to examine the nature of the trust in civil law and the provisions of the civil law of trusts which affect the investment of funds given in trust for religious or other charitable purposes.

A trust is "a fiduciary relationship in which one person is the holder of the title to property, subject to an equitable obligation to keep or use the property for the benefit of another." [22] According to their purpose, trusts are classified as private or public. A private trust is one which is to benefit a known, specified individual or individuals. In a public or charitable trust property is devoted to the accomplishment of purposes which are beneficial or supposed to be beneficial to the community.[23]

A charitable trust has been defined as "a fiduciary relationship with respect to property arising as a result of a manifestation of an intention to create it, and subjecting the person by whom the property is held to equitable duties to deal with the property for a charitable purpose." [24] Among the purposes considered as "charitable purposes" are included the relief of poverty, the promotion of education, the advancement of religion, the promotion of health and many other purposes whose accomplishment is of benefit to the community.[25] Donations of property to the Church for its essential or incidental purposes are obviously to be considered as made

position of the trustee of charitable trusts. The judgment concerning the best manner of giving legal effect to donations with attached obligations will depend on a variety of factors, differing with the particular type of fund and obligation involved, and differing also in some degree among the jurisdictions of the various states. A study which does enter upon these considerations regarding mass foundations has been made by Kenneth O'Brien: "Foundations for Masses Should Never Create Trusts," *The Jurist,* IV (1944), 284-315.

[22] Bogert, *Handbook of the Law of Trusts,* § 1, p. 1.

[23] Scott, *Trusts,* III, § 348.

[24] *Restatement, Trusts,* II, 1095, § 348. See also Bogert, *Handbook of the Law of Trusts,* § 75; Scott, *Trusts,* III, § 348.

[25] Scott, *Trusts,* III, § 368.

for purposes within the comprehension of the expression "charitable purposes" in its civil law understanding. This is true in almost all the states even for so particularly Catholic an arrangement as the conveyance of funds for the celebration of masses.[26]

In conveying property for charitable purposes the motive of the one conveying the property is of no significance.[27] Thus, if a person were motivated by vanity or family pride in advancing charitable purposes, this motive would in no way affect the legal complexion of his action. The civil law is interested in the effects of his action, not in the motives that lie behind it. In the event that funds are given in trust for charitable purposes, the civil jurisdiction is charged with enforcing the trust and insuring that it is carried out. This protection of charitable trusts rests with the Attorney General, who may bring suit to compel the trustee to execute properly the trust with which he is charged, although one of several trustees or other persons with special interests can maintain a suit to enforce the trust.[28] It is evident that ecclesiastical individuals may be charged with the duties of trustees either as individual trustees or as administrators of ecclesiastical bodies in which the legal title of the trust property rests.

The investment and other administrative duties incumbent upon trustees of charitable trusts are generally the same as those applicable to private trustees.[29] These trustees are responsible for a certain degree of skill and prudence in the administration of the trust property committed to them. It has been required that trustees exercise the same care and diligence with which "men of prudence, discretion, and intelligence manage their funds, considering the prob-

[26] Bogert, *Handbook of the Law of Trusts*, pp. 279-282.

[27] "Courts, in determining whether or not a gift is charitable, will not look to the motives of the donor, but rather to the nature of the gift and the object which will be attained by it." *In re Graves' Estate,* 242 Ill. 23, 29, 89 N. E. 672, 24 L. R. A., N. S., 283, 134 Am. St. Rep. 302, 17 Ann. Cas. 137. See also Scott, *Trusts,* III, § 368.

[28] *Restatement, Trusts,* II, § 392.

[29] *Attorney General* v. *City of Lowell,* 246 Mass. 312, 141 N. E. 45; *City of Boston* v. *Curley,* 177 N. E. 557, 276 Mass. 549; *Bellows Free Academy* v. *Sowles,* 57 A. 996, 76 Vt. 412. See *Restatement, Trusts,* II, §§ 379 and 389.

able income, as well as the probable safety of the capital invested." [30]
This early formulation of the "prudent man" rule is reflected in the
formulation given by the *Restatement*. Herein it is declared that
"the trustee is under a duty to the beneficiary in administering the
trust to exercise such care and skill as a man of ordinary prudence
would exercise in dealing with his own property, and if the trustee
has greater skill than that of a man of ordinary prudence, he is
under a duty to exercise such skill as he has." [31]

It is to be noted that more than simply the care of a prudent
man in handling his own property is required. For such a prudent
man could take the calculated risks entailed, for example, in speculation. The prudent man rule regarding the investment of trust
funds involves the special quality of preservation of the fund and
care of the trust capital. In *Miller* v. *Pender* [32] a new trial was
granted because the trial court had adopted as its rule the standard
of the care and skill of a man of ordinary prudence in managing
his own property rather than that of a prudent man with the special duty of conserving the property.

In making investment of trust funds the trustee must, in the
absence of provisions in the terms of the trust or of a statute providing otherwise, make only such investments as a prudent man
would make of his own property, having previously in view the
preservation of the estate, and the amount and regularity of the
income to be derived; and he must conform to the statutes, if
any such exist, which govern investments made by trustees, and he
must conform generally to the terms of the trust.[33]

There are other more specific guides as to what standards and
requirements are demanded under the rather general "prudent man
rule" regarding investment practices. First of all, it is almost always
the duty of a trustee to use productively the trust property.[34] Bank

[30] *Harvard College* v. *Amory*, 26 Mass. 446, 9 Pick. 446, 461 (1831).

[31] *Restatement, Trusts*, I, § 174. In II, § 379 it is indicated that this rule
is applicable in the case of a charitable trust.

[32] 93 N. H., 34 A. (2d) 663 (1943).

[33] *Restatement, Trusts*, I, § 227.

[34] *Foscue* v. *Lyon*, 55 Ala. 440; *Wight et al.* v. *Lee*, 126 A. 218, 101 Conn.
401; *Jennings' Executors* v. *Davis*, 5 Dana (Ky.), 127. See *Restatement,
Trusts*, I, § 181.

deposit at interest for an unreasonably long time is not regarded as satisfying this demand.[35] In view of the necessity of preserving the *corpus* of the trust, speculative investments are not permissible in view of the risk normally attendant upon them.[36] Proper diversification of investments is required in order to protect the *corpus* of the trust from destruction through the failure of any one investment.[37] Types of securities must be diversified, and also the localities upon which the securities depend.[38]

The trustee must keep the trust property separate from his own property and separate from the property of other trusts, and this rule applies in making investments, and, to effect this, trust property must be properly marked as such, so that it cannot indeliberately or deliberately be confused with the personal property of the trustee or other property.[39] It is to be noted that the settlor of the trust may give broader discretionary power to the trustee than that allowed by law normally, and this broader power may involve permission to mingle the property of various trusts for investment purposes.[40]

Among the factors to be considered by a "prudent man" in making investment is the "seasoned" quality of a security.[41] "Seasoned in the market" refers to a quality of an investment by which its

[35] *Restatement, Trusts,* I, § 180.

[36] *Dickinson's Appeal,* 152 Mass. 185, 25 N. E. 99, 9 L. R. A. 279 (1890); *Cornet* v. *Cornet,* 269 Mo. 298, 190 S. W. 333 (involving the bonds of an untried bridge company); *English* v. *McIntyre,* 51 N. Y. S. 697, 29 App. Div. 439 (involving buying stock on margin); *Murphy-Bolanz Land and Loan Co.* v. *McKibben,* Tex. Com. App., 236 S. W. 78 (involving speculative purchase of realty). See Bogert, *The Law of Trusts and Trustees* (7 vols., St. Paul: West Publishing Co.; Vol. III, 1946; Vol. IV, 1948; all other volumes, 1935), III, § 612; Riddle, "Trust Investments: Their Extent and Some Related Economic Problems," 5 *Law and Contemporary Problems* 339, 343 (1938).

[37] In *City of Boston* v. *Curley,* 177 N. E. 577, 276 Mass. 549, it was held prudent to have not more than one-fifth of a trust fund in one investment.

[38] *In Re Ward's Estate,* 121 N. J. Eq. 555, 192 A. 68 (1936).

[39] Bogert, *Trusts and Trustees,* III, §§ 596 and 612.

[40] *Restatement,* I, § 179 e.

[41] *Aydelott* v. *Breeding,* 64 S. W. 916, 111 Ky. 847, 23 Ky. Law Rep. 1146; *Robertson* v. *Robertson's Trustee,* 113 S. W. 138, 130 Ky. 293, 132 Am. St. Rep. 368.

price is characterized by stability. This price stability comes through the passage of time and it is partly the result of wide distribution among permanent investors.[42] It is opposed to the more volatile quality of securities whose price fluctuations are frequent and which are involved in a great deal of speculative trading. Another factor that must be considered is the liquidity of the investment.[43]

An even greater degree of specificity in norms that are mandatory in the making of trust investments is to be found in statutory indications of what investments are permissible for trust funds. These statutes vary greatly as to the scope of permitted trust investments. In some of the states certain classes of securities are designated as permissible for trust investments, while other states go so far as to list specific approved securities; some states have established constitutional provisions forbidding the legislature to permit trustees to invest in certain types of securities, or constitutional provisions prescribing the permitted investments; in some states the statutes are merely permissive, while in others they are exclusive.[44]

The limitations imposed by statute upon a trustee in making investments can be avoided by terms of the trust which enlarge the scope of permissible investments.[45] In this way greater discretionary power can be conferred upon the trustee by the settlor in freeing the former in varying degrees from statutory restriction.

In the administration of charitable trusts trustees are ruled by a large complex of legislated and judicially imposed norms. It has been the intent of the present exceedingly limited study merely to indicate general areas in matters of investment selection and administration pertaining to charitable trusts wherein norms of the civil law are applicable. Only the more prominent factors regarding investment have been indicated. These and many others will have

[42] Taylor, *Investments*, p. 44.

[43] *In re Blake's Will*, 263 N. Y. S. 310, 146 Misc. 780. *In re Frank's Estate*, 291 N. Y. S. 44, 160 Misc. 903.

[44] *Restatement, Trusts*, I, § 227 n. The statutes of all the states respecting investments permitted for trusts are to be found in Prentice-Hall, *Wills, Estates, and Trust Service*, Vol. IV, §§ 15, 301

[45] *Restatement, Trusts*, I, § 227 s.

to be examined by the trustee of a charitable trust in the light of the terms of the particular trust, of the local statutory provisions affecting trusts, and the judicial construction placed upon these in the jurisdiction concerned. Only through such a study can the trustee be aware of all the enforceable duties for which he is liable.

ARTICLE 4. FUNDS OF CHARITABLE CORPORATIONS AND THE CIVIL LAW

The nature of the legal title by which charitable corporations hold their property has been the subject of much judicial deliberation. Property may be devoted to charitable purposes not only by means of its transfer to a trustee in order that it be used for charitable purposes, but also by means of its transfer to corporations specifically organized for the accomplishment of charitable purposes.[46] There has arisen the question whether the property given to charitable corporations is to be considered as being held absolutely, or whether it is to be considered as held in trust for the purposes or some of the purposes for which the corporation was organized.

If the property is considered as held in trust by the corporation, the provisions of law regarding trust funds, including the provisions affecting investment, will be applicable. A variety of court decisions has appeared in answer to the various forms in which the question has been raised at different times and in the different jurisdictions of the various states. Some of these decisions have unequivocally denominated gifts to charitable corporations as conveyances of mere legal title to the corporation as trustee.[47] Others have regarded such gifts as held by the charitable corporation without the character of a technical trust.[48] The *Restatement of the Law of Trusts* has adopted this latter position.

The *Restatement* declares that when property is given to a charitable corporation, a charitable trust is not created, and that this is

---

[46] *Restatement, Trusts, II, Introductory Note to Charitable Trusts*, p. 1093.

[47] See Scott, *Trusts*, III, 1948 Supplement, p. 34, note 3, for an extensive list of decisions in this tradition.

[48] See Scott, *Trusts*, III, 1919, note 3, and also the 1948 Supplement, p. 34, note 3, for a list of cases decided in this fashion.

true although the corporation is directed by the terms of the gift to hold the principal forever and to devote only the income to the accomplishment of the purposes of the corporation; it is also true when by the terms of the gift the corporation is directed to use the property for a particular one of the corporation's purposes.[49]

It is not within the scope of the present study to examine this broad question as to whether a charitable trust is created by a gift to a charitable corporation.[50] Furthermore, it seems that a general principle establishing a charitable corporation either as an absolute owner of funds given to it or as a trustee cannot be reached, but that what must be decided in each case is the question whether a particular rule which is applicable to trustees is applicable to charitable corporations with respect to restricted or unrestricted property.[51]

Among the various rules relating to the investment of trust funds which may or may not be applicable to the investment of funds pertaining to charitable corporations are the following: the necessity of following legal lists or other statutory or judicial guides for investments, the prohibition against the merger of funds even for investment purposes, the enforceability of restrictions placed by the donor regarding the manner of use of the property given. Among such restrictions placed by the donor, of particular significance regarding investment is the restriction that the property must constitute an endowment, i.e. the principal must be preserved intact and the income alone is to be spent. If these restrictions are enforceable at civil law, the charitable corporation will therefore be required to keep the property intact and invested, the income alone

[49] *Restatement, Trusts,* II, Introductory Note to Charitable Trusts, p. 1093.

[50] Discussions of the history and development of the problem are to be found in Blackwell, "The Charitable Corporation and the Charitable Trust," 24 *Washington University Law Quarterly* 1-45 (1938); Lincoln, "Gifts to Charitable Corporations," 25 *Virginia Law Review* 764-795 (1939); Taylor, "A New Chapter in the New York Law of Charitable Corporations," 25 *Cornell Law Quarterly* 382-400 (1940).

[51] Scott, *Trusts,* III, 1948 Supplement, p. 35.

being used for the purpose of the corporation or for the one specific purpose for which the property was given.[52]

These rules, as has been indicated, apply to trusts. Aside from the general question whether any donation to a charitable corporation is to be regarded as creative of a trust, it is necessary to examine whether and to what extent these rules for trustees are applicable to charitable corporations. To the extent that these rules, legislatively or judicially established, pertain to contracts as mentioned in canon 1529, they will be given canonical effect by that canon.

It is to be noted in the treatment of charitable corporations that their funds are essentially of two kinds, viz., those given unrestrictedly for the general purpose of the corporation, and those given for some specific purpose among those for which the institution was incorporated.

A. Legal Rules on Investment and on Merger of Funds

Trustees are obliged to follow any extant statutory directives regarding the investment of trust funds. They are also obliged to keep each trust fund separate and to invest it separately, unless they have been freed by the donor from these restrictions. Statutes frequently apply similar restrictions to the funds of charitable corporations.

Oregon provides statutes indicating permissible investments that may be made by either trustees or charitable corporations with funds that have been given for charitable purposes.[53] Pennsylvania has statutory enactments whereby, unless it is otherwise provided in the trust instrument, the directors of a charitable corporation shall have power to invest in such investments as in the honest exercise of their judgments they may, after investigation, determine to be safe and proper investments; they are required to keep accurate accounts of all trust funds, separate and apart from the other funds

---

[52] It is to be noted that in this section only the obligation rooted in civil law is being considered. It is quite obvious that even when there might be no obligation in civil law to respect the intent of the donor, the more stringent canonical provision of canon 1514 must be observed in this matter.

[53] Oregon Code, 1930, § 32-803 as cited by Scott, *Trusts*, III, 2052, note 5.

of the corporation.[54] California has authorized by statute the establishment of common trust funds[55] by charitable corporations.[56] Pennsylvania has authorized by statute the establishment of common trust funds for all non-profit corporations.[57]

The applicability of statutes must be examined in the light of different legislative enactments for different categories of corporations. The classification "charitable corporation" is commonly understood as signifying bodies incorporated for charitable purposes, including corporations for eleemosynary, religious, and educational purposes.[58] This term, however, is not an effective guide in all jurisdictions when there is question of establishing statutory provisions. Various statutes may be applicable to different corporations in accordance with the various classifications of these corporations in the law.

By way of example, the law of New York State legally classifies corporations as public, stock, or non-stock corporations, with each having various subdivisions. Non-stock corporations are subdivided into religious corporations, membership corporations, and any corporations other than a stock or public corporation.[59] Pennsylvania classifies corporations as profit corporations[60] and non-

[54] *Purdon's Pennsylvania Statutes Annotated,* Titles 13-15, Constables-Corporations (St. Paul: West Publishing Co., 1938, with 1947 Cumulative Annual Pocket Part), tit. 15, § 2851-306.

[55] A common trust fund is "a group of securities set aside by a trustee for investment by two or more trusts operated by the same trustee. . . . The purposes of such a common or investment fund are to diversify the investments of the several trusts and thus spread the risk of loss, and to make it easy to invest any amount of trust funds quickly and with a small amount of trouble. Such a common trust fund cannot legally be operated without statutory sanction. . . ." Uniform Common Trust Fund Act, Prefatory Note, in Bogert, *Trusts and Trustees,* III (Pt. 2), 357, note 57.1.

[56] California Civil Code, § 606.5 as added by Laws of 1947, c. 850, as cited by Scott, *Trusts,* III, 1948 Supplement, § 389.

[57] *Purdon's Pennsylvania Statutes Annotated,* tit. 15, § 2851-318 (1947).

[58] Taylor, "A New Chapter in the New York Law of Charitable Corporations," 25 *Cornell Law Quarterly,* 382, note 1 (1940).

[59] *McKinney's Consolidated Laws of New York, Annotated,* Book 22, General Corporation Law (1943, with 1946 Cumulative Annual Pocket Part), § 2.

[60] *Purdon's Pennsylvania Statutes, Annotated,* tit. 15, § 3.

profit corporations,[61] among which are to be numbered what are commonly termed charitable corporations.

The Religious Corporations Law of New York does not provide any statutory enactment limiting or restricting the investment of funds of religious corporations.[62] By contrast, perpetual care funds held by cemetery corporations or by religious corporations controlling a cemetery are quite rigidly restricted as to permitted investments, which are limited to those appearing upon a legal list.[63]

Different ecclesiastical groups may be incorporated in various civil forms with statutes peculiar to each form. The civil charter also of each corporation must be looked to for further indication of legal restrictions and limitations upon its financial operations.

In the absence of statutory provisions respecting investment powers of charitable corporations, there does not seem to be available any judicially established norm as to whether the restrictions upon trustees apply also to charitable corporations both as regards the choice of investments and also the merger of funds.[64] Scott has declared that it seems that the rules applicable to investments by trustees are not necessarily applicable in the case of a charitable corporation.[65] He further declares that regarding *unrestricted* funds it seems that a charitable corporation can make investment of these in accordance with the general rule of prudent management. However, when funds have been given to the corporation to be used as an endowment,[66] or when their use has been specified for some par-

[61] *Ibid.*, tit. 15, § 2851-2.

[62] *McKinney's Consolidated Laws of New York, Annotated,* Book 50, Religious Corporations Law, 1918, with 1946 Cumulative Annual Pocket Part.

[63] *McKinney's Consolidated Laws of New York, Annotated,* Book 34, Membership Corporations Law, 1941, with 1946 Cumulative Annual Pocket Part, § 92.

[64] Blackwell, "The Charitable Corporation and the Charitable Trust," 24 *Washington University Law Quarterly,* 1 (1938).

[65] *Trusts,* III, § 389.

[66] "The term endowment has been defined as the bestowment of money as a permanent fund, the income of which is to be used in the administration of a proposed work." *St. Joseph's Hospital* v. *Bennett,* 281 N. Y. 115, 22 N. E. (2d) 305, at 306. See also Scott, *Trusts,* III, 1948 Supplement, p. 60, n. 5.

ticular corporate purpose, it is not clear whether there are applicable the stricter rules for investment by trustees, if such rules exist.[67]

There is also the question whether these *restricted* funds of a charitable corporation must be kept separate from unrestricted funds. Trustees are ordinarily not permitted to mingle funds of different trusts.[68] Scott declares that no authority has been found on the question of the applicability of this rule to charitable corporations. It is his belief that, when the terms of the gift establish no restrictions in this matter, it would not be improper for the charitable corporation to so mingle these funds.[69]

B. *Legal Status of Donor's Directives Establishing Endowment*

Investment implications are involved in the question whether and in what manner the charitable corporation is legally obliged to carry out the expressed intent of the donor regarding the preservation of principal and expenditure of income alone. The answer to this question will determine the legal necessity of maintaining such property in productive use as opposed to expending the principal. There is an obvious psychological appeal to charitable donors to declare such an intention as a means of perpetuating their name or influence. What is the legal status of such a restriction upon the gift?

Those court decisions which have declared that gifts, even restricted, to charitable corporations are held absolutely by the corporation without the quality of any attached trust [70] may possibly point toward the establishment of a principle that denies legal validity to the restrictions which require the principal to be maintained intact. This specific corollary has been drawn and established in *Corporation of Chamber of Commerce* v. *Bennett*,[71] wherein it was held that the restrictions of the donor upon a gift to a corporation in requiring that income alone from the property be used were invalid on the ground that the absolute owner of property cannot be restricted in its use.

[67] Scott, *Trusts*, III, 1948 Supplement, p. 60, n. 5.
[68] Bogert, *Trusts and Trustees*, III, §§ 596 and 612.
[69] Scott, *Trusts*, III, 1948 Supplement, p. 60, n. 5.
[70] See p. 166, note 48.
[71] 143 Misc. 513, 257 N. Y. S. 2 (1932).

On the other hand, when the courts have declared that certain gifts to charitable corporations are impressed with a trust,[72] the way is laid open for the further corollary that provisions placed by the donor in restricting the use of the property to a specific one of the several corporate purposes, or in requiring the maintenance of principal with the expenditure of the income alone, are enforceable as trust provisions. This conclusion was established in *Lehigh University* v. *Homer*,[73] wherein the court declared that, if a gift is made to a charitable corporation for its general purposes, the corporation is not a trustee, but if the gift is made to a charitable corporation for specific purposes, the corporation holds as a trustee.[74]

This application of the trust complexion to certain funds held by charitable corporations was similarly made to endowment funds in *Hobbs* v. *Board of Education of North Baptist Convention*,[75] wherein it was declared that unrestricted gifts and those which permitted the principal to be expended become the absolute property of the corporation, but all endowment funds are held as charitable trusts. Thus, when the donor has clearly created a trust or the courts construe that a trust was created, the restriction respecting expenditure of income and preservation of the endowment will evidently be enforceable as a trust provision.

In *Lutheran Hospital of Manhattan* v. *Goldstein*,[76] the restriction placed upon a charitable corporation, namely that the property be used for endowment, was presupposed as enforceable in this case as a technical trust provision, and thereafter the court refused to exercise its *cy pres* power to permit the endowment principal to be spent for current expenditures.[77]

In this vein Scott declares that restrictions to use for specific purposes and to maintenance of endowment seem to be valid in the

[72] See p. 166, note 47.

[73] 159 Pa. Super. 84, 46 A (2d) 516 (1946).

[74] See also *Van Reuth* v. *Mayor and City Council of Baltimore*, 165 Md. 651, 170 A. 199 (1934); *Mayor and City Council of Baltimore* v. *Peabody Institute*, 200 A. 375 (Md. 1938).

[75] 126 Nebr. 416, 253 N. W. 627 (1934).

[76] 182 Misc. 913, 46 N. Y. S. (2d) 705 (1944).

[77] See also *Application of Brooklyn Children's Aid Society*, 269 App. Div. 789, 55 N. Y. S. (2d), 323 (1945).

case of charitable corporations in the same way as they would be valid if the property were given to individual trustees for charitable purposes.[78] So too Bogert declares that it is important to determine whether a donor intended to make an absolute gift to a charitable corporation or wished to make the charitable corporation a trustee, because of the consequences that in the first instance the corporation can merely be forced by the Attorney General to act within its corporate powers, while in the second instance the Attorney General can compel obedience to all the terms of the trust.[79]

There is another position in civil law regarding the legal status of a donor's expressed intent. It is the position midway between a charitable corporation holding a gift absolutely and holding it in trust. It developed in New York's evolving judicial history of the status of charitable trusts and of the title enjoyed by charitable corporations to property given to them. In *St. Joseph's Hospital* v. *Bennett* [80] the court gave an answer to the question whether a charitable corporation could freely dispose of property given to it with the restriction that the principal be kept and the income alone be expended.

In this case the testator devised a portion of his residuary estate to a charitable corporation which operated St. Joseph's Hospital to be held as an endowment with the income to be used for the ordinary expenses of maintenance. The charitable corporation instituted proceedings in order to obtain a declaratory judgment as to whether it could use the entire property, both principal and interest, in partial payment of a mortgage debt on its real property, or in its judgment for purposes within its corporate powers other than the ordinary expenses of maintenance specified by the testator. On appeal of the Attorney General from judgment granting the requested authorization, it was held that the fund could not be diverted from the purpose specified by the testator, nor could it be used in a manner different from the manner prescribed.[81]

[78] *Trusts*, III, § 348. 1.

[79] *Trusts and Trustees*, II, 1031, § 324.

[80] 281 N. Y. 115, 22 N. E. (2d) 305, 130 A. L. R. 1092 (1939).

[81] "No authority has been brought to our attention that a gift to a charitable corporation with the express direction that it be applied to a specific corporate purpose in a specific manner may be accepted by the corpo-

Yet, as was pointed out by the court, the gift was not established upon condition subsequent,[82] nor was the property to be considered as held in trust. It was not considered, however, as a completely unencumbered gift, for such a view would thwart the intent of the testator and would have an adverse effect upon future
gifts. The court considered the gift as something midway between
property held by absolute title and property held in trust. The
bequest was considered as absolute, the words of the testator as indicating the gift to the charitable corporation as his primary purpose,
and the specific use to be made of it as a secondary purpose. The
testator's general intent was to help the charitable corporation. By
the designation of the specific manner of use, the gift was neither
made less absolute nor was a trust created. It has been said that
the position of the court was that in effect the testator's language
resulted in an absolute gift which had attached to it certain equitable
restrictions respecting its use.[83]

Thus in the instant case the requirement that the principal be
preserved and the income alone be expended was regarded not as a
trust provision but as an equitable restriction to be enforced by the
court.

In *Knickerbocker Hospital* v. *Goldstein*,[84] wherein a testator
had left a large sum to a hospital as an endowment, the income of
which was to be used for the hospital's general purposes, it was held
that the court would permit the use of the principal if it appeared
that otherwise the hospital would be forced to close. In this case
the court permitted a deviation from the terms of the bequest establishing the property as endowment. It was stated that the court
was using the power of *cy pres,* which enables it to permit such
deviation in certain situations. The fact that such exercise of *cy pres*

---

ration, and then used for a different corporate purpose in a different manner."
22 N. E. (2d) at 308.

[82] See p. 177 for a brief treatment of a gift upon condition subsequent.

[83] 19 *Boston University Law Review* 657 (1939). Comment on the case
in 40 *Columbia Law Review* 553 (1940) regarded the gift, subject to the restrictions established, as a *tertium quid* between an unlimited gift and a technical trust.

[84] 181 Misc. 540, 41 N. Y. S. (2d) 32 (1943).

was deemed necessary indicates that the restriction established by the testator was otherwise enforceable. It should be noted that the court declared that it was not necessary to examine into whether a technical trust existed in this case. The restriction was enforceable whether it was a trust provision or not, and *cy pres* could be applied in either case. In indicating the enforceability of the restriction even if no trust existed the court referred to the *St. Joseph's Hospital* v. *Bennett* case.

In summary regarding the obligations under civil law of a charitable corporation to preserve property given as endowment, it may be said that enforcement may be made of this restriction when it is clearly creative of a trust, when courts are inclined to construe it as a trust provision, and when courts have enforced it as an equitable restriction. Blackwell has indicated not only the practical but also the legal dangers inherent in the practice of spending the principal of the funds given to charitable corporations as endowment.[85] These legal dangers have been made definite in New York, since Blackwell's article was written, by the development of judicial theory in the *St. Joseph's Hospital* v. *Bennett* case.[86] In jurisdictions where such a definite status has not been given by the courts to such restrictions, Blackwell's warning is pertinent.

Careful analysis must therefore be made of the terms of a gift to a charitable corporation if one is to determine whether or not a trust exists, or whether, if the gift is held absolutely, the nature of the attached restrictions suggest their enforceability in the light of the decisions rendered in the particular jurisdiction involved.

[85] "The liquidation of securities donated for permanent endowment in order to benefit the present generation is to be condemned, not only as inexpedient and as contrary to the best wishes of endowed education and charity, but also as a dangerous reliance upon the language of the courts where they have referred to the title of the institution as absolute. It is to be hoped that future developments of judicial theory in this field will evolve adequate restraints upon administrators without cutting too sharply into the area of proper discretion." "The Charitable Corporation and the Charitable Trust," 24 *Washington University Law Quarterly* 1 (1938).

[86] The article appeared in 1938. The critical case of *St. Joseph's Hospital* v. *Bennett* was decided in 1939, with other similar cases following.

Ecclesiastical administrators must consider the civil law attitude of the pertinent jurisdiction respecting the expenditure of funds given as endowment to civilly incorporated religious or other charitable institutions in the event that the expenditure of such endowment funds is sought. They must advert to the pertinent civil law at least in virtue of the civil enforceability which can be invoked against the charitable corporation. They must advert to the civil law also in order to see whether or not it enjoys the canonical effect given to some provisions of civil law by canon 1529. There will have to be examined both the nature of the original transfer of property to the ecclesiastical person, viz. whether or not a contract was involved, and also whether the civil law in the particular case may by any other title be said to be concerned with contracts or payments in the sense of canon 1529. If the pertinent rulings of civil law may be said to fall under the provision of canon 1529, then these rulings will enjoy canonical effect in virtue of that canon.

In addition to the consideration of the civil law in the case where it is desired to expend funds given as permanent endowment, there must also, quite evidently, be furnished full consideration to and compliance with canonical legislation respecting execution of the donor's intent [87] and any deviation from that intent.[88]

It is to be noted that the different civil law provisions which enforce the donor's designation of property as endowment are indicated in the present study merely as possibly applicable legal factors. Any suggestion of approval or disapproval of such specific factors could be made only on the basis of a study broader in scope than the present. So too, any indication of the most feasible manner of accepting endowments and other funds for specified purposes, and the consequent encouragement of benefactors to convey or grant property in that manner, can be given only on the basis of a study of the entire legal milieu of a particular jurisdiction, with proper emphasis on the matter of tort liability and other related considerations.[89]

[87] See canon 1514.

[88] See canons 1517 and 1551.

[89] See p. 160, footnote 21.

Note: Gift Upon Condition Subsequent

It is possible for a donor to effect the accomplishment of the purposes for which he makes the donation to an individual or to a charitable corporation by making his donation upon condition subsequent. If the accomplishment of these purposes is clearly established as a condition, failure to accomplish them will result in discharge of the contract with forfeiture of the property involved. Courts of equity are hostile to conditions and the forfeitures involved in them, and the certain imposition of a condition subsequent seems to require a precise establishment of the details of forfeiture and of the right to retake the property on the part of the donor or his heirs.[90]

[90] Bogert, *Trusts and Trustees*, II, § 324.

CONCLUSIONS

1. The property law of the *Corpus Iuris Canonici* appears to be characterized by the general purposes of protecting ecclesiastical tenure of productive property, of encouraging the improvement and the productive use of such property, and of encouraging its use for the acquisition of regular and periodic income in such a way that future benefit is not unduly sacrificed for present advantage.

2. Investment in its contemporary canonical significance consists in a conversion of money into income-producing forms of property. Bank deposit of funds at interest does not of itself constitute investment in its proper sense. In some circumstances, however, such bank deposit at interest will fall under rules regarding investment.

3. The proper canonical notion of investment includes both temporary and permanent investment. The exclusion of temporary investment from subjection to provisions establishing formalities for investment does not appear warranted.

4. Invested or stable capital is an expression which signifies income-producing property elements. Such elements will generally but not necessarily be subject to the rules regarding alienation. Invested capital elements which are placed in investment temporarily pending some other disposition are not by the fact of being invested therefore made subject to the restrictions upon alienation. For this effect the competent authority must designate them to be held as such on a rather permanent basis. This designation may be explicitly or implicitly made.

5. Investment is an act of extraordinary administration. As an act of administration it is an act to be performed essentially by the proper administrator. As extraordinary, it is an act to be performed by the administrator, not alone, but in conjunction with the required action of other persons as designated by law.

6. The canonical prohibition against speculative practices in ecclesiastical affairs does not rule out the consideration of prospects of possible increase or of possible depreciation in an investment's

capital value as a legitimate investment factor. Nor is the prohibition to be regarded as inhibitory of the liquidation of an investment when that investment becomes a poor investment, and when a better investment may be made. Such liquidation and reinvestment is not necessarily speculative; it is an operation of investment management which is canonically legitimate.

7. The requirement in canon 533 of the local ordinary's consent for the investment of the funds specified in nn. 3 and 4 of that canon reflects the equitable interests acquired by persons or pious causes within the local ordinary's jurisdiction as a result of the donations indicated in nn. 3 and 4.

8. The investment of surplus funds made under canon 1523, 4°, does not of itself constitute these funds as ecclesiastical patrimony subject to alienation restrictions.

9. Canon 1516, § 2, simply requires a safe disposition of trust property; it does not imply that an investment of the property is always mandatory.

10. Investment of money pertaining to the dowries of women religious is limited by canon law to investment in securities.

11. There is no barrier immediately canonical in its origin against the commingling or consolidation of funds constituting different endowments of pious foundations or different dowries of women religious. Administration of such funds, especially in investment management, can generally be more efficiently conducted through the combining of such funds. Such funds must, however, be kept segregated and distinct from other property held by the ecclesiastical moral person concerned.

12. The American civil law of trusts has many implications and effects in the ecclesiastical administration of property given for religious or other charitable purposes. Certain provisions of the civil law as canonized by canon 1529 variously establish norms regarding the segregation of such property, the standards of care in administering it, the permissible investments which can be made for the purpose of rendering this property productive of income, the faithful execution of the donor's intentions, and other matters having investment implications. Many pertinent provisions are to be found in the laws and judicial constructions regarding trusts for

charitable purposes and regarding the property of charitable corporations. The relation of such civil prescriptions to canon 1529 must be examined.

13. The purposes of the American law of trusts and of charitable corporations appear to consist chiefly in giving effect to the wishes of the donor. Although there is no opposition between such an end and the ends of canonical legislation, it is, of course, presupposed that the canonization of canon 1529 has effect only when there is no conflict between the specific provision of civil law and the postulates of divine law or canonical legislation. The law of the secular jurisdiction as compared with the more general tenor of the ecclesiastical law, is frequently in a position to give more specific directives, and more effective safeguards, in financial matters in order to give full effect to the donor's intentions.

BIBLIOGRAPHY

SOURCES

Acta Apostolica Sedis, Commentarium Officiale, Romae, 1909—

Acta et Decreta Synodi Dioecesanae Toletanae Primae, privately published, 1941.

Bouscaren, T. Lincoln, *Canon Law Digest,* 2 vols., Milwaukee: Bruce, 1934-1943.

Bruns, H. T., *Canones Apostolorum et Conciliorum Saeculorum IV, V, VI, VII,* 2 vols., Berolini, 1839.

Codex Iuris Canonici, Pii X Pontificis Maximi iussu digestus Benedicti Papae XV auctoritate promulgatus, Romae: Typis Polyglottis Vaticanis, 1917.

Codicis Iuris Canonici Fontes, cura Emi Petri Card. Gasparri editi, 9 vols., Romae (postea Civitate Vaticana): Typis Polyglottis Vaticanis, 1923-1939 (Vols. VII-IX, ed. cura et studio Emi Iustiniani Card. Serédi).

Canones et Decreta Concilii Tridentini ex Editione Romana A. MDCCCXXXIV Repetiti, edidit Josephus Pelella, Neapoli, 1859.

Collectanea Sacrae Congregationis de Propaganda Fide, 2 vols., Romae, 1907.

Corpus Iuris Canonici, ed. Lipsien. 2. post Aemilii Ludovici Richteri curas instruxit Aemilius Friedberg, 2 vols., Lipsiae: Ex Officina Bernhardi Tauchnitz, 1879-1881. Editio anastatice repetita, Lipsiae: Tauchnitz, 1922.

Corpus Iuris Civilis, Vol. I, Editio Stereotypa Quinta Decima, Berolini, 1928; Vol. II, Editio Stereotypa Decima, Berolini, 1929 (Vols. I et II recognovit et retractavit Paulus Krueger).

Decretales D. Gregorii Papae IX suae integritati una cum glossis restitutae, cum privilegio Gregorii XIII, Pont. Max., et aliorum principum, Romae, 1582.

Decretum Gratiani emendatum et notationibus illustratum una cum Glossis, Gregorii XIII, Pont. Max., iussu editum, 2 vols., Romae, 1582.

Jaffé, Philippus, *Regesta Pontificum Romanorum ab condita Ecclesia ad annum post Christum natum MCXCVIII,* 2. ed., correctam et auctam auspiciis Guglielmi Wattenbach, curaverunt F. Kaltenbrunner, P. Ewald, S. Loewenfeld, 2 vols. in 1, Lipsiae, 1885-1888.

Mansi, Joannes, *Sacrorum Conciliorum Nova et Amplissima Collectio,* 53 vols. in 60, Parisiis, 1901-1927.

McKinney's Consolidated Laws of New York Annotated, 68 Books, Brooklyn, N. Y.: Edward Thompson Company; Book 22, General Corporation Law, 1943, with 1946 Cumulative Annual Pocket Part.; Book 27, Insurance Law, 1940, with 1946 Cumulative Annual Pocket Part.; Book 34, Membership Corporations Law, 1941, with 1946 Cumulative Annual Pocket Part.; Book 50, Religious Corporations Law, 1918, with 1946 Cumulative Annual Pocket Part.

Monumenta Germaniae Historica, Leges, 5 vols., Vols. I-IV ed. G. Pertz;
   Vol. V, edd. G. Pertz-G. Waitz-H. Brunner, Hannoverae, 1835-1889; reprinted in Leipzig, 1925.

*Normae secundum quas S. Cong. Episcoporum et Regularium procedere solet
   in approbandis novis institutis votorum simplicium,* Romae: S. C. de
   Prop. Fide, 1901.

Potthast, A., *Regesta Pontificum Romanorum inde ab anno post Christum
   natum MCXCVIII ad annum MCCCIV,* 2 vols., Berolini, 1874-1875.

Purdon's Pennsylvania Statutes Annotated, Titles 13-15, Constables-Corporations, St. Paul: West Publishing Company, 1938, with 1947 Cumulative
   Annual Pocket Part.

Prentice-Hall, *Wills, Estate, and Trust Service,* Vol. 4.

Synodus Altunensis Prima, privately published, 1923.

Thesaurus Resolutionum Sacrae Congregationis Concilii, 167 vols., Urbini et
   Romae, 1718-1908.

Reference Works

André, M.-Condis, P.-Wagner, J., *Dictionnaire de Droit Canonique,* 5. ed., 5
   vols., Paris, 1901.

Augustine, Charles, *A Commentary on the New Code of Canon Law,* 8 vols.,
   Vol. VI, 3. ed., St. Louis: Herder, 1931.

Ayrinhac, H., *Administrative Legislation in the New Code of Canon Law,*
   London, New York, Toronto: Longmans, Green & Co., 1930.

Bargilliat, Michael, *Praelectiones Juris Canonici,* 37. ed., 2 vols., Parisiis, 1923.

Bastien, Pierre, *Directoire Canonique à L'Usage des Congregations à Voeux
   Simples,* 3. ed., Brugis, 1923.

Battandier, Albert, *Guide Canonique pour les Constitutions des Instituts à
   Voeux Simples,* 6. ed., Paris: Libraire Lecoffre, 1923.

Berutti, C., *Institutiones Iuris Canonici,* 6 vols., Vol. III, 1936; Vol. IV, 1940;
   Taurini-Romae: Marietti.

Beste, U., *Introductio in Codicem,* 3. ed., Collegeville, Minn.: St. John's Abbey
   Press, 1946.

Blat, Albertus, *Commentarium Textus Codicis Iuris Canonici,* 5 vols. in 7,
   Romae; Liber II, Partes II et III, 3. ed., 1938; Liber III, Partes II-VI,
   1923.

Bogert, George, *Handbook of the Law of Trusts,* 2. ed., St. Paul: West Publishing Co., 1942.

———, *The Law of Trusts and Trustees,* 7 vols., St. Paul: West Publishing
   Co.; Vol. III, 1946; Vol. IV, 1948; all other volumes, 1935.

Bouscaren, T. Lincoln, and Ellis, Adam, *Canon Law,* Milwaukee: Bruce, 1948.

Cance, Adrien, *Le Code de Droit Canonique,* 7. ed., 3 vols., Paris: Libraire
   Lecoffre, 1946.

Cappello, Felix, *Summa Iuris Canonici,* 3 vols., Vol. II, 4. ed., Romae: apud
   Aedes Universitatis Gregorianae, 1945.

Chelodi, Ioannes, *Ius Canonicum De Personis*, 3. ed., Vicenza: Società Anonima Tipografica; Trento: Libreria Moderna Editrice, 1942.

Claeys Bouuaert, F.-Simenon, G., *Manuale Juris Canonici*, 3 vols., Vols. I et III, 4. ed.; Vol. II, 2. ed.; Gandae et Leodii, 1934-1935.

Cleary, Joseph, *Canonical Limitations on the Alienation of Church Property*, The Catholic University of America Canon Law Studies, n. 100, Washington, D. C.: The Catholic University of America, 1936.

Cocchi, Guidus, *Commentarium in Codicem Iuris Canonici ad Usum Scholarum*, 8 vols., Taurinorum Augustae: Marietti; Vol. III, 4. ed., 1937; Vol. IV, 3. ed., 1932; Vol. VI, 3. ed., 1933.

Comyns, Joseph, *Papal and Episcopal Administration of Church Property*, The Catholic University of America Canon Law Studies, n. 147, Washington, D. C.: The Catholic University of America Press, 1942.

Coronata, Matthaeus Conte a, *Institutiones Iuris Canonici*, 2. ed., 5 vols., Taurini: Marietti, 1939-1947.

Corpus Juris, 72 vols., New York: American Law Book Co., 1914-1937.

Corpus Juris Secundum, 58 vols., Brooklyn, N. Y.: American Law Book Co., 1936-1948.

Creusen, J., Garesché, E., Ellis, A., *Religious Men and Women in the Code*, 4th English ed., Milwaukee: Bruce, 1940.

De Meester, Alphonsus, *Juris Canonici et Juris Canonico-Civilis Compendium*, nova ed., 4 vols., Brugis, 1921-1928; Vol. II, 1923; Vol. III, 1926.

Dictionnaire de Droit Canonique, fasc. 1-22, Paris: Letouzey et Ané, 1924-1948.

Doheny, William, *Practical Problems in Church Finance*, Milwaukee: Bruce, 1941.

Emery, Henry C., *Speculation on Stock and Produce Exchanges of the United States*, Columbia University Studies in History, Economics, and Public Law, n. 7, New York, 1896.

Fanfani, Ludovicus, *De Iure Religiosorum ad Normam Codicis Iuris Canonici*, ed. altera, Taurini-Romae: Marietti, 1925.

Ferraris, Lucius, *Bibliotheca Canonica, Iuridica, Moralis, Theologica, necnon Ascetica, Polemica, Rubricistica, Historica*, ed. novissima, 9 vols., Romae, 1885-1899.

Ferreres, J. B., *Institutiones Canonicae*, ed. altera, 2 vols., Barcinone, 1920.

Fournier, Paul, et Le Bras, Gabriel, *Histoire des Collections Canoniques en Occident depuis les Fausses Decretales jusqu'au Décret de Gratien*, 2 vols., Paris, 1931-1932.

Gasparri, P., *Tractatus Canonicus de Sanctissima Eucharistia*, 2 vols., Parisiis et Lugduni, 1897.

Goyeneche, S., *Iuris Canonici Summa Principia*, Lib. II, Pars II, Romae: Tip. Pol. "Cuore di Maria," 1938.

Hannan, Jerome, *The Canon Law of Wills*, The Catholic University of America Canon Law Studies, n. 86, Washington, D. C.: The Catholic University of America, 1934.

Heston, Edward, *The Alienation of Church Property in the United States,* The Catholic University of America Canon Law Studies, n. 132, Washington, D. C.: The Catholic University of America Press, 1941.

Holdsworth, William, *A History of English Law,* 12 vols., Boston: Little, Brown & Co., 1924-1938.

Hostiensis, Cardinalis (Henricus de Segusio), *In Tertium Decretalium Librum Commentaria,* Venetiis, 1581.

Jarrett, Bede, *Social Theories of the Middle Ages,* Westminster, Maryland: Newman Bookshop, 1942.

Kealy, Thomas, *Dowry of Women Religious,* The Catholic University of America Canon Law Studies, n. 134, Washington, D. C.: The Catholic University of America Press, 1941.

Kirschman, John, *Principles of Investment,* Chicago and New York: A. W. Shaw Co., 1924.

McManus, James, *The Administration of Temporal Goods in Religious Institutes,* The Catholic University of America Canon Law Studies, n. 109, Washington, D. C.: The Catholic University of America, 1937.

Melo, Antonius, *De Exemptione Regularium,* The Catholic University of America Canon Law Studies, n. 12, Washington, D. C.: The Catholic University of America, 1921.

Migne, J. P., *Patrologiae Cursus Completus, Series Latina,* 221 vols., Parisiis, 1844-1864.

Miller, Newton, *Founded Masses According to the Code of Canon Law,* The Catholic University of America Canon Law Studies, n. 34, Washington, D. C.: The Catholic University of America, 1926.

Molina, Ludovicus, *De Justitia et Jure,* 5 vols., Coloniae Allobrogum, 1759.

Mundy, Thomas, *The Union of Parishes,* The Catholic University of America Canon Law Studies, n. 204, Washington, D. C.: The Catholic University of America Press, 1945.

Noldin, H., *Summa Theologiae Moralis,* 3 vols., Oeniponte/Lipsiae: Rauch; Vol. II, 27. ed., 1941.

O'Brien, Joseph, *The Exemption of Religious in Church Law,* Milwaukee: Bruce, 1943.

Oesterle, G., *Praelectiones Iuris Canonici,* Tomus I, Romae: in Collegio S. Anselmi, 1931.

Ojetti, Benedictus, *Synopsis Rerum Moralium et Juris Pontificii,* 3. ed., 4 vols., Romae, 1909-1914.

Panormitanus, Abbas (Nicholaus de Tudeschis), *Commentaria in Quinque Libros Decretalium,* 5 vols. in 7, Venetiis, 1588.

Pejška, J., *Ius Canonicum Religiosorum,* 3. ed., Friburgi Brisgoviae, 1927.

Pignatellus, J., *Consultationes Canonicae,* 10 vols., Coloniae Allobrogum, 1700.

Pistocchi, M., *De Bonis Ecclesiae Temporalibus,* Taurini: Marietti, 1932.

———, *De Re Beneficiali,* Taurini: Marietti, 1928.

Pollock, Frederick-Maitland, Frederick, *The History of English Law,* 2 vols., Cambridge, 1895.

Prümmer, Dominicus, *Manuale Iuris Canonici,* 4. et 5. ed., Friburgi Brisgoviae, 1927.

Radin, Max, *A Handbook of Anglo-American Legal History,* St. Paul: West Publishing Co., 1936.

Redoanus, Gulielmus, *Solemnis Tractatus de Alienationibus Rerum Ecclesiarum,* Placentiae, 1589.

Regatillo, E. F., *Institutiones Juris Canonici,* 2 vols., Vol. I, 2. ed., Santander: Sal Terrae, 1946.

Reiffenstuel, Anacletus, *Jus Canonicum Universum,* 5 vols. in 7, Parisiis, 1864-1870.

Reilly, Thomas, *The Visitation of Religious,* The Catholic University of America Canon Law Studies, n. 112, Washington, D. C.: The Catholic University of America, 1938.

Restatement of the Law of Trusts, 2 vols., St. Paul: American Law Institute Publishers, 1935.

Schaefer, Timotheus, *De Religiosis ad Normam Codicis Iuris Canonici,* 3. ed., Romae: *S. A. L. E. R.,* 1940.

Schema Codicis Iuris Canonici, Romae, 1912.

Schmalzgrueber, F., *Jus Ecclesiasticum Universum,* 5 vols. in 12, Romae, 1843-1845.

Scott, Austin Wakeman, *The Law of Trusts,* 4 vols., Boston: Little, Brown & Co., 1939; also *1948 Supplement to Vol. III.*

Scotus, A., Kahl, J., Brissonius, B., Heineccius, J., *Vocabularium Juris Utriusque,* 2. ed., 4 vols., Neapoli, 1760.

Smith, Walter, *Handbook of Elementary Law,* 2. ed., St. Paul: West Publishing Co., 1939.

Taylor, A. W., *Investments,* New York: Alexander Hamilton Institute, 1929.

Tomlinson, Lucile, *Successful Investing Formulas,* New York: Barron's, 1947.

Toso, Albertus, *Ad Codicem Iuris Canonici Commentaria Minora,* Liber II, Pars II, Romae: Jus Pontificium, 1927.

Vermeersch, A.-Creusen, J., *Epitome Iuris Canonici,* 3 vols., Mechlinae-Romae: Dessain; Vol. I, 6. ed., 1937; Vol. II, 6. ed., 1940.

Vold, Lawrence, *Handbook of the Law of Sales,* St. Paul: West Publishing Co., 1931.

Vromant, G., *De Bonis Ecclesiae Temporalibus,* Louvain, 1927.

Wernz, F.-Vidal, P., *Ius Canonicum,* 7 vols. in 8, Romae: apud Aedes Universitatis Gregorianae; Vol. II, *De Personis,* 3. ed., 1943; Vol. III, *De Religiosis,* 1933.

Woywod, Stanislaus, *A Practical Commentary on the Code of Canon Law,* 10th printing, 2 vols., New York: Wagner, 1946.

Encyclopedia

Encyclopedia Britannica, 24 vols., Chicago, London, Toronto, 1946.
Encyclopedia of the Social Sciences, 15 vols., New York: Macmillan, 1932.

Articles

Blackwell, T. E., "The Charitable Corporation and the Charitable Trust," 24 *Washington University Law Quarterly,* 1-45 (1938).

Ellis, Adam, "Canonical Terms dealing with *Bona Temporalia," Theological Studies,* I (1940), 171-174.

Larraona, Arcadius, "Commentarium Codicis," *CpR,* XII (1931), 435-442; XIII (1932), 24-35; *CpRM,* XX (1939), 8-17; XXI (1940), 26-35.

Lincoln, Alexander, "Gifts to Charitable Corporations," 25 *Virginia Law Review,* 764-795 (1939).

McLaughlin, T. P., "The Teaching of the Canonists on Usury," *Mediaeval Studies,* I (1939), 81-147.

Motry, L.-Brown, B., "Memorandum by Dean Motry and Dr. Brown," *The Jurist,* II (1942), 76-79.

Nebreda, E., "Quaestiones Selectae de Iure Administrativo Ecclesiastico," *CpR,* VII (1926), 261-271, 317-333.

O'Brien, Kenneth R., "Foundations for Masses Should Never Create Trusts," *The Jurist,* IV (1944), 284-315.

Petrinus, "A Contract Determining the Status of a Religious Parish," *The Jurist,* IX (1949), 65-86.

Riddle, N. G., "Trust Investments: Their Extent and Some Related Economic Problems," 5 *Law and Contemporary Problems* (1938), 339-354.

Scott, Austin, "Fifty Years of Trusts," 50 *Harvard Law Review,* 60-76 (1936).

Taylor, Frederick J., "A New Chapter in the New York Law of Charitable Corporations," 25 *Cornell Law Quarterly,* 382-400 (1940).

Annotations, Comments, Replies to Queries

Anonymous, "Quaesita Varia," n. 18, *Periodica,* XI (1922), (157)-(158).

Anonymous, "Quaesita Varia," V, *Periodica,* XI (1922), (23)-(24).

Anonymous, "Trusts—Charitable Donation—Gift or Trust?", 40 *Columbia University Law Review,* 550-554 (1940).

Clappers, William, "Charities—Absolute Gift to Public Charitable Corporation," 19 *Boston University Law Review,* 655-658 (1940).

Goyeneche, "Consultationes," n. 34a, *CpR,* III (1922), 266-269.

Vermeersch, A., [Annotations], *Periodica,* II (1911), 74-75.

Vermeersch, A., "Quaesita Varia," III, *Periodica,* II (1911), 89-93.

Periodicals

Boston University Law Review, 1921—
Columbia Law Review, New York, 1901—

Commentarium pro Religiosis, Romae, 1920-1934; ab anno 1935, *Commentarium pro Religiosis et Missionariis.*

Cornell Law Quarterly, Ithaca, 1915—

Harvard Law Review, Cambridge, 1887—

Jurist, The, Washington, 1941—

Law and Contemporary Problems, Durham, N. C., 1933—

Mediaeval Studies, Vols. I-III, 1939-1941, New York; Vols. IV-X, 1942-1948, Toronto.

Periodica de Re Canonica et Morali Utili praesertim Religiosis et Missionariis, Brugis, 1905-1926; ab anno, 1927, *Periodica de Re Canonica, Morali, Liturgica,* Brugis, 1927-1936; Romae, 1937—

Theological Studies, Woodstock, 1940—

Virginia Law Review, University, Va., 1913—

Washington University Law Quarterly, St. Louis, 1914—

UNPUBLISHED MATERIAL

Guilfoyle, George H., *Charitable Trusts: an attitude and a consideration of administrative patterns and policies,* Thesis (LL.M.), Columbia University, New York, 1946.

INDEX

acceptance of a foundation, 135-138

Agde, Council of, 2

Alexander III, 5

Alexander IV, 2

alienation of ecclesiastical property, 3-4, 9, 29, 47, 54, 68-69, 138-139

alienation, reinvestment of proceeds from, 39-47

annuity contracts, 15-20, 54-57

antichresis, 17

bank deposit at interest, 22-26, 37-38, 113-115, 155, 163-164

benefactors, intentions and wishes of, 86-88, 95, 102, 124-125, 160, 171-177

benefice, 5, 6, 65

benefice, endowment of, 46, 65-70

Calixtus III, 20

Celestine III, 4, 15

census, 15-20, 39

charitable corporations at civil law, 166-177

charitable trusts, 91, 161-166

civil law, American, 90-93, 154-177

civil law, given canonical effect, 56-57, 93, 154-177

collocare, 98-100

commingling of funds, 84, 141-146, 164, 171

condition subsequent, gift upon, 177

consent of local ordinary, 59, 71, 72, 82-84, 108-109, 110-130, 135-137

consolidation and segregation of funds, 84, 141-146, 164, 171

contracts, civil law of and canon 1529, 154-155, 157-159

conversion of securities, 47-53, 69-70, 128-129

council of administration, diocesan, 52-53, 66-67, 139

deposit at interest, 22-26, 37-38, 113-115, 155, 163-164

depositories, diocesan, 43

diversification of investment, 77, 143-144, 164

dowries of women religious, 72-84

ecclesiastical ownership, 2

emphyteusis, contract of, 9-11

endowment, of benefices, 46, 65-70; of other non-collegiate ecclesiastical institutes, 70-71; of foundations, 46, 138-141; at civil law, 171-175

exchange of property, 3, 15

exchange of securities, 47-53, 69-70, 128-129

executors of pious wills, 87

extraordinary administration, acts of, 35-38, 135

fideicommissum, 88, 91, 92

foundations for pious causes, 131-153

fundi, 67, 118-119

incorporation of parish with religious house, 148-149

Innocent III, 4, 7

Innocent XII, 136, 142

institutes, non-collegiate, 70-71

intentions of benefactors, 86-88, 95, 102, 124-125, 160, 171-177

investment, defined and described, 22-26

investment, temporary and permanent, 24-26, 37-38, 59-64, 114-115, 119-121

investment management through agents, 50

189

BIOGRAPHICAL NOTE

HARRY J. BYRNE was born on February 7, 1921, in New York City. He was educated in the public schools of Mount Vernon and Larchmont, N. Y., and at Iona School, New Rochelle, N. Y. He entered the archdiocesan minor seminary in 1938 and St. Joseph's Seminary, Dunwoodie, N. Y., in 1940. From the latter he received the degree of Bachelor of Arts. He was ordained to the priesthood on December 1, 1945. In the following year he entered the School of Canon Law at the Catholic University of America. He received the Baccalaureate Degree in Canon Law in June, 1947, and the Licentiate Degree in Canon Law in June, 1948.

CANON LAW STUDIES *

1. FRERIKS, REV. CELESTINE A., C.PP.S., J.C.D., Religious Congregations in Their External Relations, 121 pp., 1916.
2. GALLIHER, REV. DANIEL M., O.P., J.C.D., Canonical Elections, 117 pp., 1917.
3. BORKOWSKI, REV. AURELIUS L., O.F.M., J.C.D., De Confraternitatibus Ecclesiasticis, 136 pp., 1918.
4. CASTILLO, REV. CAYO, J.C.D., Disertacion Historico-Canonica sobre la Potestad del Cabildo en Sede Vacante o Impedida del Vicario Capitular, 99 pp., 1919 (1918).
5. KUBELBECK, REV. WILLIAM J., S.T.B., J.C.D., The Sacred Penitentiaria and Its Relation to Faculties of Ordinaries and Priests, 129 pp., 1918.
6. PETROVITS, REV. JOSEPH, J.C., S.T.D., J.C.D., The New Church Law on Matrimony, X-461 pp., 1919.
7. HICKEY, REV. JOHN J., S.T.B., J.C.D., Irregularities and Simple Impediments in the New Code of Canon Law, 100 pp., 1920.
8. KLEKOTKA, REV. PETER J., S.T.B., J.C.D., Diocesan Consultors, 179 pp., 1920.
9. WANENMACHER, REV. FRANCIS, J.C.D., The Evidence in Ecclesiastical Procedure Affecting the Marriage Bond, 1920 (Printed 1935).
10. GOLDEN, REV. HENRY FRANCIS, J.C.D., Parochial Benefices in the New Code, IV-119 pp., 1921 (Printed 1925).
11. KOUDELKA, REV. CHARLES J., J.C.D., Pastors, Their Rights and Duties According to the New Code of Canon Law, 211 pp., 1921.
12. MELO, REV. ANTONIUS, O.F.M., J.C.D., De Exemptione Regularium, X-188 pp., 1921.
13. SCHAAF, REV. VALENTINE THEODORE, O.F.M., S.T.B., J.C.D., The Cloister, X-180 pp., 1921.
14. BURKE, REV. THOMAS JOSEPH, S.T.D., J.C.D., Competence in Ecclesiastical Tribunals, IV-117 pp., 1922.
15. LEECH, REV. GEORGE LEO, J.C.D., A Comparative Study of the Constitution "Apostolicae Sedis" and the "Codex Juris Canonici," 179 pp., 1922.
16. MOTRY, REV. HUBERT LOUIS, S.T.D., J.C.D., Diocesan Faculties According to the Code of Canon Law, II-167 pp., 1922.
17. MURPHY, REV. GEORGE LAWRENCE, J.C.D., Delinquencies and Penalties in the Administration and the Reception of the Sacraments, IV-121 pp., 1923.
18. O'REILLY, REV. JOHN ANTHONY, S.T.B., J.C.D., Ecclesiastical Sepulture in the New Code of Canon Law, II-129 pp., 1923.

* All published numbers are available from the Catholic University of America Press, 620 Michigan Avenue, N.E., Washington 17, D. C., except the following: Nos. 1-114 inclusive, 116, 118, 120, 121, 122, 123, 136, 153, 162, 182 and 198. But the following numbers, now reissued, are obtainable from *The Jurist*, The Catholic University of America, Washington 17, D. C., namely: Nos. 5, 7, 11, 17, 18, 19, 26, 28, 30, 31, 34, 42, 44, 51, 52 and 61.

19. MICHALICKA, REV. WENCESLAS CYRILL, O.S.B., J.C.D., Judicial Procedure in Dismissal of Clerical Exempt Religious, 107 pp., 1923.
20. DARGIN, REV. EDWARD VINCENT, S.T.B., J.C.D., Reserved Cases According to the Code of Canon Law, IV-103 pp., 1924.
21. GODFREY, REV. JOHN A., S.T.B., J.C.D., The Right of Patronage According to the Code of Canon Law, 153 pp., 1924.
22. HAGEDORN, REV. FRANCIS EDWARD, J.C.D., General Legislation on Indulgences, II-154 pp., 1924.
23. KING, REV. JAMES IGNATIUS, J.C.D., The Administration of the Sacraments to Dying Non-Catholics, V-141 pp., 1924.
24. WINSLOW, REV. FRANCIS JOSEPH, O.F.M., J.C.D., Vicars and Prefects Apostolic, IV-149 pp., 1924.
25. CORREA, REV. JOSE SERVELION, S.T.L., J.C.D., La Potestad Legislativa de la Iglesia Catolica, IV-127 pp., 1925.
26. DUGAN, REV. HENRY FRANCIS, A.M., J.C.D., The Judiciary Department of the Diocesan Curia, 87 pp., 1925.
27. KELLER, REV. CHARLES FREDERICK, S.T.B., J.C.D., Mass Stipends, 167 pp., 1925.
28. PASCHANG, REV. JOHN LINUS, J.C.D., The Sacramentals According to the Code of Canon Law, 129 pp., 1925.
29. PIONTEK, REV. CYRILLUS, O.F.M., S.T.B., J.C.D., De Indulto Exclaustrationis necnon Saecularizationis, XIII-289 pp., 1925.
30. KEARNEY, REV. RICHARD JOSEPH, S.T.B., J.C.D., Sponsors at Baptism According to the Code of Canon Law, IV-127 pp., 1925.
31. BARTLETT, REV. CHESTER JOSEPH, A.M., LL.B., J.C.D., The Tenure of Parochial Property in the United States of America, V-108 pp., 1926.
32. KILKER, REV. ADRIAN JEROME, J.C.D., Extreme Unction, V-425 pp., 1926.
33. McCORMICK, REV. ROBERT EMMETT, J.C.D., Confessors of Religious, VIII-266 pp., 1926.
34. MILLER, REV. NEWTON THOMAS, J.C.D., Founded Masses According to the Code of Canon Law, VII-93 pp., 1926.
35. ROELKER, REV. EDWARD G., S.T.D., J.C.D., Principles of Privilege According to the Code of Canon Law, XI-166 pp., 1926.
36. BAKALARCZYK, REV. RICHARDUS, M.I.C., J.U.D., De Novitiatu, VIII-208 pp., 1927.
37. PIZZUTI, REV. LAWRENCE, O.F.M., J.U.L., De Parochis Religiosis, 1927. (Not Printed.)
38. BLILEY, REV. NICHOLAS MARTIN, O.S.B., J.C.D., Altars According to the Code of Canon Law, XIX-132 pp., 1927.
39. BROWN, MR. BRENDAN FRANCIS, A.B., LL.M., J.U.D., The Canonical Juristic Personality with Special Reference to Its Status in the United States of America, V-212 pp., 1927.
40. CAVANAUGH, REV. WILLIAM THOMAS, C.P., J.U.D., The Reservation of the Blessed Sacrament, VIII-101 pp., 1927.

41. DOHENY, REV. WILLIAM J., C.S.C., A.B., J.C.D., Church Property: Modes of Acquisition, X-118 pp., 1927.

42. FELDHAUS, REV. ALOYSIUS H., C.PP.S., J.C.D., Oratories, IX-141 pp., 1927.

43. KELLY, REV. JAMES PATRICK, A.B., J.C.D., The Jurisdiction of the Simple Confessor, X-208 pp., 1927.

44. NEUBERGER, REV. NICHOLAS J., J.C.D., Canon 6 or the Relation of the Codex Juris Canonici to the Preceding Legislation, V-95 pp., 1927.

45. O'KEEFE, REV. GERALD MICHAEL, J.C.D., Matrimonial Dispensations, Powers of Bishops, Priests, and Confessors, VIII-232 pp., 1927.

46. QUIGLEY, REV. JOSEPH A. M., A.B., J.C.D., Condemned Societies, 139 pp., 1927.

47. ZAPLOTNIK, REV. JOHANNES LEO, J.C.D., De Vicariis Foraneis, X-142 pp., 1927.

48. DUSKIE, REV. JOHN ALOYSIUS, A.B., J.C.D., The Canonical Status of the Orientals in the United States, VIII-196 pp., 1928.

49. HYLAND, REV. FRANCIS EDWARD, J.C.D., Excommunication, Its Nature, Historical Development and Effects, VIII-181 pp., 1928.

50. REINMANN, REV. GERALD JOSEPH, O.M.C., J.C.D., The Third Order Secular of Saint Francis, 201 pp., 1928.

51. SCHENK, REV. FRANCIS J., J.C.D., The Matrimonial Impediments of Mixed Religion and Disparity of Cult, XVI-318 pp., 1929.

52. COADY, REV. JOHN JOSEPH, S.T.D., J.U.D., A.M., The Appointment of Pastors, VIII-150 pp., 1929.

53. KAY, REV. THOMAS HENRY, J.C.D., Competence in Matrimonial Procedure, VIII-164 pp., 1929.

54. TURNER, REV. SIDNEY JOSEPH, C.P., J.U.D., The Vow of Poverty, XLIX-217 pp., 1929.

55. KEARNEY, REV. RAYMOND A., A.B., S.T.D., J.C.D., The Principles of Delegation, VII-149 pp., 1929.

56. CONRAN, REV. EDWARD JAMES, A.B., J.C.D., The Interdict, V-163 pp., 1930.

57. O'NEILL, REV. WILLIAM H., J.C.D., Papal Rescripts of Favor, VII-218 pp., 1930.

58. BASTNAGEL, REV. CLEMENT VINCENT, J.U.D., The Appointment of Parochial Adjutants and Assistants, XV-257 pp., 1930.

59. FERRY, REV. WILLIAM A., A.B., J.C.D., Stole Fees, V-136 pp., 1930.

60. COSTELLO, REV. JOHN MICHAEL, A.B., J.C.D., Domicile and Quasi-Domicile, VII-201 pp., 1930.

61. KREMER, REV. MICHAEL NICHOLAS, A.B., S.T.B., J.C.D., Church Support in the United States, VI-136 pp., 1930.

62. ANGULO, REV. LUIS, C.M., J.C.D., Legislation de la Iglesia sobre la intencion en la application de la Santa Misa, VII-104 pp., 1931.

63. FREY, REV. WOLFGANG NORBERT, O.S.B., A.B., J.C.D., The Act of Religious Profession, VIII-174 pp., 1931.

64. ROBERTS, REV. JAMES BRENDAN, A.B., J.C.D., The Banns of Marriage, XIV-140 pp., 1931.
65. RYDER, REV. RAYMOND ALOYSIUS, A.B., J.C.D., Simony, IX-151 pp., 1931.
66. CAMPAGNA, REV. ANGELO, PH.D., J.U.D., Il Vicario Generale del Vescovo, VII-205 pp., 1931.
67. COX, REV. JOSEPH GODFREY, A.B., J.C.D., The Administration of Seminaries, VI-124 pp., 1931.
68. GREGORY, REV. DONALD J., J.U.D., The Pauline Privilege, XV-165 pp., 1931.
69. DONOHUE, REV. JOHN F., J.C.D., The Impediment of Crime, VII-110 pp., 1931.
70. DOOLEY, REV. EUGENE A., O.M.I., J.C.D., Church Law on Sacred Relics, IX-143 pp., 1931.
71. ORTH, REV. CLEMENT RAYMOND, O.M.C., J.C.D., The Approbation of Religious Institutes, 171 pp., 1931.
72. PERNICONE, REV. JOSEPH M., A.B., J.C.D., The Ecclesiastical Prohibition of Books, XII-267 pp., 1932.
73. CLINTON, REV. CONNELL, A.B., J.C.D., The Paschal Precept, IX-108 pp., 1932.
74. DONNELLY, REV. FRANCIS B., A.M., S.T.L., J.C.D., The Diocesan Synod, VIII-125 pp., 1932.
75. TORRENTE, REV. CAMILO, C.M.F., J.C.D., Las Procesiones Sagradas, V-145 pp., 1932.
76. MURPHY, REV. EDWIN J., C.PP.S., J.C.D., Suspension Ex Informata Conscientia, XI-122 pp., 1932.
77. MACKENZIE, REV. ERIC F., A.M., S.T.L., J.C.D., The Delict of Heresy in its Commission, Penalization, Absolution, VII-124 pp., 1932.
78. LYONS, REV. AVITUS E., S.T.B., J.C.D., The Collegiate Tribunal of First Instance, XI-147 pp., 1932.
79. CONNOLLY, REV. THOMAS A., J.C.D., Appeals, XI-195, pp., 1932.
80. SANGMEISTER, REV. JOSEPH V., A.B., J.C.D., Force and Fear as Precluding Matrimonial Consent, V-211 pp., 1932.
81. JAEGER, REV. LEO A., A.B., J.C.D., The Administration of Vacant and Quasi-Vacant Episcopal Sees in the United States, IX-229 pp., 1932.
82. RIMLINGER, REV. HERBERT T., J.C.D., Error Invalidating Matrimonial Consent, VII-79 pp., 1932.
83. BARRETT, REV. JOHN D. M., S.S., J.C.D., A Comparative Study of the Councils of Baltimore and the Code of Canon Law, IX-223 pp., 1932.
84. CARBERRY, REV. JOHN J., PH.D., S.T.D., J.C.D., The Juridical Form of Marriage, X-177 pp., 1934.
85. DOLAN, REV. JOHN L., A.B., J.C.D., The Defensor Vinculi, XII-157 pp., 1934.
86. HANNAN, REV. JEROME D., A.M., S.T.D., LL.B., J.C.D., The Canon Law of Wills, IX-517 pp., 1934.

87. LEMIEUX, REV. DELISE A., A.M., J.C.D., The Sentence in Ecclesiastical Procedure, IX-131 pp., 1934.
88. O'ROURKE, REV. JAMES J., A.B., J.C.D., Parish Registers, VII-109 pp., 1934.
89. TIMLIN, REV. BARTHOLOMEW, O.F.M., A.M., J.C.D., Conditional Matrimonial Consent, X-381 pp., 1934.
90. WAHL, REV. FRANCIS X., A.B., J.C.D., The Matrimonial Impediments of Consanguinity and Affinity, VI-125 pp., 1934.
91. WHITE, REV. ROBERT J., A.B., LL.B., S.T.B., J.C.D., Canonical Ante-Nuptial Promises and the Civil Law, VI-152 pp., 1934.
92. HERRERA, REV. ANTONIO PARRA, O.C.D., J.C.D., Legislacion Ecclesiastica sobra el Ayuno y la Abstinencia, XI-191 pp., 1935.
93. KENNEDY, REV. EDWIN J., J.C.D., The Special Matrimonial Process in Cases of Evident Nullity, X-165 pp., 1935.
94. MANNING, REV. JOHN J., A.B., J.C.D., Presumption of Law in Matrimonial Procedure, XI-111 pp., 1935.
95. MOEDER, REV. JOHN M., J.C.D., The Proper Bishop for Ordination and Dismissorial Letters, VII-135 pp., 1935.
96. O'MARA, REV. WILLIAM A., A.B., J.C.D., Canonical Causes for Matrimonial Dispensations, IX-155 pp., 1935.
97. REILLY, REV. PETER, J.C.D., Residence of Pastors, IX-81 pp., 1935.
98. SMITH, REV. MARINER T., O.P., S.T.Lr., J.C.D., The Penal Law for Religious, VIII-169 pp., 1935.
99. WHALEN, REV. DONALD W., A.M., J.C.D., The Value of Testimonial Evidence in Matrimonial Procedure, XIII-297 pp., 1935.
100. CLEARY, REV. JOSEPH F., J.C.D., Canonical Limitations on the Alienation of Church Property, VIII-141 pp., 1936.
101. GLYNN, REV. JOHN C., J.C.D., The Promoter of Justice, XX-337 pp., 1936.
102. BRENNAN, REV. JAMES H., S.S., M.A., S.T.B., J.C.D., The Simple Convalidation of Marriage, VI-135 pp., 1937.
103. BRUNINI, REV. JOSEPH BERNARD, J.C.D., The Clerical Obligations of Canons 139 and 142, X-121 pp., 1937.
104. CONNOR, REV. MAURICE, A.B., J.C.D., The Administrative Removal of Pastors, VIII-159 pp., 1937.
105. GUILFOYLE, REV. MERLIN JOSEPH, J.C.D., Custom, XI-144 pp., 1937.
106. HUGHES, REV. JAMES AUSTIN, A.B., A.M., J.C.D., Witnesses in Criminal Trials of Clerics, IX-140 pp., 1937.
107. JANSEN, REV. RAYMOND J., A.B., S.T.L., J.C.D., Canonical Provisions for Catechetical Instruction, VII-153 pp., 1937.
108. KEALY, REV. JOHN JAMES, A.B., J.C.D., The Introductory Libellus in Church Court Procedure, XI-121 pp., 1937.
109. McMANUS, REV. JAMES EDWARD, C.SS.R., J.C.D., The Administration of Temporal Goods in Religious Institutes, XVI-196 pp., 1937.

110. MORIARTY, REV. EUGENE JAMES, J.C.D., Oaths in Ecclesiastical Courts, X-115 pp., 1937.

111. RAINER, REV. ELIGIUS GEORGE, C.SS.R., J.C.D., Suspension of Clerics, XVII-249 pp., 1937.

112. REILLY, REV. THOMAS F., C.SS.R., J.C.D., Visitation of Religious, VI-195 pp., 1938.

113. MORIARTY, REV. FRANCIS E., C.SS.R., J.C.D., The Extraordinary Absolution from Censures, XV-334 pp., 1938.

114. CONNOLLY, REV. NICHOLAS P., J.C.D., The Canonical Erection of Parishes, X-132 pp., 1938.

115. DONOVAN, REV. JAMES JOSEPH, J.C.D., The Pastor's Obligation in Prenuptial Investigation, XII-322 pp., 1938.

116. HARRIGAN, REV. ROBERT J., M.A., S.T.B., J.C.D., The Radical Sanation of Invalid Marriages, VIII-208 pp., 1938.

117. BOFFA, REV. CONRAD HUMBERT, J.C.D., Canonical Provisions for Catholic Schools, VII-211 pp., 1939.

118. PARSONS, REV. ANSCAR JOHN, O.M.Cap., J.C.D., Canonical Elections, XII-236 pp., 1939.

119. REILLY, REV. EDWARD MICHAEL, A.B., J.C.D., The General Norms of Dispensation, XII-156 pp., 1939.

120. RYAN, REV. GERALD ALOYSIUS, A.B., J.C.D., Principles of Episcopal Jurisdiction, XII-172 pp., 1939.

121. BURTON, REV. FRANCIS JAMES, C.S.C., A.B., J.C.D., A Commentary on Canon 1125, X-222 pp., 1940.

122. MIASKIEWICZ, REV. FRANCIS SIGISMUND, J.C.D., Supplied Jurisdiction According to Canon 209, XII-340 pp., 1940.

123. RICE, REV. PATRICK WILLIAM, A.B., J.C.D., Proof of Death in Prenuptial Investigation, VIII-156 pp., 1940.

124. ANGLIN, REV. THOMAS FRANCIS, M.S., J.C.D., The Eucharistic Fast, VIII-183 pp., 1941.

125. COLEMAN, REV. JOHN JEROME, J.C.D., The Minister of Confirmation, VI-153 pp., 1941.

126. DOWNS, REV. JOHN EMMANUEL, A.B., J.C.D., The Concept of Clerical Immunity, XI-163 pp., 1941.

127. ESSWEIN, REV. ANTHONY ALBERT, J.C.D., Extrajudicial Penal Powers of Ecclesiastical Superiors, X-144 pp., 1941.

128. FARRELL, REV. BENJAMIN FRANCIS, M.A., S.T.L., J.C.D., The Rights and Duties of the Local Ordinary Regarding Congregations of Women Religious of Pontifical Approval, V-195 pp., 1941.

129. FEENEY, REV. THOMAS JOHN, A.B., S.T.L., J.C.D., Restitutio in Integrum, VI-169 pp., 1941.

130. FINDLAY, REV. STEPHEN WILLIAM, O.S.B., A.B., J.C.D., Canonical Norms Governing the Deposition and Degradation of Clerics, XVII-279 pp., 1941.

131. GOODWINE, REV. JOHN, A.B., S.T.L., J.C.D., The Right of the Church to Acquire Property, VIII-119 pp., 1941.

132. HESTON, REV. EDWARD LOUIS, C.S.C., Ph.D., S.T.D., J.C.D., The Alienation of Church Property in the United States, XII-222 pp., 1941.

133. HOGAN, REV. JAMES JOHN, A.B., S.T.L., J.C.D., Judicial Advocates and Procurators, XIII-200 pp., 1941.

134. KEALY, REV. THOMAS M., A.B., Litt.B., J.C.D., Dowry of Women Religious, IX-152 pp., 1941.

135. KEENE, REV. MICHAEL JAMES, O.S.B., J.C.D., Religious Ordinaries and Canon 198, V-164 pp., 1941 (printed 1942).

136. KERIN, REV. CHARLES A., S.S., M.A., S.T.B., J.C.D., The Privation of Christian Burial, XVI-279 pp., 1941.

137. LOUIS, REV. WILLIAM FRANCIS, M.A., J.C.D., Diocesan Archives, X-101 pp., 1941.

138. MCDEVITT, REV. GILBERT JOSEPH, A.B., J.C.D., Legitimacy and Legitimation, X-247 pp., 1941.

139. MCDONOUGH, REV. THOMAS JOSEPH, A.B., J.C.D., Apostolic Administrators, X-217 pp., 1941.

140. MEIER, REV. CARL ANTHONY, A.B., J.C.D., Penal Administrative Procedure Against Negligent Pastors, XI-240 pp., 1941.

141. SCHMIDT, REV. JOHN ROGG, A.B., J.C.D., The Principles of Authentic Interpretation in Canon 17 of the Code of Canon Law, XII-331 pp., 1941.

142. SLAFKOSKY, REV. ANDREW LEONARD, A.B., J.C.D., The Canonical Episcopal Visitation of the Diocese, X-197 pp., 1941.

143. SWOBODA, REV. INNOCENT ROBERT, O.F.M., J.C.D., Ignorance in Relation to the Imputability of Delicts, IX-271 pp., 1941.

144. DUBÉ, REV. ARTHUR JOSEPH, A.B., J.C.D., The General Principles for the Reckoning of Time in Canon Law, VIII-299 pp., 1941.

145. MCBRIDE, REV. JAMES T., A.B., J.C.D., Incardination and Excardination of Seculars, XX-585 pp., 1941.

146. KRÓL, REV. JOHN T., J.C.D., The Defendant in Ecclesiastical Trials, XII-207 pp., 1942.

147. COMYNS, REV. JOSEPH J., C.SS.R., A.B., J.C.D., Papal and Episcopal Administration of Church Property, XIV-155 pp., 1942.

148. BARRY, REV. GARRETT FRANCIS, O.M.I., J.C.D., Violation of the Cloister, XII-260 pp., 1942.

149. BOLDUC, REV. GATIEN, C.S.V., A.B., S.T.L., J.C.D., Les Études dans les Religions Cléricales, VIII-155 pp., 1942.

150. BOYLE, REV. DAVID JOHN, M.A., J.C.D., The Juridic Effects of Moral Certitude on Pre-Nuptial Guarantees, XII-188 pp., 1942.

151. CANAVAN, REV. WALTER JOSEPH, M.A., Litt.D., J.C.D., The Profession of Faith, XII-143 pp., 1942.

152. DESROCHERS, REV. BRUNO, A.B., Ph.L., S.T.B., J.C.D., Le Premier Concile Plénier de Québec et le Code de Droit Canonique, XIV-186 pp., 1942.

153. DILLON, REV. ROBERT EDWARD, A.B., J.C.D., Common Law Marriage, X-148 pp., 1942.

154. DODWELL, REV. EDWARD JOHN, Ph.D., S.T.B., J.C.D., The Time and Place for the Celebration of Marriage, X-156 pp., 1942.

155. DONNELLAN, REV. THOMAS ANDREW, A.B., J.C.D., The Obligation of the Missa pro Populo, VII-131 pp., 1942.

156. ELTZ, REV. LOUIS ANTHONY, A.B., J.C.D., Cooperation in Crime, XII-208 pp., 1942.

157. GASS, REV. SYLVESTER FRANCIS, M.A., J.C.D., Ecclesiastical Pensions, XI-206 pp., 1942.

158. GUINIVEN, REV. JOHN JOSEPH, C.SS.R., J.C.D., The Precept of Hearing Mass, XIV-188 pp., 1942.

159. GULCZYNSKI, REV. JOHN THEOPHILUS, J.C.D., The Desecration and Violation of Churches, X-126 pp., 1942.

160. HAMMILL, REV. JOHN LEO, M.A., J.C.D., The Obligations of the Traveler According to Canon 14, VIII-204 pp., 1942.

161. HAYDT, REV. JOHN JOSEPH, A.B., J.C.D., Reserved Benefices, XI-148 pp., 1942.

162. HUSER, REV. ROGER JOHN, O.F.M., A.B., J.C.D., The Crime of Abortion in Canon Law, XII-187 pp., 1942.

163. KEARNEY, REV. FRANCIS PATRICK, A.B., S.T.L., J.C.D., The Principles of Canon 1127, X-162 pp., 1942.

164. LINAHEN, REV. LEO JAMES, S.T.L., J.C.D., De Absolutione Complicis in Peccato Turpi, V-114 pp., 1942.

165. McCLOSKEY, REV. JOSEPH ALOYSIUS, A.B., J.C.D., The Subject of Ecclesiastical Law According to Canon 12, XVII-246 pp., 1942 (printed 1943).

166. O'NEILL, REV. FRANCIS JOSEPH, C.SS.R., J.C.D., The Dismissal of Religious in Temporary Vows, XIII-220 pp., 1942.

167. PRINCE, REV. JOHN EDWARD, A.B., S.T.B., J.C.D., The Diocesan Chancellor, X-136 pp., 1942.

168. RIESNER, REV. ALBERT JOSEPH, C.SS.R., J.C.D., Apostates and Fugitives from Religious Institutes, IX-168 pp., 1942.

169. STENGER, REV. JOSEPH BERNARD, J.C.D., The Mortgaging of Church Property, 186 pp., 1942.

170. WALDRON, REV. JOSEPH FRANCIS, A.B., J.C.D., The Minister of Baptism, XII-197 pp., 1942.

171. WILLETT, REV. ROBERT ALBERT, J.C.D., The Probative Value of Documents in Ecclesiastical Trials, X-124 pp., 1942.

172. WOEBER, REV. EDWARD MARTIN, M.A., J.C.D., The Interpellations, XII-161 pp., 1942.

173. BENKO, REV. MATTHEW ALOYSIUS, O.S.B., M.A., J.C.D., The Abbot *Nullius*, XVI-148 pp., 1943.

174. CHRIST, REV. JOSEPH JAMES, M.A., S.T.L., J.C.D., Dispensation from Vindicative Penalties, XIV-285 pp., 1943.

175. CLANCY, REV. PATRICK M. J., O.P., A.B., S.T.Lr., J.C.D., The Local Religious Superior, X-229 pp., 1943.

176. CLARKE, REV. THOMAS JAMES, J.C.D., Parish Societies, XII-147 pp., 1943.

177. CONNOLLY, REV. JOHN PATRICK, S.T.L., J.C.D., Synodal Examiners and Parish Priest Consultors, X-223 pp., 1943.

178. DRUMM, REV. WILLIAM MARTIN, A.B., J.C.D., Hospital Chaplains, XII-175 pp., 1943.

179. FLANAGAN, REV. BERNARD JOSEPH, A.B., S.T.L., J.C.D., The Canonical Erection of Religious Houses, X-147 pp., 1943.

180. KELLEHER, REV. STEPHEN JOSEPH, A.B., S.T.B., J.C.D., Discussions with Non-Catholics: Canonical Legislation, X-93 pp., 1943.

181. LEWIS, REV. GORDIAN, C.P., J.C.D., Chapters in Religious Institutes, XII-169 pp., 1943.

182. MARX, REV. ADOLPH, J.C.D., The Declaration of Nullity of Marriages Contracted Outside the Church, X-151 pp., 1943.

183. MATULENAS, REV. RAYMOND ANTHONY, O.S.B., A.B., J.C.D., Communication, a Source of Privileges, XII-225 pp., 1943.

184. O'LEARY, REV. CHARLES GERARD, C.SS.R., J.C.D., Religious Dismissed After Perpetual Profession, X-213 pp., 1943.

185. POWER, REV. CORNELIUS MICHAEL, J.C.D., The Blessing of Cemeteries, XII-231 pp., 1943.

186. SHUHLER, REV. RALPH VINCENT, O.S.A., J.C.D., Privileges of Religious to Absolve and Dispense, XII-195 pp., 1943.

187. ZIOLKOWSKI, REV. THADDEUS STANISLAUS, A.B., J.C.D., The Consecration and Blessing of Churches, XII-151 pp., 1943.

188. HENEGHAN, REV. JOHN JOSEPH, S.T.D., J.C.D., The Marriages of Unworthy Catholics: Canons 1065 and 1066, XVI-213 pp., 1944.

189. CARROLL, REV. COLEMAN FRANCIS, M.A., S.T.L., J.C.L., Charitable Institutions.

190. CIESLUK, REV. JOSEPH EDWARD, PH.B., S.T.L., J.C.D., National Parishes in the United States, VI-178 pp., 1944.

191. COBURN, REV. VINCENT PAUL, A.B., J.C.D., Marriages of Conscience, XII-172 pp., 1944.

192. CONNORS, REV. CHARLES PAUL, C.S.SP., A.B., J.C.D., Extra-Judicial Procurators in the Code of Canon Law, X-94 pp., 1944.

193. COYLE, REV. PAUL RAYMOND, A.B., J.C.D., Judicial Exceptions, X-142 pp., 1944.

194. FAIR, REV. BARTHOLOMEW FRANCIS, A.B., S.T.L., J.C.D., The Impediment of Abduction, XII-122 pp., 1944.

195. GALLAGHER, REV. THOMAS RAPHAEL, O.P., A.B., S.T.Lr., J.C.D., The Examination of the Qualities of the Ordinand, X-166 pp., 1944.

196. GANNON, REV. JOHN MARK, S.T.L., J.C.D., The Interstices Required for the Promotion to Orders, XII-100 pp., 1944.

197. GOLDSMITH, REV. J. WILLIAM, B.C.S., S.T.L., J.C.D., The Competence of Church and State Over Marriages—Disputed Points, X-128 pp., 1944.

198. GOODWINE, REV. JOSEPH GERARD, A.B., S.T.B., J.C.D., The Reception of Converts, XIV-326 pp., 1944.

199. KOWALSKI, REV. ROMUALD EUGENE, O.F.M., A.B., J.C.D., Sustenance of Religious Houses of Regulars, X-174 pp., 1944.

200. McCoy, REV. ALAN EDWARD, O.F.M., J.C.D., Force and Fear in Relation to Delictual Imputability and Penal Responsibility, XII-160 pp., 1944.

201. McDEVITT, REV. VINCENT JOHN, PH.B., S.T.L., J.C.L., Perjury.

202. MARTIN, REV. THOMAS OWEN, PH.D., S.T.D., J.C.D., Adverse Possession, Prescription and Limitation of Actions: The Canonical "Praescriptio," XX-208 pp., 1944.

203. MIKLOSOVIC, REV. PAUL JOHN, A.B., J.C.L., Attempted Marriages and Their Consequent Juridic Effects.

204. MUNDY, REV. THOMAS MAURICE, A.B., S.T.L., J.C.D., The Union of Parishes, X-164 pp., 1944.

205. O'DEA, REV. JOHN COYLE, A.B., J.C.D., The Matrimonial Impediment of Nonage, VIII-126 pp., 1944.

206. OLALIA, REV. ALEXANDER AYSON, S.T.L., J.C.D., A Comparative Study of the Christian Constitution of States and the Constitution of the Philippine Commonwealth, XII-136 pp., 1944.

207. POISSON, REV. PIERRE-MARIE, C.S.C., A.B., PH.L., TH.L., J.C.L., Droits Patrimoniaux des Maisons et des Eglises Religieuses.

208. STADALNIKAS, REV. CASIMIR JOSEPH, M.I.C., J.C.D., Reservation of Censures, X-141 pp., 1944.

209. SULLIVAN, REV. EUGENE HENRY, S.T.L., J.C.D., Proof of the Reception of the Sacraments, X-165 pp., 1944.

210. VAUGHAN, REV. WILLIAM EDWARD, J.C.D., Constitutions for Diocesan Courts, X-210 pp., 1944.

211. PARO, REV. GINO, S.T.D., J.C.D., The Right of Papal Legation, X-221 pp., 1944 (printed 1947).

212. BALZER, REV. RALPH FRANCIS, C.P., J.C.D., The Computation of Time in a Canonical Novitiate, X-227 pp., 1945.

213. DOUGHERTY, REV. JOHN WHELAN, A.B., S.T.L., J.C.D., De Inquisitione Speciali, XII-195 pp., 1945.

214. DZIOB, REV. MICHAEL WALTER, J.C.D., The Sacred Congregation for the Oriental Church, XII-181 pp., 1945.

215. EIDENSCHINK, REV. JOHN ALBERT, O.S.B., B.A., J.C.D., The Election of Bishops in the Letters of Pope Gregory the Great, VIII-200 pp., 1945.

216. GILL, REV. NICHOLAS, C.P., J.C.D., The Spiritual Prefect in Clerical Religious Houses of Study, X-140 pp., 1945.

217. HYNES, REV. HARRY GERARD, S.T.L., J.C.D., The Privileges of Cardinals, XII-183 pp., 1945.

218. McDEVITT, REV. GERALD VINCENT, S.T.L., J.C.D., The Renunciation of an Ecclesiastical Office, XIV-179 pp., 1945.

219. MANNING, REV. JOSEPH LEROY, J.C.D., The Free Conferral of Offices, VII-116 pp., 1945.

220. MEYER, REV. LOUIS G., O.S.B., A.B., S.T.B., J.C.D., Alms-gathering by Religious, XII-163 pp., 1945.

221. O'DONNELL, REV. CLETUS FRANCIS, M.A., J.C.D., The Marriage of Minors, XII-268 pp., 1945.

222. PRUNSKIS, REV. JOSEPH, J.C.D., Comparative Law, Ecclesiastical and Civil, in Lithuanian Concordat, X-161 pp., 1945.

223. SWEENEY, REV. FRANCIS PATRICK, C.SS.R., J.C.D., The Reduction of Clerics to the Lay State, X-199 pp., 1945.

224. VOGELPOHL, REV. HENRY JOHN, J.C.D., The Simple Impediments to Holy Orders, XVI-190 pp., 1945.

225. BROCKHAUS, REV. THOMAS AQUINAS, O.S.B., J.C.D., Religious who are known as *Conversi,* X-127 pp., 1945.

226. GRIESE, REV. ORVILLE NICHOLAS, S.T.D., J.C.D., The Marriage Contract and the Procreation of Offspring, XVI-224 pp., 1946.

227. BOUDREAUX, REV. WARREN LOUIS, J.C.D., The *"ab acatholicis nati"* of Canon 1099, § 2, XII-110 pp., 1946.

228. BOWE, REV. THOMAS JOSEPH, A.B., J.C.D., Religious Superioresses, VIII-206 pp., 1946.

229. DIEDERICHS, REV. MICHAEL FERDINAND, S.C.J., J.C.D., The Jurisdiction of the Latin Ordinaries over their Oriental Subjects, XIV-153 pp., 1946.

230. DINGMAN, REV. MAURICE JOHN, A.B., S.T.L., J.C.L., The Plaintiff in Contentious Trials.

231. FRISON, REV. BASIL, C.M.F., M.MUS., J.C.D., The Retroactivity of Law, X-221 pp., 1946.

232. GALVIN, REV. WILLIAM ANTHONY, M.A., J.C.D., The Administrative Transfer of Pastors, XII-288 pp., 1946.

233. GORACY, REV. JOSEPH C., J.C.L., The Diriment Matrimonial Impediment of Major Orders.

234. HALE, REV. JOSEPH FRANCIS, M.A., S.T.L., J.C.D., The Pastor of Burial, X-247 pp., 1946 (printed 1949).

235. HENRY, REV. JOSEPH ARTHUR, A.B., J.C.D., The Mass and Holy Communion: Interritual Law, XII-138 pp., 1946.

236. LINENBERGER, REV. HERBERT, C.PP.S., J.C.D., The False Denunciation of an Innocent Confessor, VIII-205 pp., 1946 (printed 1949).

237. LOWRY, REV. JAMES MARTIN, A.B., J.C.D., Dispensation from Private Vows, XII-266 pp., 1946.

238. LYNCH, REV. GEORGE EDWARD, A.B., S.T.L., J.C.D., Coadjutors and Auxiliaries of Bishops, X-107 pp., 1946 (printed 1947).

239. Lynch, Rev. Timothy, M.S.SS.T., J.C.D., Contracts between Bishops and Religious Congregations, XIII-232 pp., 1946.

240. McClunn, Rev. Justin David, A.B., S.T.L., J.C.D., Administrative Recourse, VII-142 pp., 1946.

241. Lohmuller, Rev. Martin Nicholas, A.B., J.C.D., The Promulgation of Law, XII-140 pp., 1947.

242. McGrath, Rev. James, A.B., J.C.D., The Privilege of the Canon, XII-156 pp., 1946.

243. Marbach, Rev. Joseph Francis, A.B., J.C.D., Marriage Legislation for the Catholics of the Oriental Rites in the United States and Canada, XIV-314 pp., 1946.

244. Shimkus, Rev. Bernard Aloysius, A.B., J.C.L., The Determination and Transfer of Rite.

245. Smith, Rev. Vincent Michael, A.B., S.T.L., J.C.L., Ignorance Affecting Matrimonial Consent.

246. Wachtrle, Rev. Paul Anthony, A.B., J.C.L., The Baptism of the Children of Non-Catholics.

247. Crotty, Rev. Matthew Michael, J.C.D., The Recipient of First Holy Communion, X-142 pp., 1947.

248. Eagleton, Rev. George, J.C.D., The Quinquennial Faculties, Formula IV, XIV-199 pp., 1947 (printed 1948).

249. Gibbons, Rev. Marion Leo, C.M., J.C.L., Domicile of the Wife Unlawfully Separated from Her Husband, XIV-171 pp., 1947.

250. Kelly, Rev. Bernard M., S.T.L., J.C.D., The Functions Reserved to Pastors, XII-141 pp., 1947.

251. Kilcullen, Rev. Thomas J., LL.M., J.C.D., The Collegiate Moral Person as Party Litigant, X-150 pp., 1947.

252. Lafontaine, Rev. Germaine Joseph, W.F., J.C.D., Relations Canoniques entre le Missionaire et Ses Superieurs, X-117 pp., 1947.

253. Lane, Rev. Loras Thomas, A.B., S.T.L., J.C.D., Matrimonial Procedure in the Ordinary Court of Second Instance, XVI-184 pp., 1947.

254. Lover, Rev. James Francis, C.Ss.R., J.C.D., The Master of Novices, X-168 pp., 1947.

255. McNicholas, Rev. Timothy Joseph, J.C.L., The *Septimae Manus* Witness.

256. Marositz, Rev. Joseph John, M.S.C., J.C.D., Obligations and Privileges of Religious Promoted to the Episcopal or Cardinalitial Dignities, XII-180 pp., 1947.

257. Murphy, Rev. Francis Joseph, J.C.D., Legislative Powers of the Provincial Council, XII-158 pp., 1947.

258. O'Brien, Rev. Romaeus William, O.Carm., J.C.D., The Provincial Superior in Religious Orders of Men, X-294 pp., 1947.

259. Pfaller, Rev. Benedict Anthony, O.S.B., J.C.D., *The ipso facto* Effected Dismissal of Religious, XII-225 pp., 1947.

260. POPEK, REV. ALPHONSE SYLVESTER, J.C.D., The Rights and Obligations of Metropolitans, XX-460 pp., 1947.

261. RISTUCCIA, REV. BERNARD JOSEPH, C.M., J.C.D., Quasi-Religious, XVI-318 pp., 1947 (printed 1949).

262. SONNTAG, REV. NATHANIEL LOUIS, O.F.M.Cap., J.C.D., Censorship of Special Classes of Books, XII-147 pp., 1947.

263. STADLER, REV. JOSEPH NICHOLAS, J.C.D., Frequent Holy Communion, X-158 pp., 1947.

264. SZAL, REV. IGNATIUS JOSEPH, J.C.D., The Communication of Catholics with Schismatics, XII-217 pp., 1947.

265. WAGNER, REV. URBAN S., O.F.M. Conv., J.C.D., Parochial Substitute Vicars and Supplying Priests, IX-126 pp., 1947.

266. QUINN, REV. JOSEPH, M.A., J.C.D., Documents Required for the Reception of Orders, XIV-207 pp., 1948.

267. BENNINGTON, REV. JAMES CLEMENT, A.B., J.C.L., The Recipient of Confirmation.

268. BLAHER, REV. DAMIAN JOSEPH, O.F.M., A.B., J.C.L., The Ordinary Processes in Causes of Beatification and Canonization.

269. CLUNE, REV. ROBERT BELL, B.A., J.C.L., The Judicial Interrogation of the Parties.

270. COURTEMANCHE, REV. BASIL F., B.A., J.C.L., The Total Simulation of Matrimonial Consent.

271. DLOUHY, REV. MAUR JOHN, O.S.B., A.B., J.C.L., The Ordination of Exempt Religious.

272. DONOVAN, REV. JOHN THOMAS, PH.B., S.T.L., J.C.D., The Clerical Obligation of Canons 138 and 140, XII-209 pp., 1948.

273. FREKING, REV. FREDERICK W., A.B., S.T.B., J.C.L., The Canonical Installation of Pastors.

274. FULTON, REV. THOMAS B., J.C.L., Prenuptial Investigation.

275. GODLEY, REV. JAMES P., J.C.L., Time and Place for the Celebration of Mass.

276. KANE, REV. THOMAS A., A.B., B.S., J.C.D., Jurisdiction of the Patriarchs of the Major Sees, XII-153 pp., 1948 (printed 1949).

277. KENNEDY, REV. ANDREW A., J.C.L., The Annual Pastoral Report to the Local Ordinary.

278. KONRAD, REV. JOSEPH GEORGE, J.C.L., Transfer of Religious.

279. KRESS, REV. ALPHONSE, J.C.L., Contumacy in Ecclesiastical Trials.

280. MCCARTNEY, REV. MARCELLUS ANTHONY, O.F.M., M.A., J.C.L., Faculties of Regular Confessors.

281. MCCASLIN, REV. EDWARD PATRICK, M.A., S.T.L., J.C.L., The Division of Parishes.

282. MCELROY, REV. FRANCIS J., A.B., J.C.L., The Privileges of Bishops.

283. Quinn, Rev. Stephen, M.S.SS.T., J.C.D., Relation Between the Local Ordinary and Religious of Diocesan Approval, XII-153 pp., 1948 (printed 1949).
284. Schneider, Rev. Edelhard Louis, S.D.S., B.A., J.C.D., The Status of Secularized Ex-Religious Clerics, X-155 pp., 1948.
285. Thompson, Chester J., A.B., J.C.L., The Simple Removal from Office.
286. O'Brien, Rev. Kenneth R., A.B., J.C.D., The Nature of Support of Diocesan Priests in the United States, XVI-162 pp., 1949.
287. Metz, Rev. John E., S.T.L., J.C.D., The Recording Judge in the Ecclesiastical Collegiate Tribunal, X-130 pp., 1949.
288. Reinhardt, Rev. Marion J., S.T.L., J.C.L., The Rogatory Commission.
289. Ortega Uhiuk, Rev. Juan, S.J., J.C.L., De Delicto Sollicitationis.
290. Casey, Rev. James V., J.C.D., A Study of Canon 2222 § 1, XII-127 pp., 1949.
291. Allgeier, Rev. Joseph L., J.C.L., The Canonical Obligation of Preaching in Parish Churches.
292. Cahill, Rev. Daniel R., J.C.L., The Custody of the Holy Eucharist.
293. Carr, Rev. Aiden, O.F.M. Conv., S.T.D., J.C.L., Vocation to the Priesthood: Its Canonical Concept.
294. Knopke, Rev. Roch F., O.F.M., J.C.L., Reverential Fear in Matrimonial Cases in Asiatic Countries: Rota Cases.
295. Lavelle, Rev. Howard D., J.C.L., The Obligation of Holding Sacred Missions in Parishes.
296. Mickells, Rev. Anthony B., J.C.L., The Constitutive Elements of Parishes.
297. Noone, Rev. John J., J.C.L., Nullity in Judicial Acts.
298. Sheehan, Rev. Daniel E., J.C.L., The Minister of Holy Communion.
299. Statkus, Rev. Francis J., J.C.L., The Minister of the Last Sacraments.
300. Cook, Rev. John P., J.C.L., Ecclesiastical Communities and Their Ability to Induce Legal Customs.
301. Fazzalaro, Rev. Francis J., J.C.L., The Place for the Hearing of Confessions.
302. Hannan, Rev. Philip M., J.C.L., The Canonical Concept of *congrua sustentatio* for the Secular Clergy.
303. Quinn, Rev. Hugh G., S.T.L., J.C.L., The Particular Penal Precept.
304. Gallagher, Rev. John F., J.C.L., The Matrimonial Impediment of Public Propriety.
305. Welsh, Rev. Thomas J., J.C.L., The Use of the Portable Altar.
306. Waters, Rev. Joseph L., S.S.J., J.C.L., The Probation in Societies of Quasi-Religious.
307. Regan, Rev. Michael J., J.C.L., Canon 16.
308. Gallagher, Rev. Thomas V., J.C.L., The Rejection of Judicial Witnesses and Testimony.
309. Byrne, Rev. Harry J., J.C.L., Investment of Church Funds.
310. Chatham, Rev. Josiah G., Ph.B., S.T.L., J.C.L., Force and Fear as Invalidating Marriage: the Element of Injustice, XIV-183 pp., 1950.